Fellowship Baptist Trailblazers
BOOK 4

FELLOWSHIP BAPTIST
TRAILBLAZERS

Life Stories of Pastors, Missionaries and Church Leaders

BOOK 4

EDITED BY

Jonathan N. Cleland, Matthew Maw &
Christian Clement-Schlimm

the fellowship
BAPTIST PRESS

The Fellowship Baptist Press, Guelph, Ontario

An imprint of H&E Publishing, West Lorne, Ontario, Canada

fellowshipbaptistpress.com

Cover & book design by Janice Van Eck

Fellowship Baptist Trailblazers
Life Stories of Pastors, Missionaries and Church Leaders
BOOK 4
Edited by Jonathan N. Cleland, Matthew Maw & Christian Clement-Schlimm

ISBN 978-1-77484-182-2 (paperback)
ISBN 978-1-77484-183-9 (eBook)

Dedicated to the loving memory of
Frederick Austin Vaughan (1927–2010) and
Mildred Margaret Vaughan (1925–2025)

Contents

Foreword

My earliest recollection of a Fellowship Baptist gathering was at mid-sixties Muskoka Baptist Conference (MBC) in one of the original buildings—filled with men and women, celebrating and singing over coffee and cookies. Even as a child, the joy in that room and the discernible presence of the Holy Spirit made a lifetime impact on me. It was more powerful than anything else I had experienced in suburban Toronto, on TV or at school. To be sure, some of those present had been born in the 1800s, but the fellowship in that moment had overcome the discipline and hardship of the previous century.

My father was ten feet tall to me in those days. Other kids on the street owned better bicycles, and enjoyed more entertainment, but my dad was the one who casually bought a box of dynamite from a construction company and took it up to MBC to help clear the road they were building. When the church was rapidly growing in the mid-sixties, a group of bikers known as the Vagabonds took up residence in an abandoned farmhouse across the road. They would eventually join in with the Satan's Choice Motorcycle Club and later on the Hells Angels. But Fred Vaughan would visit with them and took enough genuine interest in their welfare that on Sunday mornings they would keep their motorcycles silent out of respect. Whenever I tried to "run with the pack," his strong hand would reach out and pull me back (thank the Lord).

Thistletown Baptist Church survived massive cultural and demographic changes in Toronto partly because the largely European-Canadian congregation of the sixties began to embrace the growing Jamaican and Asian communities without reservation. These were some of the happiest and most formative days of my life, when hundreds packed into Sunday school. Back in the day, church members would simply knock on doors in the neighborhood and promote the Sunday school. But this practice has become more dangerous and less welcome in the twenty-first century. I asked pastor Ken Davis how he managed visitation around Thistletown in 2010. His reply was, "Very carefully," including that he'd often attend public places like the shopping mall and strike up conversations with people. In any event, his love of people was effective.

Back in 1975, while attending junior high, and when Timothy Starr was home missions/church extension secretary, I wrote a letter asking Dr. Starr about the requirements for someone interested in pioneering a Fellowship Baptist church. He took the time to pen a thorough, serious reply—which impressed and encouraged me as a young teen. I noted that in the mid '70s, the Fellowship had more churches across Canada than McDonalds had fast-food restaurants. But there was a disconnect. Everyone knew and loved McDonalds, but not many Canadians knew anything about their local Fellowship Baptist church. Understanding the challenges of evangelism and the potential of the Fellowship in Canada became an obsession.

The late seventies and early eighties were difficult times both for me and the generation around me. Pop culture, economic decline, moral decay and increasing geopolitical forces led to higher divorce rates, suicide of friends and the abandonment of the faith. One thing that kept me together during those years was the reverence I held for certain men and women of the faith. Many of the names in this book were known to me through household conversations between my mom and dad.

Looking back, it was the fellowship of a diverse church community in the '60s that enabled me to marry into a Caribbean family in 1987 and never look back as the Lord blessed us mightily. Mom and Dad hit full retirement, but they couldn't sit still. They pioneered a fourth Baptist church in Angus, and eventually moved to the farm Christina and I had bought in 2001. Dad found an old, boarded-up Gospel Hall down the road that had been empty for twenty years and got permission from its trustees to "give it another shot." I was horrified, since he'd been through strokes and heart attacks and was clearly on the decline. But when dozens started attending, I found his recurring theme of knocking on doors still paid off! One woman up the street said it was just his genuine smile that convinced her to walk to church every Sunday.

One would expect a change in tenor between the original *Trailblazer Series* and this new volume as envisioned by Jon Cleland. Around thirty years have elapsed and the nation has changed considerably. One common thread is of ordinary men and women achieving great things for the kingdom of God through faithfulness in the local community. This book should encourage the reader to use the gifts they have been given and remain faithful—knowing that you are surrounded by a great cloud of witnesses (Hebrews 12:1). In the late sixties, I saw evangelists go into suburban neighbourhoods and create a commotion so that scores of kids would soon gather for singing and stories—followed by an invitation to join the bus to Sunday school. You might get into trouble if you tried that approach nowadays. So, evangelism has changed. Society has changed. But this book demonstrates how a newer generation of pastors, missionaries and church leaders adapted while ministering the age-old good news of the gospel.

The Lord has blessed me with living experiences in the USA and Canada. It's easy to look at—say Northern Virginia, where megachurches draw 8,000+ people to a well-produced, high-energy service. And we attend another location where a 120+ year old Baptist church with an awesome, hand-carved edifice rarely draws over twenty demoralized seniors. But when I did the math (local population versus attendance) for these two contrasting regions, I found little difference in the percentage of local population attending church on Sunday! We have our work cut out for us. Let us take courage from stories such as those in this volume and press on for the kingdom of God.

Jonathan Vaughan

Editors' introduction

I t is a great honour to be able to edit this volume. I (Jon) was first introduced to the *Trailblazers Series* in the summer of 2022, when I was helping Dr. Michael Haykin with writing the fifty-year history of West Highland Baptist Church, Hamilton, Ontario. One entry that I consulted was found in *Trailblazers* volume 1 on the life of Rev. Lambert Baptist. Pastor Baptist served for several years at West Highland and his entry was an important source for the church's history. It was at this point that I realized the historical importance of having these stories recorded.

However, I also realized that the series, though having three volumes, stopped in 2004. Twenty years later, I knew there were more stories that needed to be recorded. It is our hope that the restarting of this *Trailblazer Series* will record important stories in the history of the Fellowship. We hope that these stories will encourage young people, like ourselves, as we look to continue the ministry that has been passed on to us.

There are several people we wish to thank for their help in making this volume possible. First and foremost, we thank the contributors. It needs to be noted that all the people listed in this volume were invited to contribute by us. They humbly and gratefully submitted their entries in response to our request. While this is the fourth volume in this series, it is our hope that it will not be the last. So if you know of someone that should be included in a future volume, please let us know. We would love to invite them to be a part of a future volume.

Secondly, we are thankful to Steven Jones, Lynda Schultz and the Fellowship. Steve in particular put together a list of people for us to contact and both he and Lynda have been very encouraging of this project. We are thankful that the Fellowship cares about its history and wants to see this history preserved and passed on.

Thirdly, we thank the Vaughan family. Fred A. Vaughan, who went to be with the Lord in 2010, was the editor of the first three volumes. There would be no *Trailblazers Series* without him. Jonathan Vaughan, Fred's son, has been a great encouragement and we appreciate him writing the foreword to this volume. It is our hope to continue the work that Pastor Vaughan started. This book is dedicated to the memory of Fred and his wife, Mildred.

The people included in this book are listed as *trailblazers*, not necessarily because they have added something new to how we think about or do ministry (although they may have), but because they have, whether they believe so or not, blazed a trail for those of us who come after them. The work of the ministry does not start and end with one person but is passed on from generation to generation. May this volume encourage and inspire the next generation who look to serve Christ's church faithfully and passionately as we continue in the path that has been blazed before us.

Editors Jonathan N. Cleland, Matthew Maw
& Christian Clement-Schlimm

1 /

Steve Adams

When our neighbourhood milkman knocked on our door in the winter of 1968, I had no idea how significant and sovereign that event would be. I was growing up in a good but non-Christian home on the west side of what was then Galt, Ontario. Just two blocks away was a small Brethren assembly known as Westside Gospel Chapel. The group who started the work had a vision to reach children of young families in the neighbourhood living in small post-war bungalows.

Don Gowing, the milkman, had a simple request. He lived at the far end of our street and each Sunday morning would travel past our home on his way to the Gospel Hall where he was a member. He noticed as he passed by that my sister and I were always at home on Sundays, as my parents had no church affiliation. He was asking if he could pick up my sister who was seven and me, five years of age at the time, and take us to the Gospel Hall. My parents agreed with this proposal, and the next Sunday, Don and Dorothy Gowing carted us along with them to church.

Over the next five years, that routine continued. About one year in, my family moved to the other side of town. However, Don, ever the evangelist, had invited many neighbourhood kids to the burgeoning Sunday school, and the church leadership began renting a school bus to gather those of us who otherwise would be unable to attend based on our changing geography.

During those years, wonderful Sunday school teachers including Roy Thompson, Bruce Gowing, Gilbert Crossman, Bob Gowing, Ross Morrell and others, loved on me as they taught me great stories of the Bible. Frankly, my behaviour made me a handful. Nevertheless, the continuing, patient and unmerited love these teachers had for me left a very significant impression.

Mildred Lapsley was a dear lady in the church who had a burden for children and each summer organized backyard Bible clubs. She asked my parents if we might host one at our home, and even though my parents were not Christ followers, they agreed. In the summer of 1973 when I was ten years old, a college student working that summer as a Bible club counsellor presented the gospel in a clear and winsome way. I remember giving my life to Christ under a tree in my own backyard, and consequently had an immediate sense of my salvation in Christ.

Five years later, at the age of fifteen, I was baptized at Westside by Roy Thompson and Gib Crossman. I was the first one in my family to come to know Christ and be baptized. I continued to attend Westside until age sixteen, and then began a slow drift from the Lord.

During this time, my mother, a local politician, was on city council when an organization called Youth with a Mission wanted to set up their Canadian headquarters in Cambridge. Sadly, many misunderstood what this group was about, and that created fear and resistance. My mother agreed to visit their location in the Maritimes to better understand them. This visit had an obvious impact on her life, as she saw people who lived in complete dependence on the Lord and were people of constant prayer.

When I was seventeen, my mother passed away and our home was left in disarray. Her passing was during my last year in high school, and with my father struggling with grief and my sister in college, my future was uncertain.

With little parental input in my life regarding my future, I decided to go into the workforce and not pursue higher education. I took a job in management at a local entertainment facility that had a roller rink, arcade, mini golf etc. Interestingly, the principal owner of the facility was the son of one of the founding members of Forward Baptist Church.

While working here, I met Cheryl LaCroix, a young woman who had a strong faith in the Lord and was attending Ontario Bible College. Having grown up at Temple Baptist Church, Cheryl and her sister had recently begun attending Forward. I was interested in dating her, but she told me in no uncertain terms she would not date a boy who did not go to church. I had told her a bit about my faith background, although at that point in my life there was little evidence of faith. So, I sheepishly agreed to go with her to Forward.

After about my third visit to Forward, I was greeted by an older couple in the foyer. They introduced themselves—Don and Dorothy Gowing, my former milkman and his wife! They were delighted to see me there and had kept me continually in their prayers. What a blessing that was to hear!

Pastor Ernest Kennedy was the senior pastor at the time, and under his clear preaching I rededicated my life to Christ. At a Sunday night service in 1983, a missionary gave a presentation and handed out a commitment card. That night I signed a pledge to be available to whatever the Lord had for me in the future.

In the mid-eighties, I went to work for a major fine jewelry retailer where my father was employed. I soon got a sense that I would like to own my own jewelry store and so in 1986, at only twenty-three years of age, I purchased a small jewelry store in Kitchener. A year after the purchase, Cheryl and I were married and became increasingly involved at Forward.

In 1988, Pastor David Anderson became the senior pastor at Forward. He came from Troy Baptist Church outside of Detroit. Although he only stayed three years, he and his wife Mary had a profound impact on our lives. They had a great passion for reaching those who had little to no access to the gospel around the world. Over the next three years, our heart for the world increased significantly.

In 1991, Pastor David organized a missions work trip to visit our missionaries, the Leavers, serving in Quito, Ecuador. Cheryl and I planned on travelling together but our first son, Spencer, was born just two weeks before departure. Off I went on my own. The trip was pivotal in my Christian life.

Two weeks after I got home, Cheryl and I made the decision to prepare to go but be willing to stay. Upon making that decision, we were immediately contacted by a man interested in purchasing our jewelry store. Four months after returning from my trip, we sold our store with little clarity about what the next step might be. Needing work, a friend offered a job in his business. This hiatus lasted three years, but the Lord used it to ready my heart in needed ways before serving him in vocational ministry.

In 1993, we received an invitation from World Thrust, a missions mobilization ministry in Atlanta, Georgia, to join their staff. We began raising our support and left for this assignment in June 1994, with our son Spencer and our new daughter Riley. This was the same ministry that Pastor David Anderson joined when he left Forward.

After relocating to Atlanta, we realized the ministry we were now part of had significant issues in staff relationships. This resulted in half of the staff leaving six months after our arrival. This painful and confusing experience strengthened our dependence on the Lord and on each other.

We continued to serve at World Thrust and became members of Grace Fellowship Church. The pastor, Buddy Hoffman, had been deeply affected by the ministry of World Thrust and had a growing passion for the unreached. We became good friends, and in 1997 he invited me to become their first part-time missions pastor in this rapidly growing church. We saw the hand of God move in powerful ways during this time, as people from Grace Fellowship Church surrendered their lives to be missionaries and the church became very global in its ministry model. It was also during this time that our third child, Landon, was born.

In 1999, a chance encounter with Dr. Bill Jones led to another major life change. Bill had started a missions ministry (today known as Crossover Global) and was looking for an executive director to replace him. Bill was being prepared to become the president at Columbia Bible College and Seminary. Hence, we packed up again and moved to Columbia, South Carolina. We had the privilege of watching God bless Crossover, as the ministry grew; we bought property and built a new ministry centre across the road from the Bible college and seminary. Although I did not have an undergraduate degree, the seminary allowed me to enroll in a master's program which I was anxious to do. While serving at Crossover, travelling extensively and raising our young family, the Lord allowed me to complete my degree. Looking back, I'm not sure how it all fit!

After serving for five years at Crossover, we had a growing sense that we were to return to Canada. Through a series of nudges from the Lord, we resigned from our position and without knowing what the Lord had for us, we returned to Canada in June 2005.

Mentorlink Canada was a new ministry that had been incorporated but had yet to have someone give it "wings." I became the first director of Mentorlink Canada. We reconnected with Forward— our home church—and became increasingly active there.

Steve Adams

At the same time, I had a growing concern about the number of young adults leaving our churches. Consequently, I started a young adults Bible study and worship service on Sunday nights at Heritage College. We called it 3:16, named after Colossians 3:16. It quickly grew to 200 in attendance. One night, while giving my testimony, a young Heritage student in the audience realized it was her father who had led me to Christ in my backyard some thirty years earlier.

Eight months after our return, the existing lead pastor of Forward Baptist Church resigned. The church was in a difficult place as attendance was down, the staff was small and a few years earlier, a major building expansion had been undertaken.

The church began a lead pastor search that ultimately led to me being asked to assume the role. As I had not been a lead pastor before, providentially, Pastor Ernest Kennedy was invited to join me as my associate and mentor. How amazing that the Lord would allow me to serve alongside the man who had such a profound effect on my life twenty years earlier!

I assumed the lead pastor role at Forward on July 1, 2007. Over the next several years, we got to see the favour of God in our midst in remarkable ways. Our church started to grow, as we became increasingly focused on reaching those far from God in our community.

I eventually stepped away from the leadership of Mentorlink and handed it over to Marvin Brubacher. At the same time, we added additional staff at Forward and again God was generous in that area. At one point, we had a pastor on staff in his twenties through to one in his nineties.

Many people came to Christ, and over the next twelve years we baptized about 500 people. Again, we felt God nudging us as a church to launch out in faith. We started two additional locations in 2010, Huron Park and Forward Church Willow. Eventually Forward Willow became a standalone church known as the Church of the City. My oldest son, who was serving at Forward as our junior high pastor, eventually joined the pastoral team of Church of the City in Guelph and today is the lead pastor there. When we started the two new locations, we also started live streaming our services. We were one of the early churches in Canada to do this.

Several unique opportunities arose during those years at Forward. A local public school burned down and within three days we took the school into our facility. An initial request for an eight-week stay turned into almost four years. Again, this gave us opportunities to share the love and hope of Christ in ways we could never have imagined. We also developed a major summer camp ministry, revitalized our facility and saw hundreds of thousands of dollars given away each Christmas to bless our community and make Christ known. Our staff grew to twenty-five and became like a family to one another. What a blessing to have a front row seat for all of this!

After twelve years at Forward, we sensed the Lord might have another new ministry chapter. So once again, with uncertainty about what was next, we resigned to seek the Lord in this next chapter. Through a series of conversations with the Fellowship president Steve Jones and then FEB Central regional director Bob Fleming, I joined FEB Central part time, serving churches in leadership development, skills training and staffing issues. I am also involved in our Next Level Leadership training, our Next Level Preaching training and our interim pastor training as well.

At the same time, I started a consulting organization known as Adams and Co. Our focus is mainly around helping churches secure lead pastors and staff, and on building strong staff teams. We have served many churches—including West Park in London, Calvary in Guelph, Fairview in Lindsay and Emmanuel in Chatham, among others—in discerning and finding who their next pastor may be. We continue in this work and find it a source of great joy and blessing. In addition to this, I have also been involved in several longer-term interim preaching assignments.

Today our three children are all involved in their local churches—our daughter Riley in Sydney, Australia, our son Spencer is pastoring at Church of the City, and our son Landon is an elder at Restoration Church in Cambridge.

As I look back, my heart is filled with gratitude to God for the men and women he has brought into my life at strategic times to direct, encourage and shape me in my walk with the Lord.

Submitted by Steve Adams

2 /

Jacques Alexanian

A giant in the ministry

"In the Mission to the Americas ministry, you have always been considered like a giant, and you still are."
—*Grey Jeffreys, vice-president, Mission to the Americas*

When I was young, giants were a fantasy that fascinated me. I was impressed by Godzilla and similar creatures that had a huge impact on people. I read about them and watched them on TV. I would have never thought that, one day, I would meet a real giant. That's what happened when my path crossed Jacques Alexanian, a giant in the ministry.

Childhood

"We cannot understand ourselves if we do not know our roots."
—Jacques Alexanian

The Alexanian's family story started with the butterfly effect of the assassination of the Archduke Franz Ferdinand of Austria and his wife Sophia in Sarajevo, on June 28, 1914. The consequences of this event led to the death of about nine million people during World War I. In April 1915, a genocide was carried out against Armenian citizens in various towns and villages of Turkey. Authorities organized death marches across deserts and mountains, with the hope of eradicating these people. Young Pascal Alexanian, Jacques' father, was among the unfortunate victims of these deadly marches. He was made slave to a mean owner before he escaped. Later, Pascal arrived in Syria where he met evangelical Christians who were on an international humanitarian mission. It was through the missionaries' care, full of love and compassion, that he saw Jesus' gospel of grace.

In 1921, Pascal was transferred to Beirut where he joined the French Army. He eventually ended up in France, full of hope and a life of opportunities ahead of him. There he met Mariam who, just like him, had escaped the Turkish massacre upon their people. They got married in 1928 and she gave birth to their first child, a son, to whom they gave a very French name: Jacques. First of four siblings, Jacques was born on September 12, 1929. In the Armenian tradition, being the firstborn is a position of honour, but also one of great responsibility. His father's expectations grew as Jacques got older. Pascal's faith in God made him believe there were bigger things for his son. The son and the father soon discovered they didn't share the same dreams, leading to tensions between them. Jacques' father demanded his son excel at school in order to enter medical school. But Jacques had other dreams. Realizing that he was disappointing his dad, he became a lazy and rebellious student.

Jacques was only ten years old when the Second World War began. During this time, he started to study construction and wanted to be a carpenter. After the war, in 1949, he promptly decided to fly away to a life of prosperity in the United States of America. Among his farewell gifts, his family gave him a New Testament. Jacques was not yet converted. He arrived in Philadelphia, an English-speaking city, with a radio as his only friend. With his entrepreneurial spirit, Jacques opened a successful dry-cleaning business. Soon after, he started to work as a carpenter. His new financial success led him to a life of pleasure and luxury. Yet, his heart was not fulfilled.

Conversion and study

"Follow me!"—*Jesus*

In his adopted country, Jacques' radio provided a great deal of unexpected help: gospel radio broadcasts. One Sunday afternoon, a radio show hosting Charles E. Fuller caught his attention. Jacques felt like God was speaking directly to him. At the end of the program, he fell on his knees and asked for God's mercy and forgiveness for his sins. He began to read the New Testament he had received from his family and, surprisingly, he understood it all. That afternoon, he received Christ as his Lord and Saviour. Jacques now understood the love of Jesus through his death on the cross. He realized that God sent his son to die for all the sins of Jacques Alexanian and to redeem his life. Encouraged by a Christian friend, he joined Philadelphia's Olney Baptist Church. While he was attending a missionary conference, he felt the call to serve as a missionary.

To achieve his goal, Jacques began to study at the Philadelphia Biblical Institute where students were encouraged to join a prayer meeting to intercede for the mission and for revival in different parts of the world. The young man was convinced God was calling him to join a European mission, so he chose a group that was praying for Europe. In this group, a young woman was showing the same ambition: Loretta Mae Hanold. Both got deeply involved in this ministry and it became a pretext to meet on a regular basis and, shortly after, to enter a courtship. They got married on June 23, 1956. Their marital journey lasted until Jacques' death in 2023.

Soon into their marriage, Jacques' heart for Europe was about to take an unexpected turn. Mr. Mason, the dean of the Bible school, travelled to Quebec and he could not find a single evangelical church to attend with his family. Upon discovering this strange situation, Jacques was deeply touched. The more he pondered the idea, the clearer it became that God wasn't sending him to Europe, but to North America, to the Canadian province of Quebec. Interestingly, this province is mostly French-speaking, just like France, where he first thought he would go. At the time, the province was still controlled by the Catholic Church, which was working hand in hand with the government. State and religion were teaming up to vigorously influence the schools and almost all aspects of social life. For the Church of Rome, Quebec was the practical incarnation of its theological doctrines, deeply implanted in the lives and culture of its citizens. While preparing for the mission, Jacques pursued his studies at Wheaton College and his family moved to Illinois for the next six years. Life as a student was going well, but it was hard for the young family: Jacques who was studying for his master's degree had to write numerous papers, attend many meetings and hold a job to pay the bills. The couple was seriously stretched by this busy life. By the grace of the Lord and some help from brothers and sisters in Christ, Jacques and Loretta were able to bond like never before. This would become the basis for his being a good counsellor for many pastoral couples in Quebec.

After his studies, Jacques was still hesitating on where to serve God. Then one day he heard a guest speaker on a Chicago radio station. The man was sharing his burden for the French-Canadian church in Quebec. The guest was a certain Ernest Keefe. He and his wife Betty were initially trained to go to Africa but ended up having compassion for Quebec. Jacques organized a meeting with the couple. They shared their testimony with him and this French-Canadian province's need for the gospel. So, in 1960, Jacques decided to go serve God in Quebec. He made a short trip to Canada and, while attending a meeting in Asbestos, Quebec, he heard Lionel Gosselin's prayer for his province. This young Christian asked God's help for a Quebec "that had been living in darkness for the past four centuries." This prayer was the confirmation Jacques needed. He made the necessary arrangements with the mission, and within less than two years, the family moved to Quebec. They arrived in Asbestos in 1963, but stayed only a little while, moving again to serve in Sherbrooke, a city with a university.

Love for the local church

> "He has the unshakable conviction that the church is the place of excellency to educate and instruct the believer's character."
> —*François Picard, former president of SEMBEQ*

In Sherbrooke there was a biblical institute called Béthel. It offered French classes to the newly arrived foreign missionaries. Loretta needed to learn

French, so she did. One of the teachers, Jack Cochrane, invited Jacques to collaborate with him during some meetings. Then, Jacques became a missionary pastor of a tiny church in March 1964. It was a hard time, but Jacques and his companions tried to reach as many people as possible. They did door-to-door evangelism, started a Christian library, helped with outdoor meetings, made phone calls, distributed tracts, etc. Jacques once said, "The five first years were very difficult," but he received encouragement from a group of young Americans who came to visit for a summer festival. Youth would play a vital role in Jacques' ministry. Happily, in April 1967, a chapel was inaugurated in downtown Sherbrooke.

The 1960s in Quebec were called the "Révolution tranquille." Many factors converged to lead to this Quiet Revolution. In its desire to be modern, the province began to distance itself from the Catholic Church in the realms of education, healthcare, politics, family and economics. After centuries of control by the Catholic Church, Quebecers aspired to change. Strangely, one important factor of this change came from the Catholic Church's Council of Vatican II. Because of Vatican II, people now had the right to read the Bible, something that was forbidden until then. The mass was no longer celebrated in Latin, so people could understand what was being said. And, sins which used to be deadly, were not anymore. The population of Quebec was confused and stunned. Things changed rapidly and drastically. The Expo 67 and, later on, the Olympic Games hosted in Montreal in 1976, contributed to people searching for truth elsewhere.

In the summer of 1967, the whole world had its eyes on Quebec and its centre of attention: Montreal's Expo 67. Jacques attended the event as a spiritual guide in the Sermon of Science Pavilion, where Christian video documentaries were presented with the intention of reaching people for Christ. Jacques repeated this at Sherbrooke's Farm Fair, inspired by Dwight L. Moody at Europe's World Fair. In 1969, Jacques set up a tent where he showed Moody Bible Institute documentaries. It was here that the Desrochers, Armand and Carmen families accepted the message of Christ. They were popular singers known by the French-Canadian audience, and they were the first to record Christian albums in French.

In the summer of 1970, two tents were set up in Sherbrooke with the Desrochers in concert. More than 8,000 people heard the message of Christ at the farm fair. But that's not all! In 1972, another 8,000 people heard the message, and 1,300 wanted to know more about it. In October of this same year, sixteen people were baptized and more than twenty people answered God's calling. This was a display of Quebec's opening to the gospel. But it came with a price. Even if, by that time, no more Christians were being put in jail for their faith, as had happened in the 1950s, there was still opposition to the gospel. For instance, Claude Laverdière, a teacher, had been fired from his school board because he was no longer a Roman Catholic. But by the grace of God, and the help of the church, Claude started evangelizing among the youth in *cégep* (college) and on university campuses. Claude's example served as a model for Jacques' ministry to reach students in Quebec.

Multiplication as a tool

"His unusual vision and passion made him a man of his own."
—*John MacArthur*

Jacques was a man of vision. In 1974, he moved from Sherbrooke to Hull, near Ottawa, to begin his own ministry planting French-speaking churches. At first, he joined a bilingual church, even though his desire was to serve francophones. Shortly after, the English-speaking church invited Jacques to transition the church into being exclusively francophone. The chapel was given to the francophone ministry along with $5,000 to help Pastor Alexanian's ministry. Within just three years, the church became financially self-sufficient.

Jacques believed in youth. It is that conviction that explains why, for most of the 1970s, he saw the educational system as a great context for the growth of the gospel and, therefore, for the growth of the province's church. One key partner in this endeavor was Guy Lavoie. Jacques had asked Guy to help him reach the young people in the CEGEPs (colleges) and universities. With Guy and other teammates, youth began to be the main factor behind the growth and the health of the church. Bill Philips, one of the cofounders of SEMBEQ—Séminaire Baptiste Évangélique du Québec (Quebec's Evangelical Baptist Seminary)—was rejoicing in these words: "Campuses at all kinds of educational schools were the perfect place to touch, recruit and coach the new generation of future leaders for the ministry in Quebec."

In 1977, the idea of hiring youths for the ministry was born. The SEF program (Serviteur En Formation, "servant in training") was established.

Young believers were trained by receiving one year of theological training while serving in a local church and living by faith. For instance, André Constant was one of these first trainees, with Jacques as his tutor. In 1983, André Constant became the Hull church's senior pastor.

Jacques was convinced that church planting was both a biblical and strategic way to see the gospel grow. In June 1977, Jacques and a group of men decided to open another church near Hull, considering that among the sixty people who had been baptized, many came from nearby Gatineau. In 1978, with the help of Gatineau's church, two other churches opened: one in Buckingham and another in Casselman in Eastern Ontario. Another opened in Vanier-Orléans in 1981. The concept of a mother church and her daughter churches became clear, possible and realistic. For Jacques Alexanian, multiplication was not only a concept, but a practical application of the gospel of Jesus Christ.

SEMBEQ's snowball effect on local church ministry

"It's Christ the Lord who uses his people to train his people."
—*Michael A.G. Haykin*

Jacques believed in training men of faith. In the 1960s, Quebec was known as a "pastors graveyard," but things would rapidly change in the early '70s. The need for pastors was great, conversions were numerous and the opportunities for training were minimal. Rufus Jones, who was a program director at Wheaton College, was always repeating the same thing: "Be more numerous / Multiply yourself / Multiply the ministry / etc." Jacques' reaction to Rev. Jones' saying was: "I have never seen this before. I don't know what to do or how to do it!" It is with the Latino-American model of Ivor Greenslade that Jacques and his acolytes decided to look at as a model to train other missionaries. The main goal was to transfer the training from the seminary to the local church.

On September 3, 1973, a committee of the French fellowship made the decision to start a biblical seminary adapted to the situation and needs of Quebec's rapid growth. In 1974, the new school became a reality. More than 110 students were ready to be trained. In God's providence, Ernest Keefe was the first to come to teach the group a class on Mark's Gospel.

Jacques' vision for the seminary was clear: give the local church priority in the training of men. The seminary was not to stay independent from the local churches, but it would, instead, seek to serve them. The local church was central to training the people. André Constant said: "We have to defend the role of the church community." The training of future leaders in the church and their role as leader must concern all the members of any given church. There should be no gap between theory and practice. For Jacques, the capacity of a leader to take care of the church does not reside only in his knowledge and competency, but also in his character, in the quality of his heart.

While he was still the head pastor at the Hull church, Jacques was also serving with SEMBEQ. The ongoing flow of Quebec's new believers was huge, and its needs were getting bigger. Eventually, Jacques would get to the point where he would dedicate all his time and energy to the seminary.

Jacques was a thinker and a man of spirit. He wanted to train ministry students who think with maturity, who are not afraid to develop their capacity to establish solid convictions. In Jacques' view, students must be exposed to other theological opinions. Jacques wanted to open their vision to have compassion on those who suffer, to understand the central importance of the gospel, to develop rigour in their theological thinking and to promote a dynamic local church. The help the ministry in Quebec needed was to be echoed in the Christian world. People like Elisabeth Elliot, John MacArthur, Don Carson, Gene Getz and many more, came to Quebec to give essential and very instructive conferences and training. These collaborations showed the vast influence of Jacques Alexanian and his great vision for Quebec, a vision that he shared wherever he went. He wanted to train oaks, not pumpkins.

In the beginning, Quebec depended on outside missionaries to train Christians in Quebec. Those servants—from around the globe and from many different cultures and ideas—put aside their differences to live in harmonious cohesion to build the ministry in the province of Quebec. The man for this time was Jacques Alexanian, a man who gathered different people for a common goal: the glory of the gospel. At the start of his ministry, Jacques did not know that his mission in Christ would be for a French-Canadian province. He, an Armenian-born man, raised in France, trained in the United States in English, would then serve Canada's French population. His desire was to equip and empower future leaders with a unified, strong vision of peace and respect through the gospel. Jacques Alexanian was a father figure in the eyes of many church workers. With great affection, he often called them "my sons" and was a model for them like the apostle Paul in 2 Timothy 2:2, one of the main verses he used at SEMBEQ.

Jacques Alexanian

For Jacques, "SEMBEQ has to train disciples that are engaged in the ministry of the gospel, for a mature leadership and a healthy church." This was exactly what he did in Sherbrooke and Outaouais. And that is what he wanted for the seminary too. In a document written for the fortieth anniversary of the seminary, he said: "SEMBEQ was the 'snowball effect' that God used for his Quebec ministry to make a multiplicity of future leaders."

Jacques never stopped expanding or improving the training. He always found a way to challenge his students. Just like Jacques, the seminary was dynamic, ready to adapt and face contemporary issues with influence and competency. But he was realist: he knew that SEMBEQ belongs to the Lord. He knew it was by God's will that this expansion was going on. God made it all possible by his will, and Jacques was thankful to him. And by the grace of God, Jacques could see some special fruit of his ministry before passing away. He saw Richard Houle, who received the first bachelors degree at SEMBEQ in 1984, give a certificate to Éric Leblanc in 2011. The Paulinian circle of training was completed.

Don Carson put it like this: "He was an anchor in a great period of change."

Involved in mission until the very end

"SEMBEQ's model, linked to theological education based in the church, contributed to the ministry of the kingdom in many places around the world."
—*Rick Miller, director, Mission to America*

Jacques didn't retire. After years serving SEMBEQ and training François Picard as his successor in the ministry, Jacques continued to serve and share the blessings of God. For another decade, he travelled the world to share this model of training mission workers centred on the local church, a model he believes was found in Scripture and taught by the apostles. "We now have a story to tell," he liked to say.

His pilgrimages led him to travel to France and Belgium in Europe, Japan, Haiti, Central America and other countries, between 1990 and 2016. And in *la belle province*, he served a year as a consultant at Sherbrooke's church between 1991 and 1992. He did the same at Buckingham, between 2003 and 2009, and then served at Casselman from 2014 to 2016. He continued to help and serve from church to church, until the honourable age of eighty-six. Wherever he went, he continued to implement the gospel's culture. For him, the gospel *is* the culture of all cultures.

Conclusion

"I pray that God's Spirit leads you to write about what glorifies Jesus, so the readers will be moved by the love of Christ and will serve him passionately. When this project is finished there will be words, not about me nor you, but about Jesus and his achievements."
—*Jacques Alexanian's words to me in one of our meetings of preparation for this work in January 2022*

My mother's funeral was at the same time as Jacques Alexanian's. "Maman Lise" had the blessing of experiencing rich gifts directly and indirectly from SEMBEQ in the church of Granby, and in the French Evangelical Baptist Fellowship. In mom's funeral prayer, Richard Houle said that their deaths marked the passing of two great people who served with distinction in the mission of Christ, two spiritual giants. So, Jacques Alexanian's mission in Quebec was accomplished: training lay people and leaders in the local church for the glory of God.

Submitted by Rev. Stéphane Gagné

3 /

Dr. Kenton (Kent) C. Anderson

"He who does the work is not so profitably employed as the one who multiplies the doers."

T his quotation from John R. Mott well describes how God has led me in his service. My efforts in service to the Lord and as a life-long member of the Fellowship Baptist community have largely been about raising up new generations of leaders whom God has gifted and called to the ministry of the church. If God has been pleased to use me, it has largely been through the effect of my students and those who have benefitted from the educational systems I have designed and led. I pray that this legacy will continue long after I am gone.

It is an uncomfortable task, having been asked to describe at some length one's life and ministry. I am encouraged by the fact that I was asked to frame this writing as a kind of "testimony" of the work of God in and through me. All that I have done has been by his grace and at his call.

My journey of faith and service begins with God's work in drawing my parents to faith and service years before I was born. Both my mother, Myrna, and my father, Rodney, came to Christ through the youth group at Maple Ridge Baptist Church in the Lower Mainland of British Columbia, under the long and faithful ministry of Reverend A.J.L. Haynes, who became my pastor when I was born. Pastor Haynes served that church for forty-one years. It was through his ministry that my parents came to know and love the Lord and each other. Without their pioneering faith, I would not be who I am today.

Maple Ridge Baptist was a great incubator of pastors and missionaries during those years. I could name many of my friends who came up through that youth group in the 1960s and '70s who became engaged in vocational ministries of various kinds. These were the days before youth pastors, when we were encouraged as "young people" to take leadership for ourselves.

My first sermon was given in an evening service at that church when I was seventeen years old. I had read a book by Philip Keller about the life of Gideon. The sermon that resulted was more a poor retelling of Keller's teaching than it was my own, which was probably appropriate, given my lack of learning and wisdom at the time. But it was a launching pad from which emerged a lifetime of ministry and service. It was a conversation at Camp Qwanoes (a Fellowship camp on Vancouver Island) with Pastor John Bonham of Fellowship Baptist Edmonton that God used to confirm his calling in my life. I had been working a job pumping gas at Mussallem Motors, which kept me from attending church on most Sunday mornings. (Pastor George Dawe would make a point of running out of gas on Sundays so that he could come to encourage me while I filled his tank each time.) After talking with Pastor Bonham, I resolved myself to tell my boss that I would no longer be available to work on Sundays, even if that meant losing my job. I understand there are worse things than working on Sundays, but I recognized that at that point in my life, it was important for me to be in church. My boss seemed unhappy about it, but I was never scheduled on a Sunday again, and I was granted more shifts than I could handle. This was a small encouragement at an important time, confirming that God would take care of me if I was willing to follow his call.

From there, I ended up at Northwest Baptist Theological College, not understanding how important that school would be to my future. While pursuing my degree, I got involved in a number of Fellowship churches as an intern. I worked with Pastor Bruce Mateika at Fellowship Baptist, Fort McMurray. I spent a summer at First Baptist, Drumheller, working with Pastor Gordon Forbes. Of course, I served at my home church, Maple Ridge Baptist, with Pastors Ian Bowie and Dave Chapman. I served with Pastor Dennis Burris at Westbourne Baptist in Calgary and with Pastor John Greb at Newton Fellowship Baptist. Perhaps the most significant of these was a surprising opportunity to serve as interim pastor at Killarney Baptist in Calgary. The church was in need, and I was available. Only twenty-one years old, I served that church as its sole pastor for eleven months, preaching three times a week, working with the deacons board, visiting the sick and even publishing the bulletins on an old Gestetner machine. We didn't even have a secretary, much less an assistant. By God's grace, the church survived.

Kent Anderson

I have told my students that I learned the three most important things about ministry during that year, all of which were something a twenty-one-year-old could do: I could show up, I could be reasonably sound in my use of the Scriptures, and I could make sure they knew I loved them. That seemed to be enough.

Following my graduation the next year, I married Karen, who had come to Christ at Whispering Pines Bible Camp, a Fellowship camp near Calgary. We have now celebrated more than forty-one years of marriage. Together, we moved on to serve full-time at Campbell River Baptist and Richmond Baptist as assistant (youth) pastor, working with the senior pastor, David Fairbrother. We then moved north to Prince Rupert Fellowship Baptist, where I served as lead pastor for most of six years.

At Prince Rupert, it was my privilege to follow the amazing ministry of Pastor Lloyd Jackson, who had served there for more than thirty years. In fact, he had mentored my father when Dad was a bi-vocational pastor of a Fellowship church plant in Terrace, BC. For me to follow "Pastor J" seemed absurd, though God confirmed his call when we had dinner with Lloyd and Agnes, just after having agreed to come to Prince Rupert to serve.

"You can imagine," he said, "that after thirty years, I was praying pretty hard about who would follow me to this church. God brought someone to my mind," he said, "though I have not said a word to anyone about it until now. That person was you." You can imagine how his confidence and the sense of God's superintendence fuelled me through those years as various challenges arose. Despite my relative inexperience, God blessed us through that time. The church flourished. People came to Jesus. Our three children were born (Kelsey, Kirk and Katelyn), and together, our family took shape and grew.

My kids are amazing, each of them forging their own futures under God's care, with spouses and children (my grandchildren) of their own. My oldest daughter is a pastor's wife herself. Watching Kelsey and Matt in their ministry at 100 Mile House, BC, offers many memories of the experiences Karen and I went through in our own time up north.

Somehow, I knew that God had more for me, and after a period of prayer and discernment, I decided to upgrade my education. I returned to Northwest to earn a second Master's degree in preparation for a sojourn in Fort Worth, Texas, where I earned a PhD with a focus in preaching at Southwestern Baptist Theological Seminary. Even there, God's hand was leading me.

During our first week in Texas, someone "randomly" invited us to visit his church. When there, we realized we had met the pastor previously. My former mentor at Campbell River, Pastor Pete Unrau, had brought this Texan pastor, Harold Bullock, to be the keynote speaker at a BC Fellowship pastors' retreat many years before. Pete's son, Bevin, had served at this church some years prior. Of the thousands of churches in the Dallas/Fort Worth area, this was the church God sent us to in our very first week! It still gives me goose bumps to think on this.

Hope Church, Fort Worth, was an amazing place. Under Pastor Harold's leadership, they had planted seventy-five churches around North America (including in Canada), and they didn't even have a building of their own.

We had to check every week to see which hotel we were meeting in that Sunday—but as we know, the church is not a building.

After graduating from Southwestern, we returned to British Columbia and were given an opportunity to develop into a faculty role at Northwest and ACTS Seminaries (at Trinity Western University). They didn't have the budget to hire me outright that year, but they gave me plenty of opportunity to teach in an adjunct capacity. That year, I ended up teaching eleven courses (all for the first time), while serving as interim enrolment director. All that almost added up to a full-time salary. I relied heavily on old notes from my pastor days and a lot of youthful enthusiasm. I must have done all right because, by their good grace and the blessing of the Lord, I was offered a full-time faculty position the following summer.

What a privilege to follow in the footsteps of giants like Professor Don Hills and Dr. D.A. Carson and to work with Pastor Doug Harris and Dr. Larry Perkins. When Northwest was forced to close its undergraduate division for financial reasons, around the year 2000, I became academic dean of the school under Larry's presidency as we moved to focus entirely on graduate-level studies as part of the ACTS Seminaries consortium. Upon Larry's retirement in 2010, I was invited to become president myself.

Those were years of fruitful challenge. Often, people would ask me if I missed being a pastor. I would say that I never felt I had left my calling but that I just had a different sort of congregation. Northwest has always been fully focused on the work of the church and pastoral development. My thinking was that I could be one person, exercising my gifts in one place, or if God was pleased to give me the opportunity, I could raise up many to fulfill their gifts, exponentially reproducing my gifts in others as God led. Decades later, I am seeing that God has blessed this "multiplication of the doers." The current president of Northwest, Dr. Barton Priebe, after a long and faithful pastoral ministry, was one of those students I was pleased to have under my care. Now, he is my friend and colleague.

My primary area of teaching during these years was homiletics. I had always been affirmed for my preaching, and so I was interested to see how I might be able to advance a renewal in the work of gospel proclamation. Building on my dissertation work, I taught a form of "Integrative Preaching" intended to speak to both head and heart in a way that contemporary listeners might find compelling. These were the days of the seeker-sensitive movement, where a lot of preaching was aiming for relevance, often at the expense of solid exegesis. My suggestion was that we didn't have to make that choice, but by an integrative emphasis, we could unite deep biblical truth with a compelling engagement of the modern listener. We could integrate narrative with exposition, such that the whole person was attracted to meet and respond to God.

This has been a personal mission, as I have been privileged to teach these things to thousands at every level, from PhD to Sunday school, on four continents and in more schools and places than I could name. My four books on the subject (published by Zondervan, Baker Academic and Kregel) have spread this thinking near and far. In addition, I was privileged to join in forming the Evangelical Homiletics Society along with my mentor-from-afar, Dr. Haddon Robinson. Through that agency, I have not only been able to multiply preachers, but also other teachers of the same, who are themselves increasing the multiplying factor. Even as I write these words, I find it hard to fathom the import and impact of these efforts.

During those years, I continued serving the church through interim and guest preaching/pastor roles, and in my home churches, Parkland Fellowship and Dunbar Heights Fellowship Baptist. Pastor David Horita was not only my friend but also my pastoral mentor, from whom I learned much and saw amazing fruit. David went on to become the executive director at Fellowship Pacific during a time of dramatic reinvention of ministry and the flourishing of our churches. David might be the most transformational leader I have ever known. It has been my great privilege to serve as his colleague for so many of these years.

The early twenty-first century has not been a time of roses and sunshine for the work of theological education. Many schools have struggled deeply to understand how to serve a changing landscape. Classic forms of education have not been thriving as the expense and form of conventional education have become increasingly difficult to sell. When I was named president of Northwest, I challenged the board and faculty with the opportunity to invest our enterprise in the development of new and better ways. Through a long and varied dialogue with David and his team at the FEB Pacific office, we invented a new, mentored, contextual approach to seminary education. The *Immerse* program became the first fully competency-based Master of Divinity program accredited by the Association of Theological Schools. The impact of this work transformed our churches, allowing Fellowship Pacific and Northwest to grow and flourish in many ways. Competency-Based Theological Education

(CBTE), the subject of my most recent book, and co-authored with Greg Henson of Kairos University, has become an international movement, described by many as the most promising undertaking in the work of theological education in the last twenty years.

For Fellowship Pacific, Immerse became the go-to way of pastoral and ministry development. Through this innovative approach, our churches were able to invest in the development of their own emerging, gifted leaders rather than seeing them go on to other places and schools. The success of this movement has given me the opportunity to consult with and assist many other schools, churches, denominations and missional agencies to develop similar programs elsewhere. The legacy of this movement will resonate for a long time to the glory of God and the shape of his kingdom.

More recently, I was surprised to receive an invitation to serve as the president of Providence University College and Theological Seminary in southern Manitoba. It was hard to imagine leaving British Columbia for the Prairies, and just as hard to imagine leaving full-time service within a Fellowship institution to serve in a non-denominational ministry. After a period of discernment, it seemed good to my family and to the Holy Spirit for me to accept this exciting opportunity. To be able to take the gifts and experience God had built within me and to apply these things not only to a seminary but to a whole university environment was compelling, as was the opportunity to learn a whole new network of people, churches and organizations in the centre of our great country.

This is where I find myself at the time of this writing, serving the Lord and the 1,200 students and 12,000 alumni in the year of Providence's 100th anniversary. What a privilege (and challenge) it has been to sustain and build upon the Christ-centred imperatives of Providence. Our mission here is to see people know and love Jesus as they grow in knowledge and character for leadership and service. Here, we have developed a large new campus for international students in downtown Winnipeg, a Centre for On-Demand Education that serves leaders in their contexts both near and far while growing Providence's long-standing rural campus in Otterburne, Manitoba.

My life has not entirely focused on my work and on the professional aspects of my ministry. God has given us so many things, and I have always wanted to enjoy as many of them as I can. I have always enjoyed stories, sports and songs. In addition to guitar and golf, which I have played throughout my life, I have recently added piano and downhill skiing. One might question the wisdom of taking on a sport like skiing at my age, but if not now, when? I've even discovered a love for drawing and painting, which I could not have imagined in my younger years. One is never too old to learn and to try new things, for as long as God gives us breath, we have the opportunity to know him and enjoy his gifts.

I do not know how long I will be here at Providence. While I am now of traditional retirement age, I do believe I have much to offer for years to come, whether through my service on the board of the Association of Theological Schools, or in my first love, the local church. I have continued my membership at Dunbar Heights, a longstanding ministry of Fellowship Pacific in the heart of Vancouver, where I am on the preaching team and often lead worship. I am so grateful for the ministry of my pastor, Wes Parker, who was one of the first Immerse graduates.

It was Professor Donald Hills, who trained and was beloved by a whole generation of West Coast pastors, who convinced me of the priority of the local church. I remember when I took Theology 100 under him more than forty-five years ago while at Northwest. He had us look up every instance of the Greek word, *ekklesia*, and discern whether each use of the word was in reference to a local gathering or something else. The consensus was that more than 90 per cent of the Bible's use of the word we translate "church" refers to a local body of gathered believers who loved each other, served one another and could hold each other to account. That lesson stuck with me. Having served at Providence these years, I have come to love the work of God in many denominational families. I will not venture to say that the Fellowship is better or more faithful than the others. I will say that the Fellowship has been my home and my family, and for that, I am grateful.

Karen has walked with me on this journey now for well more than forty years. She has been my constant companion, my constructive critic and now my college colleague through this journey. It has been a privilege to watch and support her growth and ministry, first as a pastor's wife and a devoted mother and then in later life with a ministry of her own. For thirteen years, Karen served as a Baptist Housing chaplain, serving hundreds of residents and staff at Shannon Oaks and Clarendon Court in Vancouver, BC. Now, she serves as a faculty member, director of the chaplaincy program and dean of the Centre for On-Demand Education at Providence. Her love and faithfulness to me and to those others she serves inspires me to offer the same. So much of what I have described in these paragraphs is due to her support.

It has been quite a journey. Writing this has reminded me of how much influence those many leaders I have named have had upon me. It is surprising when I notice younger leaders looking to me in that same way. God will never leave himself without a witness. While the day of my influence might be lengthening, I am heartened by those generations that are coming in my stead and which, through education, I have had the privilege to shape in some way. In that, I try to embody my favourite oxymoron: *humbled confidence.* I am humbled because I acutely know my limitations, but my confidence is unbounded because I walk in the care and capacity of my Lord. It is by his grace that I stand and await his welcome into the kingdom he has established, and in which we pray will come on earth as it is in heaven.

Submitted by Dr. Kenton (Kent) C. Anderson

4 /

Rev. Doug Blair

L ooking back from a vantage point north of eighty years, I see my
life as a demonstration of "amazing grace" and a strong sense of
God's call and leading in my life.

My first recollections are of my parents' home in Nashville, Ontario, a
1929 Model A that had to be cranked to start—and church. Having been
born during a World War (no, not the first), I decided at two years of age
to follow my parents out of Toronto. This still seems to have been a good
decision.

We began attending a small Congregational church in Pine Grove. As
it turns out, it might have been smarter and more efficient to live near
the church. We pretty well seemed to be there most of the time, and my
father worked only block away. Sunday school, morning service, evening

service, Wednesday prayer meeting and let's not forget Friday kids pro-gramme—all were *de rigueur*. The church had called a graduate of Central Baptist Seminary, Harold Kettyle, and he led the congregation to join the Fellowship.

It was during our time there that the Lord began giving me the "Samuel treatment." First, he called me into his family when I was about eight years old. On a Sunday night (no, I have no recollection of the sermon), when I had gone to bed the Holy Spirit spoke to me. I did not hear a voice, but a thought came into my mind and would not leave. "What would happen to me if I died tonight?" I am pretty sure eight-year-old boys do not think of such things on their own. I remember getting out of bed and kneeling. I said to the Lord, "Lord, if I have never trusted you before, I trust you now." From that moment, God has given me the confidence that he is my Father and that I am his son.

Second, the "Samuel treatment" continued when, at eleven, I sensed God calling me into his service. We had several missionaries visit our church and they had a strong influence on my life. Essentially, all of them ended up at our place for Sunday lunch. I suspect none ever left without being better off than when they arrived at our home. One missionary family had a daughter about my age. I had the strong sense that my dad thought she would be an excellent marriage partner for me. Since neither of us had any interest in the other, I have come to be convinced that was not God speaking through my father.

As high school drew to a close, friends in my church (by then Calvary Baptist in Woodbridge) encouraged me to attend Bob Jones University in South Carolina. There a bachelor of arts degree was bestowed upon me. Afterward, I sensed a leading to attend Dallas Theological Seminary. Those were very happy days. I made many long-time friends among students and faculty, earned a ThM degree, and above all found a wonderful wife, Detra.

Detra and I met at First Baptist where we were in the same study group on Sunday evenings. After I had sensed the need to know her better, I asked her if she would like to sit with me in church. Being a proper south-ern girl, she looked at me and responded, "I don't believe we have been introduced." That must not be the end, so I came back with, "Well I'm Doug Blair and you are Detra Wade, so now we have been introduced." How could she argue with that logic? So, we got married, though not exactly immediately. It took three years to fully convince her. She has willingly, I think, followed me wherever the Lord led for well over half a century. Her ministry complemented and strengthened mine.

Just after graduation, a church in West, Texas, took me on as interim pastor. After a few months, the elders asked me to stay permanently and scheduled a church vote. Imagine! Right after graduating from seminary and being asked to take the reins of a good-sized church with a parsonage. Not only that, but the parsonage had an air conditioner in one of the windows. Pretty heady stuff for a new grad living above a garage in an apartment with no air, no insulation and a black roof for the Texas sun to beat down on. Upon visiting an older widow on a Sunday afternoon, she informed me that I would, indeed, not be their next pastor. This information did jolt me, so I enquired as to why. She informed me that there were many members who did not regularly attend but who would show up at the meeting, having never heard me, to vote "no." Her response to my next natural question, concerning a reason, indicated that my graduation from Dallas Theological Seminary would preclude any hope of acceptance. She must have been prophetic, or at least very knowledgeable. When the meeting was over, the elders came out in tears and informed me that my friendly elderly lady had been correct. As I have come upon at least a modicum of wisdom and looked back upon that disappointment, I have seen this as God's care and leading in my life. The church would not have been a good fit, and a ministry there would have led to frustration and disappointment.

While I was at seminary, a new pastor, Dave Irwin, came to Calvary, Woodbridge. He set up visits for me to three churches which were looking for a pastor. One of them had called someone in the interim and the next one wanted me to come. This invitation was delivered after the evening service the day I preached. They offered me fifty dollars a week plus an apartment in the church. When I demurred, wondering if I could live on fifty dollars a week, they quickly suggested that I wouldn't need to, as my wife could drive a school bus. After giving my answer, I hurried to my car and headed toward anywhere else.

The third church was in Pembroke, Ontario. There I was scheduled for two Sundays and the week between. They were very responsive—or perhaps desperate—and I shortly received a letter inviting me to become their next pastor. I was awarded the princely sum of $120 a week. This accounted for about fifty per cent of the church's income. So, it was time to pack up all our worldly goods and head north from Texas and back to familiar surroundings. We enjoyed the ministry there, although I am not sure that Detra has ever been warm since we left Dallas.

Shortly after arriving, a woman in the congregation commented that she hoped I would stay a while, as they had had some short-term pastors. As it turned out, she got her wish. We were there almost ten years. During that period, the church began to grow modestly, and our family did as well by the arrival of three sons.

When I arrived, I found several issues that needed to be dealt with. To start with, outgoing expenses exceeded income. I began driving a school bus on the side and committed my salary to the church. I did this for a couple of years until I had an accident. The bus owner informed me that it was no longer the Lord's plan for me to continue. Well, he didn't put it just that way, but the result was the same. By then, however, the church was able to function without that income.

I also found out that the church had reneged on a debt to a local store. As soon as I could, I grabbed—not literally—the church treasurer and we paid a visit to the store in question. When we told him the purpose of our visit he replied, "Oh I wrote that off long ago." We suggested he write it back on until we paid every farthing, which we did. It did not occur to me at the time, but in a small city the businessmen all know and talk with one another. It was years before I realized what a difference that had made for the reputation of the church in the city.

Starting my ministry there was a little like being tossed into the deep end with no lessons. I had learned the Bible, Greek, Hebrew and much more; the thing I must have missed was how to lead a church. When I started, I had to speak five times a week—adult Bible class, morning service, evening service, Wednesday evening prayer meeting and Friday night youth. They must have been a patient congregation. As the church began to bear more fruit, we were faced with the need to do something about the building. The church was meeting in an old mansion built by the founder of the city. By the time I arrived, the furnace was gas. Previous pastors had lived upstairs with the necessity of getting up in the middle of winter nights to feed coal to the monster in the basement. There was also a second stove down in the depths to heat water for the baptistry. There was a rather ingenious system of piping circulating the water. The temperature was not exactly uniform from time to time. Some may have wanted to just stay in and relax like a bath—others not so much.

It was during the early years at Calvary Pembroke that I met and soon became friends with Roy Lawson. He left as pastor of Central Baptist London to serve with the Fellowship Baptist Young People's Association (FBYPA) as the Fellowship youth director. That friendship lasted until his entrance to the Lord's presence decades later. Roy's mentoring strengthened my ministry and opened doors of service that blessed me in many ways.

Doug & Detra Blair

While in Pembroke, a phone call came through that I was not prepared to receive. When I answered, a woman suggested that while I did not know her, I would know of her brother. She had reason for assuming that. Her brother was in our local jail literally charged with an axe murder. He had killed his girlfriend's mother and six-year-old brother. She wanted me to visit and share the gospel with him. Perhaps one might understand my reluctance. I was somewhat encouraged when I went to the jail and observed that the woman ahead of me visiting her boyfriend was separated from him by a bar far enough away that they could not reach each other. My encouragement dissipated very quickly when they brought him out into a side room and then invited me in. Then, they went out, shutting the door behind the guard. It turns out that pastors and lawyers visit unsupervised—yikes! Nonetheless, he was very calm, and in due course he accepted the Lord. Although forgiven by the Lord, he was not by other inmates. Women and children are considered off limits by other prisoners—and they ended his life not long after his arrival at Kingston Penitentiary.

The church building continued to be an issue and wasn't getting better or bigger. We had a company come in and design an addition to our present building. I was ready to proceed, but the deacons were not on board. This was a difficult decision to accept. However, as it turned out, it was from the Lord. A year later we had bought another property of several acres from some nuns and sold our old building, preparing to build anew. This provided a much more lasting solution. The new facility had the potential to handle close to 500 in two services.

Early in my ministry in Pembroke, I was asked to serve on the board of what was then known as the FBYPA. The ministry was the youth work of the Fellowship but was independently operated. FBYPA also owned Muskoka Baptist Conference at the time. As time went on, FBYPA was absorbed into the Fellowship and MBC became independent. My stint on that board led to other boards, including FEB Central, the Fellowship French board and the National Council of the Fellowship. Board ministry became one of my great joys. At one point, I was chairing two Fellowship boards, Heritage College and Seminary as well as Pregnancy Care Canada.

During my years at Pembroke, I ran into a friend from university at a conference with whom I had lost contact. He invited me to speak at a summer Sunday night Bible conference at his church on Long Island. We continued visiting and preaching there annually for several decades. When he passed away, I lost a friendship that had lasted over fifty years.

It was during our time in Pembroke that the Lord blessed us with three boys. Fifty years later, they are still a blessing to us. Having lived in rental accommodation all our married lives, Detra and the boys were happy to move into the house we had just built next to a small river. However, that joy did not last long. The month after I finished the landscaping, I had a series of life-changing conversations.

In 1978, I was contacted by the Fellowship and asked to chat with Lambert Baptist of Temple, Sarnia. Lambert was chair of what was at that time the home mission board of the Fellowship, charged with planting new churches. After meeting with Temple and the home mission board, I was called to plant a church in the east end of Sarnia. Having accepted the call, Detra and I gathered our belongings and the kids and headed all the way from the eastern border of Ontario with Quebec to the western border with the USA. Both Detra and the boys, who were between four and seven, came willingly to a new challenge.

And a challenge it was! Within the month of moving, we began services at a local high school. Between Temple sending people and a few from a recently-closed church just outside the city, we began with a core group of about twenty-five the first Sunday. Before long, a number of those had left town or moved on. Growth was somewhat slow and steady for the first years. We were able to maintain a very positive relationship with the school. But after ten years, we had grown enough that we could move toward a building of our own. We had been searching for property for some time when Ontario Housing changed their priorities and placed a corner three-acre lot up for sale. God gave us a willingness to work and give akin to the tabernacle in the Bible. After constructing the new building, largely built with our own hands, we worshipped God with much excitement.

There came a point when I began to realize that if we kept on doing what we had always been doing, we would get diminishing returns on our labour. I was, by nature, very conservative and not a huge change agent, but my desire for greater fruitfulness finally overcame my aversion to change. I adapted our worship style in an effort to reach a younger audience. Unfortunately for me, I wasn't very good at it and projection technology was not well advanced. To balance that shortcoming, I suppose, it was very expensive.

But God can make a way. A friend of mine called me looking for a place for a worship pastor from his youth group who had recently graduated from Heritage College. We had no money for another pastor, but the Lord knew that. The previous week a man from Temple had called me enquiring if I knew anyone looking for work. So it was that Scott Lewis came to us on a volunteer basis. The change in worship style did lead to an exodus of around 100 people in the first year. Nonetheless, the church did not shrink. Then it began to grow strongly. Within a few years we were ministering to close to 500 people, although they did not necessarily all show up together. Scott was a great blessing to the ministry and served around thirteen years with us. Thus, it was not long before we added a part-time counsellor (Cheryl Bourgeois), followed by a youth pastor (Eric Veen) and then a children's pastor (Steve Bourque).

When Scott left to plant another church, we looked for an associate. The Lord led us to Tim Cressman and his wife Val. As my age rolled up to seventy, we began a succession process. The church accepted Tim Cressman as their pastor, and he became associate senior pastor. The next year we reversed rolls, and the following year I retired.

In retirement, I had the joy of being an interim pastor in several churches. These came in sizes small to north of 1,000. Each one was unique, and they were all a joyful experience. Detra quickly found a ministry of prayer and encouragement in each of the churches we served in this way.

Looking back on the ministries the Lord has given me, I am truly amazed at the privileges my Lord has given me. Detra and I got to travel broadly, preaching and teaching. We took several trips to Nicaragua to teach pastors and their wives. We ministered to missionaries of the Fellowship gathered in France. One trip that was a highlight was an opportunity to minister to pastoral couples in Russia. We had the joy of ministering to our French family at the AEBEQ pastorale, where I preached in French for the first time.

I believe that there is no greater issue in our day than that of life itself. That passion grew through the ministry of Detra, who served at our local Pregnancy Care Centre for about twenty years. For most of those years, she was the executive director. In due course. she was asked to serve on the national board of what is now known as Pregnancy Care Canada (PCC). Her response was a bit of a takeoff on Isaiah. She said, "Behold, here am I. Send him." That began service on the board. I continue to have the joy of chairing that board into my eighties.

Early in my ministry, I promised the Lord that I would never seek a position, but that if he opened the door, I would walk through it. Having served two churches and more than half a dozen boards, I still see God's hand over me in grace and mercy.

Submitted by Rev. Doug Blair

5 /

Dr. Rick Buck

I grew up in a loving home in the Simcoe/Waterford area of Ontario. My parents, Bob and Reta Buck, had also grown up in the area and my dad had taken over the family business, CW Buck and Sons Construction. In those days, my dad worked hard and partied hard. My mom was a socialite and loved to entertain. They were wonderful parents, but they were not believers and did not have much to do with God, even though they had both gone to church when they were young. For them, Saturday nights were usually spent partying with friends. So, while my parents were recovering on Sunday mornings, they sent me on a church bus to the Waterford Baptist Church Sunday school. That is where I first heard the good news of Jesus Christ from a Sunday school teacher: a plumber named Wayne Duesling. He shared with us the simple love story of the Bible. I listened, but it would be some time before I really appreciated all that was taught to me on those Sunday mornings. God planted the seed of his truth in my life as a young boy, but it wouldn't be until years later that the harvest came.

As I got older, sports became my main passion. The true god of my life during my teenage years was myself. The important things to me were my friends, my popularity and my performance—life revolved around me. I was very proud and puffed up. My older brother and sister got into quite a bit of trouble, and I prided myself on being the "good kid." I assure you, I had quite a list of sins, but in my mind, next to my brother and sister, I looked like an angel! During my high school years, I had success in both track and hockey, which further led to an inflated sense of self. And although I was mistaken in my estimation of my own abilities, I see how even then, God used my dedication to my sports to keep me from some of the pitfalls my brother found himself in, like alcohol and drug use.

It was during my early teens that my mom became a Christian. What a radical change God made in her life! She accepted the Lord through a Billy Graham crusade on TV, and though for the first year of her new-found faith she kept it all to herself, God began to change her from the inside out. When she was ready to tell the world she was a believer, she was on fire, sharing with her family and others about Jesus. We were all amazed, but also slightly irritated by her passion for God. Mom would repeatedly come into my room on Sunday mornings to wake me up to get me to go to church with her. In typical teenage fashion, I would often pretend I was still asleep! But sometimes, because I loved my mom and felt sorry for her, I would go with her. On the one hand I hated being there, but on the other hand I was intrigued. Our home had been a place of discord—but things were changing. What struck me most was the new peace and joy my mom had. I realize now that if Christ had not come into my mom's life, my parents' marriage or our family may not have survived. It was primarily this change in my mom's life that, years later, resulted in my dad's conversion; I would have the privilege of baptizing him.

About this time, a lady from Simcoe Bible Church invited me to their youth group. I said, "No," but she wouldn't give up asking. Finally, I said, "Yes," mostly just to get her to stop calling! At that time my hair was down to my shoulders, and I only wore T-shirts and jeans, and this was a conservative church. I definitely stood out among the kids there! But strangely, I was both repelled by and drawn to this group at the same time. God was speaking to me, and the truths of my Sunday school days were coming back as I listened to the Bible teaching. Finally, one Sunday as I was sitting in church listening to God's Word being preached, I realized that I wasn't "good" after all. My problem was my pride. I thought I was too good to really need to repent. But God was showing me my sin and that religion isn't what God wants—he wants a forever relationship, totally based on his grace and mercy in Jesus Christ. So as best as I knew how, while the pastor was preaching, I surrendered my life to Jesus Christ and told God that whatever he wanted to do with my life, I would be willing to do. I was just turning fifteen and had no idea what that would mean for the rest of my life.

Not long after that, someone from the church asked me if I would be willing to share my story with the congregation. I had told God I would be willing to do anything, but that was the one thing I hadn't really considered—nothing made me more nervous than standing up in front of people! But to keep my promise to God, and with total dependence on him, I experienced for the first time being helped and enabled to speak and point others to the greatness and goodness of Jesus Christ. It would be the beginning of learning how to let God push me outside my comfort zone and use me in ways I couldn't have conceived of. I was baptized a few months later.

In those early years as a Christian, even as a teenager, I learned the importance of feeding deeply on the Word of God to grow as a Christian. I couldn't get enough of the Bible and would listen to Christian radio programs every morning before school. I also began to realize that sports could not be the ruling passion of my life and began to pray about what the Lord would have me do. God began to put a desire in my heart to serve him in some way.

God also taught me some difficult but valuable lessons early on. The church where I became a Christian ended up in conflict over the pastor who had meant so much to me. That pastor left the church and ultimately his faith altogether. I was confused and conflicted. By this time, I had this growing passion to serve God and thought that maybe God was calling me into full-time ministry. But this church fight and the pastor's actions were disillusioning and I started to question everything. God, however, used this time as incredible preparation, helping me to understand the Christian life better. I came to realize that Christians are people of grace, and are only as good as their strong look to Christ. God reminded me to get my eyes off others and to keep them on him. At the end of the day, I will only answer for my life before God. What a valuable lesson the Lord allowed me to learn early on.

As difficult as that time was in my life as a new believer, I can see the many ways God used it to prepare me for life and ministry. Through that time, the Lord even strengthened my calling to serve him, and so, after high school, I enrolled in London Baptist Bible College (now Heritage) to begin to train for ministry. I was so blessed to have an internship at my home church during these years. I learned so many things, not only from my courses and my professors at school, like Dr. Dave Barker who really became a mentor for me, but also from Pastor Bob Snell who had recently come to Emmanuel Bible Church and was willing to work with this young, rough-around-the-edges student. God taught me so much during those years of learning and serving.

Perhaps the most valuable gift God gave me during those years was my wife! I met Jo in my final year of Bible college, and we married the following year while I was in seminary. Jo had graduated from Central Baptist Seminary (now Heritage) with her BRE and was working at Churchill Heights Baptist Church as Pastor Ian Bowie's assistant. She had a desire and passion for ministry, and we soon discovered that the Lord had led us together to serve him side by side. She and I have often joked that we were the first merger of the two schools (CBS and LBBC/LBS) that would ultimately become one (Heritage)! We spent our first year of married life at Dallas Theological Seminary for one year of graduate studies. We returned to Canada and I finished my Master's degree back at London Baptist Seminary, where I could resume my internship at Emmanuel in Simcoe.

Jo had grown up at Emmanuel Baptist Church in Barrie. Her parents, Ross and Evelyn Thompson, became members at Emmanuel in 1950, and were involved in many aspects of ministry in the church. They were also very involved at Muskoka Bible Centre, and over the years Jo's dad served on the board, and her mom served as chair of the women's committee in the early years of women's conferences. Their faithfulness in serving and giving was a great example to me who hadn't grown up in the church.

Jo is my best friend and my greatest counsellor in ministry; we have served God together for these past thirty-seven years. Jo has worked alongside me in all areas of my ministry but has also had her own calling in ministry to women, especially through leading Bible studies. She has a gift for words and editing, and used to like to remind people that my sermons would have been much longer if she hadn't helped me take out the extraneous parts! Her favourite saying to me is "Less is more!" I am so grateful for what God has allowed us to experience together in ministry as partners. There have been so many wonderful mountaintop moments in ministry, but we have experienced some very difficult moments, as well. Through all of these, God has been so gracious to

Jo & Rick Buck

us. We have also been blessed with two amazing children. Our son Jon, a realtor in the Orillia area, is married to Erica and they have three wonderful children: Eli, Everly and Eleanor. Our daughter Kristy is married to Brian Ramirez and they live and work as houseparents in Hershey, Pennsylvania, with their son Cohen and daughter Riley. I am overjoyed that my children and their spouses have authentic and deep relationships with Christ that are evident in their homes. We know it is not because of our parenting (we made lots of mistakes), but because of God's grace!

I was on staff at Emmanuel Bible Church in Simcoe all through my BTh and most of my MDiv years as an intern, but my first full-time ministry opportunity came when Calvary Baptist Church in Woodbridge invited me to come as their pastor. I was fresh out of seminary, and they really were taking a chance on this "young buck" just starting out. Our son Jon was just twenty months old, and we had lots to learn about life and ministry! Calvary had come through several challenging years, and we wondered if we had the wisdom or the experience to help them. But as I look back, I believe the Lord sent us there to be an aide to bring some healing and to begin a revitalization work. As the church began to grow, so too did our family; our daughter Kristy was born. During my time at Calvary, I developed as a pastor, learning much about ministry and being a leader. I am thankful to the Lord for the opportunity to walk alongside this church for a time. We made some important friendships there that remain to this day, and so it was a difficult decision to leave to go to Barrie six-and-a-half years later. In fact, when the leadership from Emmanuel asked if I would consider coming to be their lead pastor, I initially said, "No." But Jo and I continued to pray about God's will for us and for the Calvary church family, and when Emmanuel returned almost a year later to ask the same question, we recognized God was indeed leading us there. We had finished the work God had called us to do in Woodbridge and now the Lord would use someone else to continue that work. So, we packed up our young family and headed north to Barrie.

Our years at Emmanuel were fruitful and busy, and what a joy it was to serve there for almost twenty-four years. As lead pastor, my job was to preach the Word and shepherd the flock, which I loved doing. But I also knew that to be an effective and biblical church, we needed to empower the people to "do the work of ministry" and that it would take a team effort to do so. I had always believed in a "staff to grow" philosophy of ministry, and over the years God brought incredible men and women to be part of Emmanuel's ministry team. One of the earliest team members we added was Steve Paul. Steve and Cathy had been Emmanuel missionaries in Chad who had returned home, and what a wonderful addition Steve was to me as associate pastor for the remainder of my time at Emmanuel. Not long after Steve was brought on, we added another team member as pastor of outreach and evangelism: a retired principal, Ed Gray. Although Ed had not been a pastor before, he had a God-given gift of evangelism. His joy for sharing Christ was contagious, and through training and programs centred around evangelism, our people soon began sharing their faith. We began to look outward and not just inward as a church, and by God's grace we started to grow. In fact, it wasn't long until we went to two services, and even then, we were outgrowing our building. Some of it was transfer growth, as Barrie was also growing, and we welcomed newcomers to Emmanuel. But praise God, our church was also filling up with those who had been witnessed to and brought by our own people!

And so, we now had the joy and challenge of a church that needed more space. We were in a land-locked building in our present location, so we formed teams to explore our possibilities. In 2003, Emmanuel launched our Share the Vision Stewardship program—with the goal of raising $2.25 million over three years. It was a huge undertaking, but we each began to pray, "Lord, what do you want to do through me to accomplish your will here at Emmanuel?" As we prayed, the Lord led us to property on Salem Road in Barrie where we found land we could build on with room to spare, set on the outskirts of our city. And what a story of faith that land acquisition and building is! There were many times during this season of faith that, as leaders, we were on our knees asking for God's help and direction. It certainly wasn't all smooth sailing, but there were so many "God moments" on this journey, from the Lord changing the hearts of sellers, to providing another church to buy our old building, to miraculous provisions of money at just the right times. We acquired the land and started building in 2004 and, by God's grace, opened the doors at our new location in Fall 2005. Our prayer was that the Lord would use this new building for his purposes to win more to Christ and grow his church.

What a privilege it was to lead during this time of stretching and faith for the church family. God continued to bless in growth, not just in numbers, but more importantly in seeing peoples' lives changed. Over the years, we added many more staff members, all who had a great impact in ministry there. Although there are too many staff to mention, some of the pastors like Steve Paul, Dave Whitelaw, Jonathan Fitter and Jordan Wilcox, all who began with us on staff newly into ministry, have continued on to lead other churches. Josh Davy, who came on staff with me before I left, has stayed on to become lead pastor of Emmanuel presently. What a joy to be a part of their lives and ministries! We also had the opportunity to benefit from pastors like George Bell, Brian Baxter, Lance Johnson and Paul Kerr—all these men had years of ministry experience and agreed to join our staff, sharing their wisdom with the Emmanuel family. I personally benefitted from having these seasoned men of God serve alongside me in ministry.

It was also exciting to be part of the multiplication work God did through Emmanuel. By God's grace, Emmanuel Barrie became a multi-site congregation while I was there. We started Emmanuel Orillia and saw the beginnings of Emmanuel North Barrie (which began just after my departure). Watching God's people have the faith to launch out in these church plants has only increased the strength of God's people. I feel so blessed to have been part of these works.

Stretching myself to continue to learn and grow has always been important to me so, with the Emmanuel leadership's blessing early on in my time at the church, I began work on obtaining my Doctor of Ministry degree from Trinity Evangelical Divinity School in Deerfield, Illinois. My original plan to quickly complete the degree took a back seat to the priority of helping the church through the building program. But finally, after many years, I was thankful to finish my doctoral work, which focused on apologetics in preaching. I have since been privileged to use this training as an adjunct professor at Heritage Seminary.

Of course, there have also been very difficult times in the life of our church family, and for me personally as well. In 2018, after the sudden loss of my mother in August, our missionary family, the Blackburns, lost their daughter tragically in a car accident. That was a huge shock for our church family. Not long after that, one of our long-time church members, and a close personal friend of mine, Tony Bellavance, died suddenly in his sleep. Then, while we were walking with his family (our friends) through that, my father, who had been admitted to the hospital, had a sudden deterioration in his condition and passed away one week later. Five days after that, our daughter-in-law's father passed away from cancer (her mother had died suddenly three years earlier). I spoke at each of these funerals. These were four months we definitely were not prepared for. We were reeling in grief. Was God still good? Absolutely. But we needed some time. So, graciously, the Emmanuel family gave us a few months to heal and recover. In time God helped us to settle our hearts, find our joy in his peace and return to ministry ready for what God had for us next.

A year later, I was approached by FEB Central to consider coming on staff as their regional director, overseeing the staff who support our almost 300 Fellowship churches in Ontario and English-speaking Quebec. My first thought, again, was to say, "No," but I agreed to pray about it. And so, Jo and I took the next number of months to talk and pray. We had no intention of leaving Emmanuel. It was our home, and we loved the people and being on staff. But as we committed ourselves to following God's lead, the Lord impressed upon each of us that this was the step he was asking us to take. This was the hardest decision we had to make in ministry, but in Fall 2019, I informed the Emmanuel board of my decision, and in January 2020, we told the congregation that God was calling us into a new role. It was bittersweet. Bitter, because we loved serving alongside this family of believers. But sweet, because my new role with FEB Central would allow me to remain in the area, so Emmanuel would still be home for us. Although I spend many Sundays speaking in other churches, we love to still be part of this great family. What a gift from God it was to be given the role of leading Emmanuel for so many years! Jo and I are forever grateful for the ministry team and leaders who supported us so well for so long.

These last five years since transitioning from Emmanuel have been both a mix of joy and sorrow. In Spring 2020, I launched out to join the FEB Central team—just as the COVID-19 pandemic began sweeping across the world. It was a challenge, but also a privilege to serve our group of churches during this difficult time. As we came through the rough initial days of being unable to meet together, we were finally able to gather as a group of pastors at our annual Pastors' Conference in 2022—and what a joy that was to all be together finally! Unfortunately, what followed was many of our men getting COVID-19, myself included. For me, this resulted in infections and complications that I never could have imagined. I spent the next two years seeing doctors and specialists, trying to find an answer for the crazy variety of symptoms I was experiencing. I was unable to travel, so I took a medical leave from work, but in the end had to resign from my position. Along with the physical struggle, came a mental and spiritual struggle that I hadn't known up to this point in my life. *Why was this happening? Who was I if I could no longer be a pastor or in ministry?* It was a very long two years. I was trying to get answers and solutions for my body, while also trying to come to terms with what God was teaching me through this time. I wrestled with my sense of worth and identity, but God used this experience to remind me that the only identity I needed was that I was his child through faith in Christ. If God chose to use me further in ministry, that was up to him. It was a struggle with God I didn't know I needed. I praise him that he has restored me physically now, and although I may not be all that I used to be health-wise, he has allowed me to return to serving him by serving his church in a new role as a director of leadership advancement for FEB Central. I am so grateful for the FEB Central team who supported me so well those years and then welcomed me back. I am also very thankful those years of physical challenges are over, and I am again able to lead and encourage other pastors in their ministries. But I pray I never forget the lessons God impressed on me in that desert season in my life.

From a prideful kid from Simcoe to a "still in progress" pastor to pastors, my life story is evidence of God's amazing grace. And perhaps the greatest lesson I have learned is that, while it is a privilege to serve him, the most important thing remains my own relationship with my Saviour and Lord. Being a pastor has been my calling, but my true identity is as a follower of Jesus Christ. To God be the glory.

Submitted by Dr. Rick Buck

6 /

Rev. Jack Chen

Born to Buddhist parents in India, Jack Chen found himself asking deep spiritual questions about life, sin, death and God, very early in life. Since neither his mom nor dad had the answers to these questions, they discouraged any further enquiry.

But God is good. Since his parents knew little or no English, they sent him to learn English at the Sunday school of the historic Carey Baptist Church. The school, founded by the famous missionary William Carey, was conveniently just 200 yards away from the family's home. Jack definitely learned English, but more than that he learned the answers to his spiritual questions. At the age of thirteen, Jack discovered and joyfully received Christ as his personal Saviour, much to the chagrin of his parents.

Here, in his own words, are the "chapters" of Jack's eventful life.

Chapter 1: 1949–1976

When Dad lost his carpentry business, I had to drop out of school and began an apprenticeship to train as an electrical technician. I was only seventeen years old at the time. It was during this training that a dangerous "accident" happened. A 440-volt explosion caused by a careless worker gave me temporary blindness. Out of this accident, however, I felt God's call to proclaim the glorious gospel to the lost millions—but to *which* nation, I was not certain at this point.

Upon completing a two-year diploma course in theology at Calcutta Bible College, I answered God's call to be a full-time minister as the city director of Calcutta Youth For Christ. I could not have asked for a better introduction to full-time ministry. Working with the youth of the great city of Calcutta (now known as Kolkata), I honed my skills in leading many young people to the Lord.

Some of my exploits with Calcutta Youth for Christ include leading a delegation of 120 teenage boys and girls from Calcutta and Bangladesh to a youth convention in South India—requiring a thirty-six-hour train journey one way. Our city came away with the top prizes in vocal solos, choir, Bible quiz and preaching, beating top contenders from four other major cities—Bombay, Delhi, Madras and Bangalore.

I conducted five weekly Bible Clubs in four Christian schools and in a home that welcomed me with open arms. We taught Christian songs and shared the story of Jesus. Little did I know the impact of this experience would follow me to Canada much later in life.

Along with a musical group called The Forerunners (consisting of two guitarists, a drummer, a pianist and four vocalists), we toured two major cities, Bombay and Pune. I preached my first sermon in the Hindi language on the streets in front of the Gateway to India in Bombay. A hilarious moment was when I ran out of theological vocabulary in Hindi at which points the audience provided the words—my first interactive sermon!

On a monthly basis, we held monthly youth rallies in the city, featuring top musical groups and an innovative dance troupe who portrayed the gospel story. Many of these rallies were packed out with over 400 young people. During this time, two of my four siblings accepted Christ, and still follow him to this day.

The miracle in this chapter of my life was God's provision of a future life partner through yet another "accident"! On our way back from the youth convention in 1972, a railway worker accidentally detached our railway coach from the main train. This led to a twelve-hour wait in the hot summer sun in a midway railway station. It was during that twelve hour wait that I got to know the 120 delegates better, and got introduced to Lorraine. She said, "Yes," when I proposed to her five years down the road. With God there are no accidents.

While this stint with Calcutta Youth For Christ came to an end in 1976 with much sadness, God was preparing another door.

Chapter 2: 1977–1989

A wonderful thing happened in January 1977. I married the love of my life, Lorraine Chea, and began a new journey together with her that would last for forty blissful and fruitful years, till the Lord called her home in 2017. God blessed us with three wonderful kids: Jim, Karen and Kathryn.

Life is full of surprises. Unknown to me, my teaching and evangelistic outreach with the youth of Calcutta had caught the attention of Rev. William Peck, the American principal of Calcutta Bible College. In February 1977, he invited me to join the full-time teaching staff at the college. To appreciate the challenge of this role, one must consider lessons were prepared in a pre-computer age, when research was limited to actual paper tomes.

There were many highlights of this chapter of my life at the Calcutta Bible College. I taught a variety of challenging topics like personal evangelism, biblical archaeology and geography, homiletics and discipleship. On weekends, I lead teams of Bible college students in practical hands-on ministry work among village churches. This work included organizing tract distribution in key places in the city, such as the railway stations. Here, millions of people would come by train, from distant villages and towns, into the Calcutta each day for their jobs.

Many personal discipling relationships grew, along with a few key "Timothys." In the midst of a busy teaching schedule, this gave enduring results and satisfaction. A recent reunion of some of my former students in 2024 revealed the extent of the impact these disciples have made since graduating from Bible college. Churches have been planted, missions agencies formed and the gospel has been taken to such places near and as far as Nepal, Thailand and Myanmar (formerly Burma).

I was involved in missions during this time. John Thomas, my former Bible college teacher, invited me to be his right hand and the vice chairman of a fantastic missions organization he started in 1976. The JKPS was a national organization that proclaimed the gospel and planted churches in the 44,000 villages of West Bengal. I was involved with other cross-cultural ministries throughout the summer. I travelled with teams of students in fourteen of the twenty-nine states of India, including Jammu, Kashmir, Punjab, Orissa, Manipur, Nagaland and Nepal. Much fruit happened as the students sang and shared their testimonies. Afterward, many from the churches we visited applied to come for study at the Bible college.

The miracle in this chapter of life was the "chance meeting" with Warren Myers, a visiting worshipper at Carey Baptist Church, who was on staff with the Navigators based in Singapore. Within a few minutes of being introduced, Warren asked me if I had ever been discipled. You can imagine my great delight that, when I said no one had intentionally discipled me, he personally offered to teach and disciple me so that I would be prepared to disciple others. This chance meeting resulted in a lifelong discipline of living as a focused disciple of Christ, "making and multiplying" disciples. There are no coincidences or chances with our God, just divine appointments.

In August 1989, this chapter came to a close as God led my family and me to emigrate to Canada at the age of forty. This, too, was a divine appointment, as the next chapter of my life deepened my following of God's leading in my life.

Chapter 3: 1989–2008

During a visit to Toronto to see my parents in 1987, a Bible college classmate invited me to preach at her Chinese language congregation, Banfield Memorial Church. That speaking engagement led to an invitation to return to Toronto as the senior pastor of that congregation. Yet again another chance event led to a life changing decision. In 1989, my wife Lorraine and I both resigned from our respective jobs and set out for Canada with our three young children, Jim twelve years old, Karen nine years old and Kathryn three years old, to begin a new chapter in our lives.

Life in a new country was quite the challenge and yet, with the perspective of time, it amuses me as I see quite a few very interesting things. With Lorraine's experience in shorthand and her typewriter speed, she landed a job almost immediately with Sun Life Insurance where she worked till 2008. I daresay not many readers today know how typewriter speed could land you a job, or even what shorthand is! I had a slight setback, however.

Since our immigration process took nearly eighteen months, the Chinese congregation that invited me to be their pastor ceased to exist. Many of its members could not wait, and drifted away to other established churches. This meant I had to look for a job. No church seemed to have an opening for an immigrant pastor fresh off the boat!

Jack Chen

Overcoming challenges as new immigrants toughened us in ways we could not imagine. The first obstacle was finding a way to attend church on Sundays. Since we did not have a car, and the only church we knew was the one that had extended an invitation for us to come to Canada, it took us two hours one way by two different public buses. We would leave the house at 8 a.m. for a 10 a.m. service and be back at 2 p.m. Imagine doing this with three young children at the ages of twelve, nine and three years old! Little did we realize, God was preparing us for the next phase.

On a late Wednesday afternoon in 1990, a friend called to ask me if I was ready to preach that very Sunday. Their senior pastor had left quite suddenly and moved away to the USA. Following that Sunday's speaking engagement, Gormley Missionary Church called me to be their interim pastor until a full-time pastor could be found.

Two very exciting events happened as a result of the engagement at Gormley. First, a couple living common-law and attending the church felt convicted by a sermon on Christian marriage and family and decided to legalize their relationship by getting married. Second, a conversation with one of the elders led to an opportunity to plant a new church in Pickering, 46 kms to the east. Thus began three years of serving as the bi-vocational founding pastor of Pickering Missionary Church, meeting in Vaughan Willard Public School.

The year 1994 was one of pause. Like a modern day Job, suffering one setback after another, that year I received two "pink slips" terminating my day job at Sun Life Insurance and ending my pastoral role at Pickering

Missionary Church. Psalm 27:23 gave much comfort in that not only does God order the steps of man, but he also orders the pauses. That God was not done with us became as clear as sunlight flooding through a dark tunnel. In August of that year, while attending Churchill Heights Baptist Church (now known as Morningstar Christian Fellowship), the senior pastor John Mahaffey interviewed me over lunch and immediately extended an invitation to join him on staff at the church. He was particularly interested in my experience of launching and running small groups for Bible study. The elders confirmed that decision and in December 1994, I began my ministry at Churchill Heights as the pastor for discipleship ministries. Several highlights stand out during this ministry. The first was the challenge to start in-home Bible study groups that we called, Connections. Beginning with six groups in a church of 450 congregants, God blessed and multiplied the ministry to raise up thirty-two vibrant and growing Connections Groups by 2008.

On May 1, 2000, I had the joy of leading my eighty-six-year-old Buddhist father to Christ! This was an answer to a prayer for my parents' salvation, one I had had been praying for thirty years. Mom accepted the Lord twelve years later in 2012. God miraculously entered her life when the porcelain idol she had worshipped all her life suddenly exploded into smithereens. She witnessed this with her own eyes, even as she was bowing before it in her bedroom. She never replaced that idol and became a follower of Christ till the very end.

Another highlight during this chapter of life was when our oldest son Jim answered God's call upon his life. In 1996, after a short-term ministry trip to India with SIM, he enrolled in Bible college and subsequently went on to pastoral ministry.

The miracle in this chapter is receiving yet another call from God signalling change. The Lord had grown Morningstar Church to 1,150 regular attenders. After twenty-six years of fruitful ministry, my wife and I departed yet again for a fresh field of ministry in answer to God's call. In 2007, during a visit back to Kolkata, India, the deacons of my home church, Carey Baptist Church, extended an invitation to return as their senior pastor. This historic church had dwindled down to less than sixty members. This call was a privilege and a great challenge.

Chapter 4: 2009–present

In December 2008, my wife Lorraine and I landed back at Carey Baptist

Church. As I, the new senior pastor approached the front door, I saw emblazoned across it the famous motto of William Carey:

EXPECT GREAT THINGS FROM GOD
ATTEMPT GREAT THINGS FOR GOD

This was, at once, welcoming and daunting, as we stepped on to hallowed ground where the Serampore Trio, the mighty saints of God had trod before us.

The very first task we faced was to help the church celebrate its 200th anniversary, happening hardly two weeks after we landed. By God's grace, the event was well-attended, including the guest speaker, Jack Hannah from Toronto. Even though he was recovering from a heart attack just three weeks before, Jack left for Kolkata and blessed our church.

The task ahead of us was formidable, and seemed like something that both Nehemiah and Ezra would have done in Jerusalem, rebuilding both the walls of Jerusalem and the temple. In our case, the walls were the actual physical walls on four sides of the campus which were crumbling. This posed a threat to life on the streets outside should a collapse occur. The constant refrain I heard from the deacons was, "We don't have the money to do it." To me, that refrain was as loud as a clarion call to trust the Lord. We did, and the Lord provided. The cumulative cost of rebuilding the walls was over 300,000 rupees (about CDN $5,172 at the time)—money the church did not have. It was an opportunity to challenge this small church to trust the Lord to provide the much needed funds, and he did.

Eventually, giving literally went through the roof. When we arrived, the average offerings were around 25,000 rupees a month. Soon God blessed us with givings that amounted to an average of 25,000 rupees per week. One especially touching gift of 44,000 rupees came from a young man. He had promised God he would give his first month's salary to the Lord when he answered his prayer for a job with IBM.

Rebuilding a "temple of praise" involved bringing up the very attendance of the membership to a respectable size. In this regard, I am grateful for the wise counsel of my friend, Pastor Booshanaraj Thomas. He was the very first Indian national pastor of Carey Baptist Church. In an email of congratulations on my new role as pastor he said, "Jack, preach the Word of God and the people will come." I did, and the people came in droves. Church attendance grew to an average weekly of 150 worshippers. On some Sundays, we had to put in additional chairs along the aisles and back rows, totalling over 200 people in attendance!

The church had two other congregations for Hindi and Bengali speakers, with pastors speaking their own language. By God's grace, these congregations also grew rapidly. The Hindi service outstripped the English congregation in size. Sunday school attendance grew as well, as we invited children from the neighbourhood, including the slums. We also started an adult Sunday school class. Soon, baptisms were taking place and new members were added to the rolls of the church.

We also revived the church's Christmas Day dinner party. Many of the new believers were the only Christians in their homes and had no celebrations of their own. The church Christmas dinner became their family event. In 2008, only thirty attended our first Christmas dinner. In our final year, in December 2013, we sold over 300 tickets and had to have two pastors' wives stand at the gate to turn away non ticketholders! One government employee tried to bulldoze his way in by flashing his government ID.

The church was involved in outreach and missions as well. The annual English and Hindi language Vacation Bible Schools in the month of May together attracted over 500 children, mostly from non-Christian homes in the neighbourhood. In 2013, a new national couple, Tapan and Rina, were adopted as our very own missionaries. They ministered to children in Rupamari village in the Sundarbans area near the seashore. This was Carey Baptist Church's first missionaries since the last missionary, George David, was appointed to the Andaman Islands in 1955!

Fifty-eight years since the last missionary was sent out, a weekly morning devotional half hour was started on the factory premises of FREESET, an NGO ministering to sex workers. These women were given jobs in the factory making jute bags for export. The only condition was that they would voluntarily leave the sex trade. This led to a monthly Saturday morning worship at the church for these women. The first Saturday morning service was packed with nearly 200 attending! More than forty of these dear ladies accepted Christ as their Saviour, over the five years that we were at Carey Church.

As a returning alumni of Calcutta Bible College, I was invited to teach the homiletics class. This I thoroughly enjoyed, because now my lessons were enriched by many years of preaching experience in two contexts, that of North America and India. I was also involved in starting statewide

training for village pastors, lay leaders, evangelists and church planters in the Bengali language. By God's grace, a movement was started.
Between 2009 and 2014, a first cohort of fifty men and women were
trained. From 2014 to 2019, a second cohort of 155 people were trained.
From 2023 to 2024, over 1,500 people went through a disciple-making
training program.

If there are two things I attribute any of my success to, it would be the
Lord himself and my dear wife, Lorraine. She discovered her niche in
service by truly being a partner ("helpmate" in KJV language) with me
in all my ministerial endeavours. From the early Youth For Christ days,
through Calcutta Bible College, onward to Canada in church planting,
Morningstar, and then, finally back to India, she has been faithful. It was
at Carey Baptist Church she discovered yet another facet of her capa-
bility as the wife of the senior pastor. She became the church's beloved
worship leader, the "aunty" to countless kids in the congregation and the
"mother" to homesick seminary students from out of town studying in
Calcutta. Most importantly, she stood with me through all the challenges
of pastoring in an environment that was at once familiar and strange. It
was familiar, because we grew up in this church, and strange because
we returned to a vastly changed situation where people were so different
from what we knew nearly twenty years earlier when we had left India.

In 2012, my wife Lorraine started a slums project called KHRIS (Kolkata
Hope Rising In the Slums) whereby we cared for over a dozen kids from
the slums. These children had dropped out of school, due to their inability to pay school fees. We helped them complete their education and
enrolled them in career courses. Four of them completed their BAs, two
are enrolled in their MA course and seven are gainfully employed, including two girls who got employment at the Marriott, a five star hotel.

In 2017, personal tragedy struck when my wife Lorraine was diagnosed
with kidney cancer, which went on to claim her life. In the midst of personal grief, came victory and hope, as friends and relatives packed out the
church building of Morningstar Christian Fellowship for the celebration
of her life. Their outpouring of love through donations in lieu of flowers
proved sufficient to move six families out of the slums into apartments.

Throughout my ministry, my family has given me so much support
and encouragement. It is with their support that I have been able to
continue the work God has called me to. My son Jim is married to Bea
and they have a fourteen-year-old son Liam now studying in grade 9. Jim

has been a youth pastor since he graduated from Bible college in 2000. He currently serves as an associate pastor at Forestbrook Community Church in Ajax. My daughter, Karen, is an IT specialist with Sun Life Insurance. Kathryn, my youngest, is a schoolteacher along with her husband Richard. They have a son Ethan, who is ten years old, and a daughter Bethany, who is seven years old.

Conclusion

A popular old hymn goes, "All the way my Saviour leads me," which echoes what Isaiah wrote, "Your ears will hear a word behind you, saying, 'This is the way, walk in it,' whenever you turn to the right or to the left" (Isaiah 30:21 NASB).

While God is speaking to us all the time, we must learn to attune our ears to *hear* his voice in the midst of all the deafening cacophony of a world chasing its own unholy grail of materialism and pleasure. My prayer is that the Lord will help me constantly adjust my sails to catch the wind of the Holy Spirit wherever he blows. As the Scottish reformer John Knox famously cried, "Give me Scotland, or I die." My prayer is, "Lord give me *Bengal*, before I die." As Jesus himself said, "We must carry out the works of Him who sent Me as long as it is day; night is coming, when no one can work" (John 9:4). The final chapter of my life will be written by those who follow after.

Submitted by Rev. Jack Chen

7 /

Rev. Dennis Bruce Christensen

I was born into a godly home to parents who loved the Lord and served faithfully in the local church. I was the third of four boys. My father had an abattoir and meat market, and so I learned the trade at a young age. I recall grinding hamburger when I was six, and by the age of twelve was able to cut up a whole carcass of beef. My father also owned a freezer locker plant, which had over 400 rental units. This was in the days before there were freezers. All that to say, these early lessons taught us how to deal with the public and to remember people's names.

I attended Hammond Elementary and then graduated from Maple Ridge Senior High School. At school, I was a good athlete, excelling in soccer, basketball, volleyball and baseball. The only reason I did not play hockey was that there were no ice rinks to play on.

I accepted the Lord at the age of six at an after school Good News Club, and was baptized a short time later. I grew up attending Burnett Fellowship Church in Maple Ridge, BC. Even though baptized at a young age, it was my line drawn in the sand and a stake that kept me through my teenage years.

When I turned sixteen, I was elected president of our church youth group. I had zero experience at leading, but our group was small, so surely it couldn't be that hard. I led our youth for seven years, and what started out as a handful turned into a significant group of young people. It was here that I met my future wife (we dated for almost seven years). Our youth became very active in outreach and various ministries. The group led services in seniors homes, in hospitals and in our own church. The group did all kinds of activities from sports to hiking, excursions, Stanley Park and Youth for Christ events. It was an exciting time for the youth at Burnett. We had a great group of leaders.

After graduation, I worked at an abattoir for a year, before leaving that profession and embarking on a new adventure in the electrical world. A gentleman from our church asked if I would come and work for him and he would teach me all I needed to know about the electrical world. For three years I served in the electrical field, becoming a journeyman electrician. There were no apprenticeships when I started so I learned the trade as I worked.

At this point, I sought a new adventure and decided to leave home and begin a new job as an inspector of highways with the paving crew. Here I designed asphalt for roads. I found myself working in some remote areas. It was while here that the Lord made a call on my life to go to Bible college.

In 1967, I made a decision to attend Northwest Baptist Theological College in Vancouver. I signed up for one year, just to learn more about the Bible and to strengthen my faith. I enjoyed the year so much, it turned into three years. In the summer of 1969, I was asked to serve the Interior churches in BC, and specifically to serve at Sunnybrae Bible Camp. During that summer, I served in seven churches, spending a week or two in each church, then six weeks at the camp. It was a full summer leading backyard clubs, meeting with youth groups, leading meetings in seniors homes and preaching every Sunday. At the camp, I put my electrical skills to work wiring up a new cabin that had been built, cut up beef that had been donated to the camp, led a cabin of twelve boys, served as the handyman when the girls camps were in progress and, at the family camps, led the youth and children's work. It was a fertile learning ground for what was to follow.

When the summer ended, I returned for my final year at Northwest Baptist Theological College. After graduation in 1970, I went to Houston, BC, in an effort to plant a church with the Fellowship. Upon arriving in Houston, I looked for a job as an electrician or as a meat cutter. That summer it seemed the whole province was on strike and there were no jobs available.

In August, April and I got married and a new chapter began in our lives. In October, we were invited to go to Barriere and preach for a call at Bethany Baptist Church. Barriere is situated in the interior of British Columbia, about an hour's drive from Kamloops. My first pastor, Pastor Foster, had once pastored there. It was a very small struggling church of about twenty people. This church had one of two choices: it could close, or it could decide to do something significant. The church was supported by the Fellowship's church planting committee, so we were considered church planters. Upon arriving, April and I set our hands to the plow and began to care for this community of about 1,000 people. I became the volunteer ambulance driver for four years. I also put my meat cutting skills to work, as I cut all the meat for the local food market. This was a great way to meet people and connect with the community. The local electrician also had so much work he called on me to do service calls for him; interestingly, no one turned me away because I was a Baptist pastor. They were all glad to see me and I was able to plant seeds everywhere I went.

One month into our ministry, a teenage girl committed suicide and we were thrust into the depths of ministry. I had never done a funeral before, nor had I ever met with a grieving family. This was all so new and frightening. Many in the community came to the service and heard the gospel and some responded. The church grew and we needed to go into a building program to double the size of our building. We added washrooms that they never had before (only an outhouse), a kitchen, nursery, classroom and larger auditorium. It was soon full and overflowing. We could sense the Spirit at work. What a wonderful way to begin one's ministry! To this day, we look back and see the hand of God at work in that community. At one point, 10 per cent of the community attended Bethany Baptist Church.

It was while we were in Barriere that we began our family. Our first two sons were born, and life took on a new look as we became parents. It was just after our second son was born that Armstrong called.

After four years at Barriere, we accepted a call to First Baptist Church in Armstrong. This church was also in BC's interior, south of Barriere in the beautiful Spallumcheen Valley just north of Vernon. We began our ministry there in 1974 and served there for seven years. This church had an attendance of just over 100, but was well established and in good health. Both churches were connected to Sunnybrae Bible Camp.

During these seven years, we saw many people come to the Lord and many young people go to Bible school. These were the days of crusades, and over the years we had the privilege of having Dr. John Moore, Dr. Doug Harris, Dr. Jack Pickford, Pastor Manville Bedford and Pastor Ian Bowie all speak at week-long meetings. Each year, we saw a harvest of souls come to know the Lord Jesus Christ. During Pastor Bowie's ministry, we saw almost twenty young people come to the Lord. That fall seventeen of them went to Bible college. These were exciting years of ministry.

It was at this time that Sunnybrae needed a camp director, so I took on that responsibility for two years while still pastoring at Armstrong. This meant buying all the food, organizing leaders for the camps and opening and closing the facility. This was a huge job, on top of caring for the work of the church. My wife and I directed three camps: boys, girls and family camp.

The church grew and we bought more property so we could accommodate all the cars on a Sunday. It was amazing that when the church decided to buy the property, money came in to pay for it all on *one Sunday*. Praise God from whom all blessings flow!

It was here that our third son was born and our family was now complete. After seven years, our home church called and asked us to come and be their pastor. It was a very sad day for all of us, but especially for our boys. It was hard for them to say goodbye to their friends and a community and church that loved them. To this day, they still have gifts that the church gave to them at our farewell.

A new chapter was beginning in 1981 as we came back home to the church where my parents, uncle and aunt, former Sunday school teachers and friends all attended. There were those who told us, "You should never go back and pastor your home church." As it turned out, April and I had a three year start on any other pastor whom they could have called. We knew the culture, the people, the community, and we were excited to begin this new chapter with our boys.

We served at Burnett Fellowship Church for twelve years. We saw the church grow, sell and buy new property and pay for a new building. The Lord gave to us some phenomenal leaders, and the church grew. It was the seniors who pushed us to relocate and rebuild. The new building cost was over one million dollars, and within two years it was all paid

April & Bruce Christensen

off. We had to go to two services and our staff expanded to five. People were being saved, baptisms were held often and the membership grew. These were some of the most wonderful days of our entire ministry—and it was all done in our home church.

In 1993, the BC/Yukon Fellowship approached us to take on the role of regional director. This was overwhelming and I felt so inadequate. I initially said, "No," but my wife told me I needed to listen to the advice I gave to others—to at least go and look, not just say, "No." Therefore, I sought counsel from Pastor Peter Teichroeb. Peter had fulfilled this role for a number of years before he retired. We spent an afternoon in the Scriptures and in prayer. The next day I met with the search committee and accepted the role of regional director for BC/Yukon.

The next fourteen years were both challenging and rewarding. One of the first things I did was hire Pastor Dan Chapman to oversee church planting and ethnic ministries. Dan is a good friend, one who had served for several years in Colombia before returning to Canada and planting two churches. I believe this was the best decision I made in all my years as regional director. We worked well as a team for our region and for the Fellowship across Canada.

Into my twelfth year as regional director, I began to struggle with my health. I went to the doctor and within one week, I was having open-heart surgery. I had major blockages that were corrected with quintuple bypass surgery. After recovery, I made a number of changes in my life. I changed my eating habits, did more exercising, but I could not change the job. The demands were too great and the pressure relentless. So, after fourteen years, in 2007, I tendered my resignation.

At this time, Dallas Barnhartvale in Kamloops invited us to come and lead the congregation. The church was slowly recovering from the loss of their former pastor's wife. We told them that we would give them five years. The next five years were extremely busy, as the church undertook to send a container of goods to our missionaries in Haiti. Although a small work, the church managed to raise over $40,000 and sent a forty-foot-high shipping container to Haiti. This was just after the earthquake in 2010. We sent medical supplies, clothing, food, bikes, generators and a myriad of other things. It was exciting to see how this group of people poured their hearts into this ministry. We next did some major renovations to the grounds and the church building. The parking lot was paved and a hockey/basketball court was built for our community to use. It was exciting to be a pastor of this congregation.

In 2012, just before the five years were up, Dr. David Horita asked us to come back to work with the Fellowship and do pastoral care. This involved meeting with pastors, assisting search committees and working with David in dealing with churches in crisis. The next six years seemed to go by so quickly, and at the age of 73 I decided it was time for a younger person to do this job.

But retirement was not in the picture yet. Tim Paquette from Sunnybrae Bible Camp invited us to become camp hosts for the camp. They provide us with a house and utilities and we could do whatever we wanted. What a way to retire! For the next five years, starting in 2018, we served at the camp in many ways. I did all the electrical maintenance, plowed snow in the winter and looked after the grounds by doing things like cutting grass and planting flowers. April also cared for the grounds and we both cared for the many horses, along with the other animals at the camp. It was wonderful. On top of this we had the joy of working with Millar College of the Bible in mentoring students. Our house was available to students and staff who often came for visits. After five incredible years, we felt it was time to move back closer to our kids and grandkids, so we gave our notice to the camp and informed them we would be moving back to the coast to be closer to our family. This past year has been precious, as we have the joy of being close to our grandkids and watching them do sports and once again participate in their daily lives.

God has been so good to us all these years and we give him all the glory. Our verse for our lives is found in Psalm 16:6–7a (ESV):

The lines have fallen for me in pleasant places;
    indeed, I have a beautiful inheritance.
I bless the LORD...

Submitted by Rev. Dennis Bruce Christensen

8/

Rev. Dr. Darryl Dash

E ven *I* thought it was ridiculous for a five-year-old to want to be a pastor.

I came to faith in Christ at the age of four or five. My mother was a Christian; my father wasn't. My father had been married twice before, and my parent's marriage began to unravel. At an early age, I saw the contrast between my mother and my father, and I wanted whatever my mother had. I knew I wanted Jesus.

Almost immediately, I wanted to be a pastor. My uncle was a pastor, and I appreciated the ministry of my pastor at Calvary Baptist Church in Brampton. He was academic, serious and deep, and I wanted to be like him. My earliest years were shaped by the people in this church, a church that leaned in a fundamentalist direction, but in which people really loved Jesus and cared for our single-parent family.

But I still thought it was strange that I wanted to be a pastor, so I didn't tell many people until I finished high school. Then I couldn't get to seminary fast enough.

I was baptized at Calvary Baptist on June 29, 1980, just before my thirteenth birthday. When I graduated high school, I got a job at a factory for a year to save up money for school. Finally, in September 1987, I moved to east Toronto to begin my studies at Central Baptist Seminary on Jonesville Crescent.

Seminary

My seminary years were meaningful for a few reasons. First, I got to attend a healthy church, Wishing Well Acres Baptist Church in Agincourt, pastored by Ron Unruh. The church was full and Ron preached the Word with power. It was a larger church, and I began to see what it looked like for a church to thrive in a city like Toronto.

Second, I loved my studies. I thrived learning from professors like Stan Fowler and Michael Haykin. I couldn't get enough of studying theology, Scripture, church history and related topics.

Third, I also got ministry experience. I spent summers as a student pastor at churches in North Bay (Fellowship Baptist Church), Toronto (Runnymede Baptist Church) and Markham (Centennial Baptist Church). As I gained experience, I also received affirmation of my calling. I grew in my love of preaching the Word.

Finally, I got to meet my wife, Charlene, at Wishing Well Acres Baptist Church in October 1988. In the middle of my last year of studies, just before Christmas 1990, Char and I were married. We began to look at options for my vocational ministry upon graduation.

Barry Duguid, who had pastored extensively in Toronto, once challenged me to consider devoting my whole ministry to Toronto because so many pastors tend to leave the city. While I never consciously committed to serving only in Toronto, Barry's encouragement planted a seed in my mind.

Early ministry

I was barely twenty-four, newly married, with an undergraduate degree in theology. I knew very little, and yet I filled out my profile for a pastoral position and sent it out to churches. One of the churches that received my profile was Park Lawn Baptist Church in West Toronto, a small church of thirty people. Ernest White, the godly head of the search committee, picked up my resume and saw how short it was. Somehow it caught his attention. "Finally," he said, "someone without an 'I' problem."

I interviewed at the church and was called as their pastor. I began my ministry there in September 1991. Those years were joyous. The church was small and quirky, and they loved us. I tried my best to help the church grow and we saw some growth and baptisms. I learned how to preach week by week, and how to lead alongside the other leaders to accomplish the church's mission.

In November 1994, our daughter Christina was born. I continued to pastor, learned to parent and also took distance education classes to further my education.

We did go through one period of struggle for reasons that I don't yet understand. A deacon decided that he didn't like me and one day, at the start of a deacons meeting, he came close to punching my face before storming out of the meeting. But we weathered that storm. The church grew a little, to around 50 people, but not as much as I would have liked.

In my immaturity, I think I began to grow impatient with the slow growth and longed for a bigger church. After seven years, in 1998, I got that opportunity and resigned my position at Park Lawn.

Difficult years

In July 1998, I started as senior pastor of Richview Baptist in West Toronto. Richview was much larger. It had been led for twenty-three years by Dr. Gordon Freeland, the church's first long-term pastor, who helped build a new building and two seniors' residences. The church was shocked to go from an older pastor with a long history to a young thirty-year-old pastor. Seniors worried about changes, while some younger people were eager for new things.

Soon after arriving, in March 1999, our son Josiah was born.

I began with high hopes, but knew it would be tough. I made too many changes for some older members and not enough for the younger ones. I worked hard to change the church's culture, but struggled to see the changes I wanted.

Around year seven, I wondered if it was time to move on, but we stayed another six years. I also served as moderator of FEB Toronto, the Toronto Association of Fellowship churches at that time.

Char struggled with postpartum depression after our son was born, and those were tough years. Still, God was gracious to me. On Stan Fowler's advice, I enrolled in a doctor of ministry program in preaching under Haddon Robinson. The course content, Robinson's example and my relationships with fellow students, helped me become a better preacher.

Around the same time, I discovered Tim Keller's ministry. He was the pastor of Redeemer Church in New York City and showed me how to be solidly orthodox and reach secular people in an urban context. I also found a book called *The Heart of a Servant Leader* by C. John Miller. It reopened my eyes to the beauty of the gospel. All of this began to shape my ministry in significant ways.

I also began to write more and to teach preaching at Heritage College and Seminary in Cambridge, Ontario.

It's hard to evaluate my time at Richview. Outwardly, many things seemed okay. Many in the church weren't aware of any tensions or my dissatisfaction. It seems God was at work during that period, but it felt like something was off.

Looking back at my sermons and some of my actions, especially in my early years, I see how my lack of experience and wisdom played a role. I had a lot of growing up to do.

In the end, I realized I probably wasn't the best fit to continue pastoring the church, and some elders agreed. I began to explore leaving, and concluded my ministry at Richview in January 2012.

Church planting

We left Richview feeling battered. I wasn't sure if I wanted to pastor another church, especially an established one. For a while, before leaving Richview, it seemed like I might become a professor at a seminary. We waited for that possibility for almost a year. During that time, I increasingly felt a desire to plant a church in downtown Toronto.

My desire began with my work as moderator of FEB Toronto. I noticed that the Fellowship churches in Toronto were placed like an inverted U around the downtown core. We had churches west, north and east of downtown, but very few in downtown Toronto. Every time I went downtown, I saw new condos being built, and I felt burdened about reaching those people with the gospel.

I started praying to the Lord of the harvest to raise up church planters for downtown Toronto, never expecting that it would be me. I thought

I was too old and too hurt to be a church planter. But over the course of that year, while waiting for the professorship job to materialize, I began to wonder if I should try planting a church in downtown Toronto.

Darryl Dash

The only good reason I could come up with to say "no" was fear, but I became convicted that fear was not a good reason. I submitted my name to FEB Central so I could be assessed for church planting, figuring they would say no. To my surprise, I was accepted.

In January 2012, soon after leaving Richview, we began the process of planting a church downtown. We wanted a place that met three criteria: first, it had to be in downtown Toronto; second, it needed to be a growing community; third, it had to have no churches. We kept exploring different neighbourhoods, but Liberty Village kept rising to the top.

I began to plan for what the church would be. I spoke at countless churches to share the vision and raise support. We prayed. We gathered a group of people to meet as the launch team. Along the way, we met two women (a mother and a daughter) who lived near Liberty Village, and who had prayed for years that God would send someone to start a church in that community.

In December 2012, we moved into Liberty Village to be part of the community. Soon after, Nathan and Sarah Fullerton, a couple who had lived north of Toronto, also moved into the neighbourhood to help us. In September 2013, we held our first official service as Liberty Grace Church in Liberty Village.

Church planting is the hardest and most joyful ministry we've ever done. We saw God work in remarkable ways. We saw him answer prayer and provide for us. We saw unbelievers coming to Christ, and we saw God reach people who were otherwise nowhere close to a gospel-preaching church.

It was also hard work. As someone has observed, church planting is a long, hard slog. We faced resistance and spiritual attack, and often had to depend on the Lord for provisions and wisdom in facing situations we'd never faced before. We also faced difficulties in our family as our daughter began to struggle with her faith.

Planting downtown is unique. People are transient. We learned that around 80 per cent of people move every two years. This transience accelerated during the COVID pandemic. Sometimes planting in our community felt like building a sandcastle. It looked good, but then the tide would come in, and we had to start all over again. It's also expensive, and meeting locations are difficult to find. Still, we saw God answer prayer after prayer, and we rejoiced in what he was doing. During this time, I also began to work with FEB Central Church Planting, helping to train other church planters. I was so encouraged as I got to see God raising up people who are willing to sacrifice much to start churches where none existed.

During these years, I began writing for a short time every day. These books eventually became *How to Grow: Applying the Gospel to All of Your Life* and *8 Habits for Growth: A Simple Guide to Becoming More Like Christ*, both published by Moody Publishers. We were able to use both these books as discipleship tools within our church.

It felt like we'd hit our stride. We loved seeing God at work, and we loved our church. Still, I kept my eye out for someone younger who could continue the work after me. Despite a few attempts, we couldn't seem to find anyone.

Eventually, in 2023, I got more serious about finding a successor. For one thing, I was getting tired of doing some of the administration work by myself. I also realized that, humanly speaking, if I didn't move soon, it would be difficult for me to make a move later as I got older. I would be in danger of staying too long for the church's good. I felt like the church could benefit from somebody else's leadership. I also became convinced, based on a book called *From Strength to Strength* by Arthur Brooks, that I should shift my energies from doing to investing in others as I got older.

I knew that transition would be tough because I had a much better sense of where I fit in ministry. Liberty Grace fit me perfectly; it would be hard to find such a good fit elsewhere. And it would be hard to find someone to come and replace me at this young church.

Surprised by grace

Early in 2023, I was asked to speak at Grace Fellowship Church East Toronto, a church that had started just a few years earlier than Liberty

Grace Church. One of the elders asked me to apply to become senior pastor.

Initially, I resisted. Char and I met with the elders to explain why we wouldn't be applying. As we left the meeting, my wife and I looked at each other. The meeting had gone much better than we thought. We had the sense that God might be calling us to go to this church, which was soon confirmed as I went through the interview process.

On September 24, 2023, we held our farewell service at Liberty Grace Church. On October 15, 2023, I began my ministry as the new pastor of Grace Fellowship Church East Toronto. It's a very different church from any other church I've pastored. Like Liberty Grace, it's both a young church and has lots of younger people. Like Richview, it meets in the inner suburbs of Toronto. But unlike any other church I've pastored, it's a church that has serious theological convictions and hunger. I also get to work with a strong ministry team, which I'm enjoying.

In May 2024, GFC East Toronto joined the Fellowship. In July 2024, Liberty Grace Church called a new pastor, Godfrey Paruthivilai.

When I was young, I wanted to do great things for God. I suppose I still do, depending on one's definition of greatness. When I was young, most of the great things I envisioned also coincided with me becoming a big deal. My ambitions overlapped with my pride.

As I get older, my goals are changing. I want to become a godly, gracious old man who loves the Lord and loves people. My prayer is that I will stay faithful at Grace Fellowship Church as long as God would have me there, and that I'll continue to serve him and love him after that.

I want to stay faithful to the end.

Submitted by Rev. Dr. Darryl Dash

9 /

Rev. Bob Flemming

I've always appreciated the African proverb, "It takes a village to raise a child." Reflecting on my story, there are countless believers who, in one way or another, influenced me and discipled me in Christ. Yes, the Lord saved me by his grace—and he used many faithful servants of his to do it! And not just individuals but, at times, entire congregations. I'm going to take the risk of naming some, and if I miss you, I apologize.

Montreal

My mother Agnes (born in Glasgow, Scotland) and my father Ted (born in Aroostook Junction, New Brunswick) both served in WWII. My dad with the Canadian Armed Forces and my mom with the British Army. After the war, they got married and moved to the suburbs of Montreal.

A pastor doing door-to-door visitation knocked on our door. My mother not only opened the door but eventually opened the door of her heart and gave her life to Christ. It wasn't too long afterward that my father was converted as well. Thus, Ted and Agnes began building their lives and their family on the solid rock of Jesus Christ.

Being raised in a Christian home was an incredible privilege. My dad liked the saying, "Values are caught and not taught." Of course, my parents taught us, but most significantly, they modelled what they believed. The consistency of their lives, living out their faith in Christ at home, at work, in our community and at church, was deeply effective. I remember some years later, making a rep hockey team, and my dad said to the coach in the dressing room in front of the entire team, "That's great he made the team, but Bobby won't be able to make Sunday practices or games because we go to church—is that alright?" I just about died (my faith wasn't as strong), but the coach didn't bat an eye; "That's not a problem, Mr. Flemming, we'll take him when we can get him." And that was my dad; he was very straightforward and open but not overbearing. He had a winsomeness about him that made him irresistible and enabled him to say what needed to be said. You can't teach something like that; you watch, and you learn. My two older brothers, Rodger and Richard, also followed the Lord, and they, too, positively impacted my spiritual journey.

Church has always played a central role in our family. Whether at home, on holidays in Cape Cod during the summer or in Clearwater, Florida, during March break, we went to church. During the final moments of the 1971 Grey Cup (Sunday night), when Argo running back Leon McQuay slipped and fumbled the football on the Calgary Stamper's 7-yard line and lost the game, my dad said, "Ok, it's over, let's go to church!" And we did. In Montreal, our family attended Strathmore Baptist Church in Dorval (it later merged with West Island Baptist church). It was a small church with a profound influence. I recall having our Sunday school class in the furnace room—primitive, but it worked. I had just started public school and was excited because the church was having a special Vacation Bible School. Frank Wellington was the guest evangelist and came with his full array of puppets—fantastic! Puppets and ventriloquism were cutting-edge stuff—surpassing even flannel-graph. The week was mesmerizing, and by the final night, after a simple gospel presentation, I went home and told my mom that I wanted to accept Christ as my Saviour. She was thrilled, took the time to explain again the fundamentals of salvation, and had me kneel by my bed and receive Christ. It was that simple and that amazing.

Toronto

My father was a lifelong branch manager for the Prudential Assurance Company of England. In the early '60s, the company moved its head offices to Toronto. So we moved, settled in the suburbs of north Toronto (Thornhill) and in no time, immersed ourselves in the life and ministry of Willowdale Baptist church. It was 1963, and for the next fifteen years, Willowdale became the place for me of significant spiritual formation. Pastor Gord Stephens was the lead pastor, and later, Barry Duguid became the associate pastor. Families like the Havercrofts, Hayes', Skinners, Stephensons, Whittingstalls, Hansons, Warrens, Stouffers' and a host of others, all blended as the body of Christ befriending us as a family. And more specifically, they began ministering to me in a variety of ways. In my early days, it was Sunday school, VBS and Christian Service Brigade. Later, it was youth, college and careers, retreats and service opportunities. Mike and Debbie Noble were our faithful youth leaders. My first sizeable ministry involvement was in the bus ministry. My older brother Rodger and Associate Pastor Barry Duguid had two buses already operating—picking up kids and bringing them to Sunday school. I become the bus captain for the "Bunny" bus. One Sunday, I announced to the kids, "If we get fifty on the bus next week, everybody gets a hamburger." We hit fifty-two kids, and so on the way home, we made a stop at the Red Barn, bought fifty-five burgers at a whopping 35 cents each, and passed them out to the kids. I'll always remember handing out the first one to a little girl, with all the kids overly rambunctious, and her saying to me, "Can I get one with no mustard?" I responded, "Not today, dear, not today." Although the bus ministry, at times, was very challenging, we did see spiritual fruit. Individuals like MacTier Wall, serving with Fellowship International in France, and Joel Gordon (including his family), board chair at Willowdale, were first contacted through the bus ministry.

Pastor Barry Duguid was a key influence in my life and calling to ministry. As older teenagers, he would organize Bible studies, prayer times, and various events, but most significantly, encouraged us to "follow Christ." Like Paul told the Thessalonians, Barry was "delighted to share not only the gospel of God but our lives as well." He spent time with us and took many of us through the SHARE program, a twelve-week

Bible study tool encouraging ongoing discipleship. On one occasion, after hearing me captivate my friends with a story, he said to me, "Bobby, have you ever thought that the Lord could use you in the ministry?" I'm sure it seemed like a passing comment, but it stuck with me, and the Lord used it to plant a seed in my heart. God was growing within me a conviction regarding lifetime service.

In my later years of high school, my faith weakened. I began to lack the conviction and boldness I once had—straying aimlessly. I was living the classic double life, going to church, while at the same time masking my relationship with the Lord to my school friends. It was during this wandering time that God intervened in a mighty way. Revival had come to Saskatoon, Saskatchewan, and it was coming to Willowdale and it was coming to me.

Pastor Bill McLeod of Ebenezer Baptist Church in Saskatoon had invited Ralph and Lou Sutera to conduct meetings in the church. Revival came, and hundreds, if not thousands, were transformed by the Holy Spirit. A lay couple, who had been impacted by the revival, were invited to speak at a Sunday evening service at Willowdale and to give their testimony. The Spirit of God moved in a mighty way, and many responded to the invitation to go forward for prayer, salvation and renewal. I vividly remember sitting at the back of the church and stubbornly resisting. After the service, I jumped in the car with Paul Havercroft, who had gone forward and was now driving us to a youth meeting at his house. We were headed south on Leslie Street, and Paul, discerning my obstinacy, pulled the car over to the side of the road and left the vehicle. I ran out after him, and when I had caught up, he looked at me with discerning eyes and said, "Bobby, did you respond to the invitation tonight?" I confessed that I hadn't. Paul exhorted me to get "right with the Lord" and not put it off any longer. After I assured him I would, we went back to the car and drove to the youth meeting. It was there in that car, alone, that I cried out to the Lord for forgiveness and surrendered my life to his leading. The Spirit of God mercifully and miraculously revived my heart—praise the Lord!

This spiritual rendezvous had dramatic repercussions for my life. First, I embraced the calling of the Lord to follow him in vocational Christian service. I had been accepted at Western University for studies in business, but now submitted to his calling to the ministry. Second, I regained my conviction and boldness. Bill McLeod held follow-up meetings at Forward Baptist in Toronto for any who had been touched by the revival. Without hesitation, I took two of my non-churched high school friends, and when an invitation was given to share, I went to the front and gave my story of renewal. Later, on another occasion, I confessed to a large gathering of my non-churched friends that I hadn't been open with them about my faith. I shared the gospel with them and my personal testimony. Although surprised, they said they knew there was something different about me. The Lord still had many things to teach me, but I was well on my way.

Bob Flemming

An interesting note about this revival experience: Years later, I would serve as a youth pastor at Forward Baptist Church, where revival follow-up meetings were held. Plus, I have had the opportunity to speak at the FEB Prairies Regional Conference, held at none other than Ebenezer Baptist Church, Saskatoon, Saskatchewan. During those years, Willowdale saw many people enter vocational ministry: Robert Cousins, Rob Hayes, Barry Howson, Paul Havercroft, Paul Whittingstall and Richard Flemming, to name a few.

Enrolling and attending Central Baptist Seminary was a great experience. The school met at 95 Jonesville Crescent, in the northeast part of Metro Toronto. Faculty taught us faithfully, lifelong friendships were forged and field experience was emphasized. During my seminary years, I mainly served at Wilmar Heights Baptist Church. Dr. Ted Barton was the lead pastor (he also taught at the seminary) and had John Crozier, Ted Stimers, Cedric Raymond and me serving as student interns at the church. Pastor Barton engaged us in every aspect of the ministry, from teaching Sunday school to preaching sermons to conducting baptisms. It was a crucial learning experience, and the Wilmar church family embraced us wholeheartedly. Their love and affirmation of us left an indelible mark on our lives. In my last year at Central, I remember Dr. Jack Scott (chancellor) calling me into his office and basically saying, "Bob, there's a church in Sydney, Nova Scotia, that needs a summer student intern. This is a great opportunity, and I know you'll be blessed in going." And that was that! So off I went to Cape Breton and served that summer as a student intern with Pastor Ken Kimbley and the congregation of Faith Baptist Church. Once again, the people of faith were amazing—praying for me, encouraging me, having me in their homes and giving me my first taste of lobster. At the end of the summer, in addition to giving me a generous love offering, a family donated a car to me! I had lost mine in an accident and felt overwhelmingly grateful—not just to the church family but, more importantly, to the Lord. It was a life lesson in trusting God for all my needs.

It was during seminary days that I met and began dating Rhonda Ciona, who attended Calvary Baptist in Oshawa. After getting engaged, I remember meeting her grandfather, who was visiting from Kelowna, BC. We talked for a while (Rhonda's mother was interpreting because he only spoke Ukrainian), and then he said, "He looks like a nice young man, but does he love Jesus?" I passed the test, and we got married in 1978.

After graduating in 1979, I served as youth pastor at Forward Baptist Church in the east end of Toronto. Once again, families like the Simpsons, Mollers, Strathdees, Wrights and many more, adopted us as their own. Paul Kerr was the lead pastor and led multiple staff with encouragement, openness and infectious joy. Forward was a big church with many ministries and, in addition to being a youth pastor, Paul took the time to mentor me and give me various serving opportunities. On one occasion, the church was hosting a week of student training meetings with George Verwer, founder of Operation Mobilisation. Upon arrival in Toronto, I was driving George to his hotel, and he said to me, "Bob, I won't be staying in the hotel. I'll just sleep in the pastor's office." Although initially taken aback, that's where he stayed and had an effective week of meetings!

We threw ourselves into the youth ministry, building relationships, organizing events, doing Bible studies, discipling and reaching out to some non-church young adults in the community. I remember Rhonda and I taking the youth group across the border to a theme park. After looking at everyone's ID, the immigration officer took me aside and said, "Look, you've got a young adult who is wanted for a misdemeanour in the state of New York. I'd suggest you leave him here for a day and pick him up on the way back." That's what we did, and we continued to minister to any who came to our youth group. Although we served at Forward for just over three years, we cherished our time there and praise the Lord for the love and support of this caring church family. It was at the end of our time there that our first daughter, Jessica, was born.

Stouffville

William Cowper's words, "God moves in a mysterious way, His wonders to perform," certainly applied to my calling to Springvale Baptist Church in Stouffville in the spring of 1982. While at Forward Baptist, I had agreed to appear on a cable TV show that one of the members utilized as an outreach. While the show aired late one night, John Montgomery, a deacon who was on Springvale's search committee and former member of Willowdale Baptist Church, couldn't sleep and turned on the television. He saw me on this rather obscure cable TV show and thought to himself, "I remember Bobby Flemming from Willowdale days; maybe he'd be open to coming to Springvale as pastor." And that was how the search team contacted me. Eventually, I accepted the call.

Tom Hamilton, an American, had been the previous pastor of Springvale and had an excellent ministry, bringing spiritual renewal to the church and attracting younger families. Building on his ministry of revitalization, we experienced countless blessings from the Lord over the next twenty-eight years! In 1983, we had our second daughter, Hannah, and our family grew along with the church.

Stouffville transitioned from a rural community to a bustling commuter town close to the city of Toronto. Bruce Hisey, a former pastor of the church, had exhorted me to "go ahead and build" if the facilities were full. Heeding his words, we saw the Lord lead us through three building expansions: one in 1984, another in 1991 and a final one completed in 2008. Land, too, needed to be acquired. In 1987, when the church couldn't afford the twenty-five acres of farmland that bordered the south of our property, nineteen members formed the Stouffville Conference Centre and purchased it with their own money. Their vision, faith and sacrificial commitment to securing the property, paved the way for future expansions. Later, through generous arrangements, the church was able to buy the property and go forward with the building. Teams of people volunteered to assist with all aspects of these expansion projects, freeing me to fulfill my pastoral responsibilities. It was amazing to see the church family come together, each one giving and participating as the Lord enabled.

The pastoral staff also expanded. With a rich history in Youth for Christ ministry during the '50s, there was a conviction that we should first focus on youth. In 1987, Byron Stewart began his ministry as associate pastor with an emphasis on youth. Events like the MAZE, a Halloween outreach, drew some 4,500 students from across the region, with dozens making professions of faith. His initiatives, including a robust youth internship program and Youth Shine Ministries, created a "leadership pipeline," producing ministry leaders locally and beyond. In 1995, Brian Simcoe, a youth intern, joined our staff as youth pastor, and then in 1999, Jay Sandiford (Byron's son-in-law) joined as well. Two other youth interns, Alex Street and Ben Bartosik, eventually served with the youth team. The youth ministry had a major impact on the spiritual climate of Springvale, resulting in many conversions, baptisms and equipped leaders following the Lord in a variety of capacities. The Lord continued to complement the growing ministry at Springvale with other excellent ministry staff. Drawing from our own membership, we utilized individuals like Bill Smith for visitation, Bill McGilvary as our first music director, Karla Kammerman as counsellor and Sharon Russell as children's director. Although part-time, they served wholeheartedly, and serving alongside them was delightful! In 1996, Bill and Heather Thornton joined our staff, Heather taking over the music director's position and Bill taking the role of associate pastor. This couple immediately fit into the church family and was used by the Lord to take us to even greater heights of effectiveness. As I reflect over the years, I praise the Lord for providing such gifted servants on our ministry team.

The people of Springvale were loving and supportive and fostered a spirit of "going all in" as they planned outreach ministry events. Hundreds would come, many from the community, to Christmas and Easter musical and drama productions, special women's events, regional youth worship nights, Victoria Day BBQ and fireworks and fundraising auctions. Banquets and food abounded! On one occasion, I remember Byron Stewart getting a young and upcoming Mark Lowry (Gaither Vocal Band) to come help us celebrate a church anniversary. Truly a memorable night with the church packed. Another ministry initiative that the church fully embraced was short-term mission trips. Emmanuel International had its offices next door and this helped fan the flames for overseas ministry. Staff and church teams travelled to places such as Haiti, Jamaica, Poland, Tanzania, Malawi, Russia, Kazakhstan and the Philippines. Teams also served on Manitoulin Island (First Nation), running a week of ministry for women or a sports camp for young men. These events and short-term mission trips had a spiritual impact not only on those served, but also on those serving.

Cambridge

In 2010, after serving at Springvale for twenty-eight wonderful years, we sensed the Lord releasing us from our role. While attending a FEB Central regional conference, I was discreetly asked by some regional board members if I'd consider the regional director position. The Lord solidified this call, and after resigning from Springvale and taking a few months off, we moved to Cambridge. I commenced serving as the FEB Central regional director in the fall of 2010.

It was a big step, but several factors made the transition smoother. First, the regional board had adopted *Ministry Plan 2010*. This revised vision for the Ministry Centre gave birth to new positions such as leadership development director, association shepherds and district shepherds. It called for staff to work more proactively with pastors/leaders, associations and congregations—to be readily available to assist our churches as needed. It also called for the development of a strategy to raise funds. From this new plan, goals were set and the way forward was clarified. Secondly, Lance Johnson, my predecessor, who had wholeheartedly endorsed *Ministry Plan 2010*, made himself available to me. Being at the top of my speed dial list, Lance would answer my every call and give me valuable information, insight and much-needed wisdom whenever I needed it. And thirdly, the Ministry Centre staff made serving as the incoming regional director truly a pleasure. Tom Haines was the church planting director, Godfrey Thorogood was the leadership development director (a new position), and I, in addition to my director responsibilities, served as the church health director. Although we didn't know each other, we connected very quickly and morphed into an effective ministry team. Enhancing our efforts were our specialized ministry leaders such as Judy Cairns (Women's Ministry Institute), Heather McKenzie, and later Jenn Martin (women's ministry), and Jeremy Best (youth ministry). Through retreats, events and training, these part-time servants were used by the Lord to see first-time professions, spiritual growth and renewal and renewed commitments to serve the local church.

It was in September 2011 that we moved our Ministry Centre from south Cambridge into the newly renovated Heritage College and Seminary. This gave us higher visibility with our churches, closer proximity to the students and affirmed our commitment to Heritage as being our central training centre for those going into vocational ministry. The leadership at the school were very accommodating—we established a partnership agreement and held various meetings and training events in their facilities. Additionally, the regional student internship program, revised and implemented by Godfrey, grew rapidly and produced many successful placements and full-time ministry positions within our churches.

As the staff travelled extensively, we could see that although there were encouraging ministries going on in a particular church, collectively, we were still disconnected and detached from each other. This prevailing spirit of independence, coupled with the pressing need for financial support from our churches, led to the implementation of our *Stronger Together* initiative. In 2012, a task force comprised of Bill Thorton, Dwayne Cline and Aaron Rock wrote the first draft of *Stronger Together*, outlining our vision, core values, benefits to member churches and a financial plan to help support it. For the next year and a half, the staff and board spent countless hours visiting pastors, associations and church leaders, gaining valuable feedback and making document revisions. *Stronger Together* was approved at our Regional Conference in 2014—truly a historic affirmation! We praise God for churches participating and donations, as of the writing of this, surpassing $900,000. But most significantly, a new spirit of interdependence and cooperation was emerging. A better sense of family was being established, and churches were coming together more effectively, seeking to reach the millions of people in our region for Christ.

Another special highlight was seeing what the Lord was doing in church planting. Tom, along with his wife Tammy, who served as the church planting administrative assistant, were experiencing a virtual explosion of couples being led to plant churches. It was unprecedented to see seven new church plants a year, and some years nine or ten. Tom worked tirelessly, along with Tammy, recruiting new planters, training and supporting them. This outward focused vision became infectious, and the Lord used Tom to establish and multiply our church planting ministry to this day. It was a joy for Rhonda and me to spend time with many of these treasured church-planting couples on retreats or at the Exponential Conference.

When Godfrey Thorogood transitioned back into pastoral ministry, Tim Strickland came on as our new leadership development director in May 2018. A year or two earlier, Tim and I attended a conference on the theme of church revitalization. Although the conference was mediocre (I may be exaggerating), we realized that the emphasis on church renewal was exactly what we needed. Tim quickly blended into our team. His experience as a lead pastor, coupled with a DMin in church revitalization, enabled him to impact many of our churches in renewed health and vitality. Through consultations, new curriculum, networks and training, Tim has helped countless churches increase their effectiveness to make disciples for the Lord.

I counted it a privilege to serve as regional director: overseeing staff, working with a supportive board and executive, conducting dozens of consultations, organizing regional and pastors' conferences, connecting with the other regional directors at Fellowship meetings (facilitated by our national president, Steve Jones) and representing the region in countless ways in our churches.

In 2020, I resigned my position as regional director. For the last four years, first under Rick Buck (who had to step down for health reasons in 2022) and now Tom Haines, I've continued serving with the region in a part-time capacity. It's encouraging to see continued growth and advancement. Serving God's people, the church, has truly been—and continues to be—the honour of my life!

Submitted by Rev. Bob Flemming

10 /

Richard & Brenda Flemming

When we look back over our lives, we see what seems to be various chapters. At first glance, they might appear to be disparate or isolated periods of time and events. But truly, they are not. One builds on the other, each one necessary for the subsequent chapters, slowly building the story and plot, line by line, chapter by chapter. The ending is still being written from our vantage point, but the Master knows every letter and paragraph of it. It's truly all been about serving him and building his kingdom.

Chapter 1: The early years—the foundation
The initial chapter sees the hand of God graciously placing both of us into families who loved and followed Jesus from day one of our existence. This

foundation provided us with security, love and the opportunity to see in the flesh what trusting God looks like. Richard's parents, Ted and Agnes Flemming, were new Christians when their second son, Richard, was born on February 27, 1953, in Montreal, Quebec. Their lives had been dramatically transformed when the gospel began to reach anglophones in that region of Montreal. They never looked back.

As a young child, Richard simply believed the Good News that he heard and responded to it. He can't identify specifically at what age he made this initial commitment to Christ, so he has simply chosen to say he was eight! Young though he was, faith has been central to his life.

Because of some of the language tensions between anglophones and francophones in the province of Quebec in those years, and as many companies began to leave Montreal to settle in Toronto, Richard's family also left and settled there. Later on, Richard would, in some ways, regret his parents' decision because it would mean learning to speak French as an adult—a much tougher assignment!

The Flemming family soon settled into Willowdale Baptist Church (north of Toronto), and there Richard made many close friends and spent the rest of his childhood and teenage years. Though faith came at a young age, there also were a number of times when he struggled to have an assurance that his faith was genuine. He often jokes that he probably went forward to "give his life to Jesus" dozens of times, much to his mom's embarrassment! Nonetheless, he served in many capacities as he grew up there. One area of service was the bus ministry, where volunteers would visit certain high-density populations and invite families to allow their children to be bused to the church on Sunday mornings for Sunday school. At one time, Willowdale had hundreds of unchurched kids coming each week. One of those children was McTair Wall, who many years later would become a fellow co-worker in France.

When Richard was in his later teens, his youth pastor, Barry Duguid, took him and a number of other young people under his wing and discipled them. This was a turning point in Richard's life and settled the issue of faith for him. Besides his family, the Lord used many others at Willowdale to influence and shape Richard for what would become a life of service in missions. After a year and a half of university and a number of odd jobs, including a few weeks as a vacuum cleaner salesman, Richard sensed God calling him to attend Central Baptist Seminary in Toronto, and he began a four-year bachelor of theology degree in 1976.

Brenda was born on March 26, 1958, in Sarnia, Ontario, the third daughter of Ralph and Joyce Harrett. Her childhood was spent in the small community of Corunna, located south of Sarnia on the St. Clair River. Her upbringing was simple, humble and unpretentious. Brenda's dad spent most of his life working in a factory, and her mom stayed at home caring for her family. Life revolved around the little Fellowship congregation, First Baptist Church, in Corunna, of which her parents were founding members. It was normal to be present for Sunday school, Sunday morning and evening services, as well as Wednesday night prayer meetings. As Brenda moved into her teens, youth activities were added to the weekly schedule. There was nothing that predicted the kind of life and global exposure she would someday experience.

Brenda was a good kid, a great student and extremely conscientious in everything she did. But somehow, in spite of all of this, the idea of personal faith and God's grace and forgiveness came more slowly to her. Brenda finally quietly placed her faith in Christ at sixteen, while attending a Christian camp that summer. As she neared the end of high school, even though teachers encouraged her to pursue studies at university, she became convinced that God wanted her to choose theological education. In September 1977, she began a three-year Licentiate in Theology at Central Baptist in Toronto. This was a life-changing choice.

Chapter 2: Preparation

The years spent at Central Baptist Seminary were significant, essential years for both of us. For Brenda, the world began to expand for this small-town girl. An especially important event was a mission trip over the Christmas break to Saltillo, Mexico, with Operation Mobilization. On that team was a certain Richard Flemming. Significant? Yes. But equally significant was the fact that God used this experience and exposure to plant the seed of missions in Brenda's heart. God had already done the same for Richard through a two-month mission trip to Haiti just prior to his studies at Central. This alignment of our hearts for missions was one of the factors that drew our hearts to each other.

Following our graduation in May 1980, Richard began serving as a youth pastor at Dovercourt Baptist Church in Toronto. We were engaged in July and married on October 4 of that same year. The location at Bloor and Dufferin, and the ethnic diversity of the youth, provided an introduction to working with and living among people from different cultures. We did not recognize at the time the significance of this ministry for us and for our future ministry. In the same way Richard had been heavily invested in by his youth pastor, we sought to devote the majority of our time and energy to discipling young people. Though we did hundreds of studies with them, we also sought to simply share our lives with these kids, most of whom were first-generation believers. Years later, one of them told us that although they really didn't remember all the Bible studies, they were deeply impacted by our lives. Arc Da Silva became a key individual whom we invested in, and he eventually became pastor of this congregation, continuing until his death in 2024.

During this time, our family expanded with the birth of Matthew (1982) and then Lindsey (1983). We were accepted as career missionaries by Fellowship International in 1983, with the objective of church planting in France. Once support raising was completed, we packed a container and our little family moved to France in October 1985. As parents and grandparents now, we recognize and are thankful for the sacrifice of our parents in letting us go, along with their many prayers and support for us throughout their lifetime. They never put extra pressure on us or questioned our call to serve God globally.

Chapter 3: Phase 1—Cross-cultural ministry

Once a home base was set up in the town of Lognes, a suburb to the east of Paris, our first task was learning French. For Richard, who had not retained any of the French he had learned in his early childhood days in Pointe-Claire, Quebec, this was a challenge! Years later, as our ministries evolved and expanded in the francophone world, he saw this endeavour as one of his greatest achievements. Over the course of the following year, he took the train daily to Paris to participate in French classes at Sorbonne University. Because of the ages of our young preschool children, Brenda took two month-long courses, but otherwise studied at home. There was an urgency and sense of "do or die," and the motivation to learn to communicate in French was great. We believed and had committed ourselves to long-term service there; we thought this was where we would spend the rest of our lives. We didn't know God's future plans for us, but obeyed him in taking the next step. Two years in, our third child, Jesse, was born in Montfermeil, France, in October 1987.

Early on, we began to attend a very small, young church plant in Lagny-sur-Marne, 26 kms east of Paris. They had no pastor at the time, so their little board of leaders took turns preaching. Little by little, as language skills increased, we became involved in ministry, and this would become our church home for thirteen years, the majority of our time in France.

As Richard took on more and more leadership within this local church, it became obvious that the rented facilities we were using in the basement of a Catholic school were vastly inadequate and were stunting any real growth. The church, though

Brenda & Richard Flemming

still very small in the number of core families, dove into a ten-month building project. With a Christian contractor from America, Dick Grant, and 100 volunteers coming from Canada, the USA and Ireland, the Lagny church building was completed in 1991. Dick preached the first Sunday in the building on the theme, "God is Never Late," a truth that has resonated and encouraged us many times in the years since. Within months of completion, the church doubled in size with its new visibility in the community.

Knowing how few evangelical churches there are in France, we were eager to begin the process of planting a new church in another area close by. The church board was hesitant to release us, so a proposition was made to hire a French intern under Richard, who would eventually take over the shepherding responsibilities of the Lagny congregation. This was when Thierry Cochet came into the picture. Thierry and Sylvie were first-generation believers, like most of the members of the church, and he soon excelled in teaching, preaching and discipling. This allowed us to begin to consider where God would have us begin the next church.

During the World Cup of Soccer that took place in France in 1998, we planned many opportunities for outreach in surrounding communities. There didn't seem to be many direct results from what we did, but as we continued praying, God brought Thierry Hirschy and his wife, Rebecca, into our lives at just the right time. Indeed, God is never late; he's always just on time!

In January 1999, we launched our second church plant in Claye-Souilly in a rental room on the main street of this very beautiful town, a dozen or so kilometres from Lagny. We had moved our family there the previous year. Several families from Lagny joined us to help form the core of this new church being birthed.

We had built a life we loved in France. But our plans were about to be interrupted. Several times in the late '90s, when Paul Kerr, the director of Fellowship International, passed through France, he began sowing the idea of Richard replacing him as director of the mission when he retired. Brenda rejected the idea out of hand, but gradually began to realize that Richard was interested by this potential. After an extended time of prayer and a visit back to Canada to meet with the mission board, we believed that God was indeed bringing us back to Canada for this role. We remained in France to complete the two-year internship process that we had promised Thierry at Claye, and then in June 2000, we packed up our home and life with three teens in tow and moved to Guelph, Ontario.

In France, our years in Lagny and Claye gave us on-the-ground experience in church planting. We didn't feel as though we were the most gifted in this work, but God was gracious. These congregations have continued faithfully in our absence, and the Lagny church has planted four other churches in the years since we left. Some of the young people have become pastors, church planters, elders and missionaries, and we would like to believe that our time there has borne fruit for Christ's kingdom.

Chapter 4: Phase 2—Global perspective

When we arrived back on this side of the Atlantic, Richard's feet hit the ground running. For fifteen years, our one focus was one area in France. Now, God expanded our vision and began to open our eyes to what he was doing in our world on a global scale. Richard devoured every book he could find on missions, and that thirst for growing and constantly learning continues to this day. Our family dynamic changed dramatically. Richard was frequently travelling overseas to visit our Fellowship missionaries in various countries across the globe and speaking in churches everywhere in Canada. Brenda loved when she was able to accompany him on visits with missionaries, to help with debriefing their ministry and seeing them in their different cultural contexts. Our experience in church planting in France was valuable asset because it gave credibility to the advice we shared and the questions we asked. We, too, had lived the missionary life. For us personally, we loved best of all when we were able to do this ministry together. It also kept our passion for cross-cultural mission burning, even as we tried to establish some new roots in Canada. Certainly, in those early years, we greatly missed the churches in France and found becoming Canadian again a bit of a challenge. We were not the same people as before; our world had expanded and forever transformed us.

In Fall 2003, we took the Perspectives on the World Christian Movement mission course. We had little idea how significant those fifteen weeks would be as we continued down the road. We went from being students to being instructors in Toronto, at Heritage, and since COVID, online and in French in Montreal.

For Brenda, one comment made during the final lesson became an anchor for her faith in the months ahead during a major trial. An instructor made a passing comment that mission candidates in their mission were required over the year of their training to read the entire Bible every month for those twelve months. A seed was planted. So, on January 1, 2004, she committed to reading her Bible in its entirety that month. She had no way of knowing what lay ahead or why this decision would be significant for her. As she neared the end of the month, she was reflecting on her "takeaway" from this challenge. This was it: the incredible, great, unwavering love of God that constantly pursues his people, providing opportunities again and again to come or to return to him. His plans could sometimes seem unfathomable, but ultimately, for our good. On the 29th of the month, as she neared the end of the New Testament, we were in a car accident in Longueuil, Quebec, and Brenda suffered a C-2 neck fracture. But prepared in her heart that God is always in control, ever in charge, and secure in God's love for her, she experienced his peace throughout the many months of recovery, particularly the first five when she wore a halo 24/7. What was clear to her was that God had preserved her life and her capacity to move, and so he wasn't done with her yet. There was more life and more ministry ahead.

When we left France to return to Canada, we both believed it was just for a time, that it was a chapter but not the final one in our ministry. So, we kept our minds and hearts open to what the next chapter might be. Brenda often joked that after every overseas trip Richard made during those years, he would come back with a new possible location.

Chapter 5: Phase 3—Mission coaches

By 2007, as our children were growing into adulthood and independent lives, we began to pray in earnest about our next phase of ministry. We knew that this time, we would no longer be going as a family but as a couple. Unlike most families at our age and stage of life, this meant not the kids leaving home but us, the parents. At the time, the location was not clear, but we began to consider criteria we believed to be important as we considered different potential contexts.

With this in mind, we came up with a list of four main criteria we believed we needed to consider for our next ministry location. The first was that it would be a francophone setting.

Because we had added French to our skill set, we believed God wanted us to use it. Secondly, we felt that the specific ministry had to be strategic in nature. God had, through the years and responsibilities we had experienced since leaving France, opened our eyes and hearts to kingdom need and work on a global scale, and we didn't want to narrow our focus to something too small. Thirdly, and for obvious reasons, it also needed to be a ministry where the two of us could be involved, each of us using our skills and God-given gifts. Lastly, we desired that it would be in a less affluent context than either Canada or France.

To follow through on this, we accepted an invitation in 2008 to go to Kinshasa, Democratic Republic of the Congo, to explore an option for future ministry with a large Baptist church association (C.B.CO). The purpose of our week with these Congolese leaders was to discern if God was opening up the next chapter of our lives to serve him there. We discovered that the roots of this church association dated back to 1878, and the sacrificial work of British and American missionaries. Although many churches had been established and leaders trained, these same churches had not yet engaged in missions. Though they had recently put a mission department in place, they didn't know what to do from there. They needed mission coaches, people who could help them learn about missions, and help them understand the gospel needs, and develop vision, strategies and training for their missionaries. We saw that this was where we could help. Our role would not be to tell them what and how they would need to do the work. On the contrary, we would walk alongside them, asking questions which would help them determine for themselves what God was asking them to do and how they would do it the African way with African means. This was in striking contrast to the message many of them had internalized: that mission work was done by wealthy, white Westerners. Since they didn't tick any of those boxes, they believed they could not do missions.

For us personally, the week we spent there was one of determining if this was what God wanted for us. We were encouraged by our many discussions, but to be completely honest, the thought of moving to and living in this deeply broken context was a serious challenge and struggle. We knew from experience that this move would be the most challenging of our lives—and we were not wrong. But God moved in each of our hearts, and on the third day of our weeklong visit, God showed us individually that this would be the next chapter of our lives. Every one of our criteria had been checked, so how could we possibly refuse? We returned to Canada to prepare for our departure.

Even when we're certain God has led in a particular direction, it doesn't mean that everything is straight sailing. As we were preparing for our departure, our daughter announced she was pregnant with our first grandchild. Leaving felt a little harder! Then, at five months pregnant, we learned that this grandchild had a life-threatening congenital heart condition. If the child was to survive, he would require a number of risky heart surgeries. We made the decision to remain in Canada to accompany our daughter and son-in-law through those initial challenges. Though there were many touch-and-go moments, ambulance rides, lengthy hospitalizations, ORNGE helicopter flights to Sick Kids in Toronto, two surgeries and several catheter procedures, our grandson entered a more stable phase, and so we moved forward. It was a hard thing to leave our family.

For four years, between 2010 and 2014, we lived in Kinshasa, DRC. We worked with Congolese leaders of many different denominations, sharing the many things we had learned and were continuing to learn concerning God's mission. Early on, we used some of the aspects of the Perspectives course that we had taken to give them a way to introduce the importance of the mission to their church leaders. Initially, we did this training, but soon, the members of their mission team were able to pass on this message, something that they continue to do to this day. We believed the blessing the church had received in the Congo was not to be held onto, but they, like Abraham, were to be a source of blessing to other francophone Africans.

As mission coaches, we never planned on remaining long-term in Congo. We thought that once we had helped them to get up and running in missions themselves, God might move us on to another francophone setting on the continent to do it all over again. God had a bigger, better plan in mind. But the years we lived there, travelling to other provinces with the team for training, and dealing with the many challenges of just living in a context of extreme poverty, allowed us to understand on a practical level the difficulties they faced and to build relationships with some key individuals. We didn't know, at the time, whom God would use in amazing ways in the coming years. Once we were no longer living in Kinshasa, we continued as non-residential missionaries, travelling to Congo several times a year, coaching, training and helping them assess their mission endeavours.

Chapter 6: Phase 4—Catalyzing movements in francophone Africa

It was during our time living in Kinshasa that we began to discover a global mission phenomenon happening in our day—disciple making movements. As we read about how God was drawing many unreached peoples to himself, using biblical and replicable principles, we saw how this could be the key to the African church as they became involved in missions.

Near the beginning of the COVID pandemic, a Congolese pastor, Jacques Mayala, called us in Canada. He had just finished reading about these catalyzing movements in a book that Richard had given him a few weeks previously during a visit to Kinshasa. It was like a Macedonian Call. This man and his wife, Rose, wanted to be coached in these concepts so they could better fulfill church planting among the Pygmies. In Kinshasa, Matthieu Gbawe had been practicing some of the principles of catalyzing movements. He, Jacques and Rose asked Richard to coach them online. Soon, Jacques' son, Jerry and his wife, Esther, missionaries in francophone West Africa, also joined these sessions. There was little to indicate what this decision would lead to in the following years. But once again, God gave us the opportunity to invest in the lives of key leaders. God would begin to do through them what we had dreamt of: African francophone leaders doing missions and training leaders in unreached francophone contexts across Africa. We would not be the ones entering these places, but we would coach Africans who would do this work better than we ever could.

These last few years represent the most fruitful time of ministry of our entire lives to date. God is doing exceedingly more than we could ever have asked or imagined. Hundreds of churches are being planted in seventeen francophone countries in Central and Western Africa, among many unreached peoples. God is using Jacques, Rose, Matthieu and Jerry to train and coach many more African leaders, who, in turn, are training others in catalyzing movements, and it is a beautiful thing! We could never have written the story of our life the way God has. We don't know if or what chapters might still be ahead, but we are so grateful for the incredible life that God has allowed us to live, one chapter at a time. To God be all the glory!

Submitted by Richard & Brenda Flemming

11 /

Rev. Jack Flietstra

I was born in Galt, Ontario, to Ynze and Cathy Flietstra. I was the eleventh child, the fourth son, in a family of twelve. My parents had immigrated to Canada as Baptists from the Netherlands with eight children, and I was the second child born in Canada. I was born on a Tuesday and was in church on Sunday. In my early years, we attended a number of Fellowship churches in the Cambridge area. The two main ones were Forward Baptist Church and Temple Baptist. For my first seven years, we lived outside of Cambridge on a mini farm, as my father was a gardener landscaper.

When I was seven, we moved into the city of Galt/Cambridge. In the summer of 1967, when I was eight, through the ministry of Child Evangelism Fellowship, I came to faith in Christ as my Lord and Saviour.

That fall, I went forward at Temple Baptist and publicly declared my faith in Christ by being baptized by Dr. Sid Kerr.

When I was nine years old, my life changed forever. My dad went to Central Baptist Seminary and graduated in May 1968. In September 1968, Temple Baptist commissioned our family as missionaries. I remember being up on the platform at Temple and having Dr. Sid Kerr lay hands on my dad and mom and pray for us as we were about to head to Belgium as missionaries. I'm not sure of the timeline, but we went to a station to take the train to Montreal. From there, we boarded a ship for an eleven day trip over to the Netherlands. As we were driving to the train station, my brother John told a joke that I never forgot. He asked, "Why do they put a fence around the graveyard?" as we passing a fenced graveyard. The answer, of course, was, "Because everyone is dying to get in." We had so many emotions going through our young minds, and my brother John was doing his part to lighten the mood. On our way, we had a brief stop in Toronto and got to see our sister Sietske and her husband John Bellsmith. There were tears, and on we went. We were sent off by a crowd at the train station, brothers and sisters in Christ, and notably, Dr. Kerr who had prayed for us. The eleven days on the ship on the ocean was filled with all kinds of fun and excitement.

Moving to Belgium was a major change in my life. When we first arrived in the Netherlands, we visited both my father and mother's families, people whom I had only heard about. I was nine when I first met my grandparents, but I could not understand them. They all spoke Dutch, and I spoke English. After a few days with family, we drove four hours south to Genk, Belgium, and moved into a home with the pastor's family. The very next day, I went to a Belgian school and had to learn a new language on the fly. A year in, I came to the point that I was illiterate in two languages! This became apparent when I was trying to write a letter to my brother back in Canada, and I asked how do you spell "I."

Our early years in Belgium were difficult on several fronts. People were causing great difficulties for my father, the missionary. We had a couple of moves. My dad's father died, and we could not attend the funeral as we did not have a car big enough for the whole family. When I was fourteen, I had a crisis of faith. I was angry with God because my family was scattered all over the world. Most were in Canada, we were in Belgium, and my sister Sietske and her family were in Thailand. I was angry because we would never all be together again. But, I was wrong and in 1982 at my brother John's wedding, we were all together for a day.

My call to ministry was interesting. When I was ten years old, I would gather all my sister Cathy's dolls and set them up on chairs in rows and I would preach to them. Then, I would baptize them holding some of them under water until there were no more bubbles. Thankfully, I don't do that to humans. At ten, when I told my teacher at a Christian school that I wanted to be a pastor when I grew up, she told me I was too dumb to be a pastor. That may have been true, but when I was seventeen, during a sermon my father was preaching at Bethel Baptist in Genk, God moved in me and called me to be a pastor. At that time, I believed it was to serve in Belgium. At twenty years of age, I went to Greater Europe Missions Bible College in Zaventem, Belgium. My intention was to move to a community without a gospel witness and start knocking on doors. Robert Holmes, the Fellowship Foreign Missions Secretary at the time, came to visit and convinced me to come to Canada so I could return to Belgium as a full-fledged missionary.

In 1982, I came back to Canada for my brother John's wedding, planning to head back to Belgium. Shortly after I returned to Canada, Rev. Robert Holmes retired, and a new Foreign Missions Secretary took over. He said I needed to get a seminary degree, so I enrolled at Central Baptist Seminary. In early 1983, I met Dedee Messina. We got engaged and married on August 11, 1984. Dedee enrolled in a one-year certificate at Central and graduated in 1985. I finished my LTh in December 1985 and graduated in 1986. When I approached the Fellowship Foreign Secretary, he wanted me to get two years of ministry experience in Canada first. Upon my return, I would have been the lead missionary on the field in Belgium, as my father was scheduled to retire, so this made sense.

While I was in seminary, I served as a part-time youth pastor at Wilmar Heights Baptist Church in Scarborough, Ontario, for two years. John Crozier was the lead pastor. Our youth group grew from three to over fifty kids. Willmar Heights went on to hire their first full-time youth pastor, Byron Steward, and I served with him for the last few months as I completed my seminary degree. During my time at Central, there were times that I worked three jobs: part-time at the church, part-time at Ragland Welding and delivering the early morning edition of the *Toronto Star*.

In December 1985, two significant things happened. Dedee and I moved from Scarborough to Burlington, where I became the youth pastor at Calvary Baptist Church under the leadership of Rev. Earl Clemens.

Within days of moving to Burlington, Rebecca Joy was born on New Year's Eve. I worked part-time for the church and part-time as a warehouse clerk for Pioneer Clubs. I served there for two years. In May 1987, our oldest son Ynze Ryan was born, and in December of 1987, I accepted a call to First Baptist Church in Cochrane, Ontario, for six months as an interim pastor. It was at this time that Dedee and I applied to the Fellowship to serve as missionaries in Belgium. The application was a six-month process, and with the church looking for a new pastor and needing some assistance during the winter months, this worked well.

We moved to Cochrane on January 12, 1988, a stormy winter day. Three months into our six months commitment, the church had looked at three ministry couples, and the church kept saying they wished we would stay. After three months, it became clear to Dedee and me that the Lord was closing the door to Belgium. We told the church in Cochrane that we were willing to stay, and we got a 101% vote in favour of us staying.

We served in Cochrane for seven years minus ten days. These were great years. The church was small but strong and growing. We grew from fifty to about ninety people. Most of the people in the church when we got there in 1988 were professionals from southern Ontario. I kept emphasizing the need to reach people born and raised in Cochrane, because sooner or later the southerners would move back closer to family. By God's grace, we were able to reach local people. During my ministry there, we celebrated the church's 80th anniversary and that same weekend May 22, 1993, I was ordained with the Fellowship of Baptist Churches of Canada.

While we were in Cochrane, two more children were added to our family: in August 1989, Joshua Jack was born, and in October, 1991, Thanksgiving Sunday, Chrissy Ann was born. Those were busy years, with a young family and lots of ministry responsibilities. Then the recession hit in the late '80s, early '90s, and most of the young professionals moved back south to their families. This was to be expected. The reality for the church and for my family became clear: the church could not afford to continue to support a pastor. I was not able to go back to a bi-vocational role at that stage in my life. FEB Central churches helped us out with a one-time gift to extend my ministry at the church for one extra year. What a tremendous blessing!

It was now Summer 1994 and I had put my name out there looking for a possible move. I contacted a church outside of the Fellowship, a non-affiliated Baptist church called Lansing Avenue Baptist in Sudbury.

I told Dedee that they would never consider me as they were associated with Toronto Baptist Seminary and I graduated from Central Baptist in Toronto. They called me, however, and I spoke at the church four times over two weekends in August. I preached again in November when they were going to vote on me. The vote was a unanimous "Yes," with all twenty-four members voting for me to come and, on January 2, 1995, we moved to Sudbury.

Jack & Dedee Flietstra

We spent twenty-seven years in Sudbury. We arrived in Sudbury on a very cold day in January, and I hit the road running. With hindsight, I probably should have done things differently. My first five years at Lansing were a time of rebuilding. Lansing had gone through a major split just prior to my arrival, which led to the former pastor resigning. For the first three years, my ministry was primarily about caring for the flock and encouraging healing. This meant no major changes. We had people come and go—they liked the preaching, but the worship style was too "old school." Although I told them I agreed that changes needed to come, it was not yet the right time. But those changes would come.

In my third year at Lansing, my ministry was almost cut short. But by God's grace, he gave me wisdom beyond my years which helped me survive. We started to see changes taking place. In our fifth year, we had a number of significant things happen. We started a church plant, we hired our first youth pastor, and we started the process of changing our worship style. Sending twenty-five people and a significant amount of support to the plant, along with the changes in our worship style, however, led to some unrest.

At one point, one of the deacons asked me, "How many more seniors did we need to lose?" To which I replied, "All of them, if that is what it takes." When we brought drums into the church, there was a movement of people who left for Berean Baptist. They believed we had brought the devil's music into the church. We were seeing young people coming to faith like never before. A lovely couple, Bill and Marg Swain, were being pressured to leave. I love Bill and Marg. The pressure was on them to leave, but as they looked at all God was doing, they said, "No, we are staying." They didn't like the music; at times I didn't like the music either, but God was moving.

In that fifth year, we also brought on our first youth pastor Tim Cressman. This was the best decision I ever made in my years at Lansing. We did not have any money, but Tim was willing to trust the Lord with us, and the Lord provided. Tim laid a foundation for our youth and college and career ministries for years beyond his time with us.

The next years were full of all kinds of adventures. We brought Mark Smith on as our next full-time youth pastor in 2006 and, two years later, we expanded our ministry from two to three full-time pastors. Mark moved into an associate pastor role. That was a learning curve for all of us.

Chris Douglas was one of our own young men who had gone to Heritage Bible College and, after graduation, came to serve with us as youth pastor. Chris was with us until June 2013. In September 2013, Ynze Flietstra, my son, came on as our youth pastor and served at Lansing until May 2021.

In 2009, Mark Smith was clear he was looking to stay on at Lansing for the long haul. So, we started the process toward Mark becoming the lead pastor and me serving alongside him. In 2017, Lansing made this official and in April 2019, Mark became the lead pastor and I moved into a supportive role.

In 2017, Bob Flemming asked me to become a district shepherd for FEB Central. This followed the publication of my first book, *Freeing Your Pastor to Serve with Joy*, and a ministry business I had called The Shepherd's Lounge. As a result of Bob's request, I started as the first district shepherd for FEB Central in September 2017. It started off as one day a week, but is now a half-time ministry. I love serving our pastors in this way.

I served at Lansing as lead pastor for twenty-four years and then assisting Mark Smith for another three years. I am now serving at Grace Baptist in Alliston, Ontario. I was asked by the then regional director of FEB Central, Rick Buck, if I would be interested in going to serve at Grace. At that time, it was a church that was needing to be restored, and the Lord has been good in doing this work. I thank the Lord for the people at Grace. I have the privilege to serve with Trevor Tristram, who is a great administrator and has a huge heart for the Lord, his Word and his people.

I'll finish off with some personal reflections on family. Dedee and I were married over forty years ago. We have four biological children and two long-term foster children. We now have fourteen grandchildren: seven grandsons and seven granddaughters. Life has not been without its ups and downs. In my second book, *God of Pain*, I talk about some of those ups and downs. The Lord has been faithful through it all, though, and I have no intention of hanging up my skates. I want to continue to serve until either the Lord returns or I go to him.

Submitted by Rev. Jack Flietstra

12 /

Rev. Lance C. Johnson

One of my goals is to write a Johnson family history which I would title, *From Norway to Heaven Via Canada*. An explanation is warranted.

In 1913 my paternal grandmother, Minda Fridheam, emigrated from Norway to begin a new life in Canada as bride to my grandfather, Karl Johansen. Eventually, my grandparents chose to change their surname to Johnson. I suppose they viewed Canada as a melting pot when, in fact, Canada has become a mosaic. When the story behind the change of surname from Johansen to Johnson is shared with my children, they show disappointment as they feel that Johansen had some personality, while Johnson comes across as being somewhat boring. However, I can assure you that life among the Johnsons is not, and has never been, boring.

My grandparents' wedding took place in the home of one of my grandmother's sisters in Brantford, Ontario, in 1913. Over the course of the next number of years, they lived in Brighton, where my father, the oldest of five children, was born in 1915. When my grandparents moved to Brantford, my grandmother was blessed to have a neighbour, a Mrs. Shellington, who chose to love her for Jesus' sake. Although a Lutheran at the time, my grandmother had just a marginal familiarity with the gospel. Mrs. Shellington invited her to a Bible study in Hamilton, where my grandmother came to understand the gospel and received, in faith, Christ Jesus as her Lord and Saviour. The grace of God was making its entrance into the Johnson family.

It has been said that God has no grandchildren, only children. The blessings of the gospel have continued throughout our family, as up to the fifth generation they are now also receiving Christ Jesus as Lord. Thus, my goal is eventually to write my family's history with the title, *From Norway to Heaven Via Canada*. It is a story of the grace of God!

The grace of the God of the Bible is amazing and unique. God's grace is God reaching down to us. It is not us seeking to impress him with our good works. God's grace is his unmerited, undeserved and unearned favour. "For it is by grace you have been saved, through faith—and this is not from yourselves, it is the gift of God— not by works, so that no one can boast. For we are God's handiwork, created in Christ Jesus to do good works, which God prepared in advance for us to do" (Ephesians 2:8–10 NIV). For our eternal salvation, faith must be placed in Christ Jesus alone. "For God so loved the world that he gave his one and only Son, that whoever believes in him shall not perish but have eternal life" (John 3:16).

As a young man, my dad moved to Montreal where he met and married my mother, and where I was born on December 2, 1945. My older sister, Shirley, and younger brother, Andrew, were born in Montreal as well. In 1949, my parents relocated to Brantford where my next two brothers, David and James, were born. Brantford was home throughout my childhood and into young adulthood.

The year before my parents were married, my dad was involved in a car accident that resulted in the loss of vision in one eye. My dad chose to never drive again. As a result, when we moved to Brantford, a house was purchased that was a half a block from an elementary school, two-and-a-half blocks from a high school, four blocks from Central Baptist Church and a twenty-minute walk for dad to get to work. We were a family of walkers! In all of this, the sovereign hand of God was evident in directing our family to Central Baptist, whose pastor was Dr. Donald A. Loveday. Yes, my closed Brethren parents were to become Baptists, and our family was to enjoy many years of spiritual nourishment and mentoring at Central.

My salvation experience occurred at the age of eight. In May 1954, Central Baptist Church conducted a week-long series of children's meetings. It was during those meetings that I too received Christ Jesus as Lord. My journey in grace and in Christ had begun. There was and is no turning back. God's glory and goodness are my constant companions.

My dear parents were Haakon and Jean Johnson—two very ordinary and yet profoundly special people. I don't recall my dad being on any church committee, but he was rock solid spiritually. The testimony to my parents is five children who all came to faith in Christ, and who have faithfully followed him.

In my later high school years, while considering a career in architecture, I sensed a call to pastoral ministry. My dad, though a blue-collar worker, had a keen sense of the expectations and pressures on pastors. His counsel was one of caution but full support.

I applied to the London College of Bible and Missions (LCBM) and in 1965 was accepted into the bachelor of theology (BTh) program with a pastoral major. The journey at LCBM was an interesting one, as the College merged with the Toronto Bible College (TBC) in 1968 to form Ontario Bible College (OBC), now called Tyndale University in Toronto. The move from pleasant London to a campus on Spadina Road in Toronto was a challenge, which I met, graduating in 1969 with my BTh.

At the end of my third year at LCBM, I was elected president of the student body for the next year which, as it turned out, was the merger year with TBC. As a result, the merger year was marked by co-everything at OBC. I therefore shared the responsibility of student body president with Paul Hope who had been elected at TBC.

The highlight of my college experience was to meet the love of my life, Marilyn Ormiston of Toronto. On August 29, 1970, we were married in Marilyn's family's church, Northminster Baptist Church, Toronto. Her pastor, Rev. Arnold McNeill, officiated and my pastor, Dr. Donald Loveday, gave the message. We have now been married fifty-five years!

I must say this: Pastoral ministry can be very challenging and there can be a lot of stress placed on a spouse and family. I have been blessed with Marilyn as my partner in life and ministry. As Proverbs 31:10–12 states, "A wife of noble character who can find? She is worth far more than rubies. Her husband has full confidence in her and lacks nothing of value. She brings him good, not harm, all the days of her life." To top it off, Marilyn plays piano, as well as keyboard and organ. Her giftedness has been a blessing in our ministry partnership, particularly in the early years. God has blessed Marilyn and me with two sons, David and Darren, and a daughter, Sharon, ten grandchildren, five great-grandchildren— and still counting!

After graduating from OBC, I attended Trinity Evangelical Divinity School in Deerfield, Illinois, for a master of arts in New Testament studies. It was a one-year residency, followed by a thesis to be completed within two additional years. My eighty-page thesis entitled, "The Angelology of Hebrews 1 and 2," was my attempt to answer why the writer of Hebrews felt it was necessary to prove the superiority of Jesus to the angels. I graduated in 1972.

My thesis was researched and written while I pastored at Hope Baptist Church in Niagara Falls. The Niagara Falls pastorate, from 1971 to 1975, was my first in full-time vocational ministry. We lived in the church's manse with utilities provided, and an annual salary of $3,750 including car expenses. Marilyn and I enjoyed fifty months of ministry in the Falls, which included new challenges and a special connection with the youth of the church. Numerical growth was experienced in a facility built on a single-housing lot with on-street parking available on only one side of the street. I have often said to friends that I took my young bride to the honeymoon capital of the world—and left four years later with our two sons who were born there.

The first Sunday evening of 1975 stands out in my mind. It was apparent that there was more than the regular evening congregation in attendance. I preached from 1 Peter 5:1–4 on the role of the pastor/elder, in front of what I later discovered was the pastoral search committee from Huron Park Baptist Church in Woodstock, Ontario. Apparently, the committee members had been encouraged to travel to Niagara Falls to view my ministry, but did not choose to coordinate who would be going and when. As it turned out, the whole committee arrived the same evening, bringing family and friends with them. The whole group numbered seventeen. I knew something was up.

The pastoral search committee had been prompted by Dr. Hal MacBain, the interim preaching pastor at Huron Park, to go and hear the young pastor in Niagara Falls. At that time, Dr. MacBain was also heading up the foreign missions department of the Fellowship of Evangelical Baptist Churches in Canada and, a few weeks before, had preached a missions Sunday for me at Hope Baptist. He suggested to the Huron Park committee that I could meet the demands of a larger challenge. Little did he or I know, this would result in the next twenty years of my pastoral ministry.

In April 1975, my ministry began at Huron Park. Marilyn and I were able to buy our first home. It was our homestead for all the years we were there. A challenging and most exciting experience occurred in our home on January 8, 1978. We were expecting our next child and anticipated visiting a hospital soon. However, at 2 a.m. that Sunday morning, with hardly any warning, our daughter Sharon came into the world with the help of two neighbours and a couple of paramedics. True to the pastoral culture of the era, I preached both morning and evening services later that day!

In the twenty very good and spiritually prosperous years God allowed us to live and minister in Woodstock, our three children were able to attend the same elementary school and the same high school from start to finish. It is not often that pastoral families have that stability, and we value that experience.

I was privileged to enjoy the hand of God's blessing as the church grew from about 150 to close to 400. Two building expansion programs were undertaken in 1982 to 1983 and 1990 to 1991. Each summer, the church conducted an outdoor program of musical groups and preaching in Southside Park on Sunday evenings. The programs attracted crowds of up to 1,000 people. This outreach, as well as others, were instrumental in our community evangelistic efforts. I was pleased to have had the joy of preaching at most of these outdoor programs.

I was blessed with the associate pastors who joined me on pastoral staff. The directors of youth and Christian education called by the church were: Rick Eby, Steve Baxter and Darin Dees. In addition, I was asked to oversee the planting of a new church in neighbouring Ingersoll. David MacBain came on staff as the Ingersoll church planter.

In the early 1990s, I was honoured to be one of the local church pastors in a study conducted by a pastoral colleague who was pursuing his doctorate through Dallas Theological Seminary. The study explored what made a local church leader effective in ministry. Being a participant afforded me the opportunity to evaluate my leadership style and priorities. The conclusion of the study was to show how a healthy church needs to be a worshipping people, on mission and unwavering. Making disciples is the church's God-glorifying mission (Matthew 29:19).

This study occurred during a time of change in local churches. As I pointed out, we had called staff members to be directors of youth and Christian education. My pastoral training had been heavy on a Christian education approach to ministry. Much of Christian education was buying into programs developed by different evangelical organizations such as Christian Service Brigade, Pioneer Girls and Word of Life. However, a new day of revisioning ministry and strategic planning was dawning. I was about to be reinvented.

I say reinvented because that is what life and ministry often requires. I have found that as my ministry grew, or as I changed from one ministry to the next, my own reinvention had to take place. Reinvention is the gracious work of God that sharpens one's spiritual gifts for a new and challenging opportunity.

As a local church pastor, I was also pleased during the 1980s and early 1990s to serve on several boards and committees of the Fellowship and the Central Region of the Fellowship of Evangelical Baptist Churches in Canada (FEB Central) in the area of church extension. These opportunities further expanded my growth in Christ and my vision as to what God could do through our Fellowship, both regionally and nationally.

When I was asked to become the regional director of FEB Central in the latter part of 1994, the region was composed of approximately 270 Ontario churches and Quebec anglophone churches. I sensed I was being asked to become the regional director because of what God had done at Huron Park in my partnership with a wonderful congregation. At this time, the region was relatively young. Although the nation-wide Fellowship began in 1953, composed of the Ontario and anglophone Quebec churches (along with some Manitoba churches), and although Fellowship churches in the other parts of Canada were already regionalized, FEB Central as a region was not founded until 1986. In one sense, we were the oldest and the youngest region, at the same time. It was imperative that the region continue to establish its identity. That identity grew with increased participation of the churches and financial giving. In fact, when I started, the region had a financial deficit of over $50,000, which we were able to eliminate and we ended my first year with a small surplus.

As regional director, I had the responsibility of overseeing all regional ministries and staff, and of being available to help the churches in a wide range of needs. In a movement of independent Baptist churches, my role was rightly defined as having no authority over the churches. Instead of authority, I had cherished opportunities to influence churches toward spiritual health and vitality.

Lance & Marilyn Johnson

Among the issues within the region that needed to be addressed was identifying a clear mission. The region's mission statement became: *FEB Central as a movement exists to be a community of spiritually passionate, disciple-making, and church planting churches.* Another issue was prioritizing the heart of our mission, namely, church planting, which was the driving force in FEB Central becoming a region. Since then, church planting has been at the heart of FEB Central's ministry DNA. During my tenure, there were two church planting directors, first Paul Percy and then Tom Haines, who were successful in building a distinct philosophy of ministry, a growing program and a great team. A further issue was responding to the Vineyard Movement. The Vineyard Movement, particularly in Toronto, was in its heyday. I am grateful that the doctrinal extremism of that movement was easily identified by the churches that responded with biblical accuracy and specifically concerning the person and ministry of the Holy Spirit.

At the mid-point of my fifteen-year tenure, the FEB Central required revisioning again, amid change within society and in approaches to ministry. The need for change has been and will always be a challenge. I believe that change needs to be viewed as God moving us out of our comfort zone and into new faith adventures. The mission statement of the region became: *FEB Central Ministries exist to assist pastors and congregations to journey effectively through the changes which God is creating.*

New initiatives during my tenure were FreshFaith, a ministry of spiritual renewal for pastoral couples; the Women's Ministry Institute

(WMI), a structured program to equip women for leadership in their local churches; and Peacemaking, a program to assist conflicted churches in their revitalization. These new initiatives were in addition to a number of excellent resources, which included church planting, youth, seniors, ministry families, leadership development, worship resources and stewardship. Churches responded well to these resources and to the FEB Central personnel available to assist. God blessed me with an amazing team.

In 2011 I had the privilege of writing a 317-page book, *Pastor Search 411*, with the help of two friends to whom I am most grateful. The back cover of the book states, "It might feel like an emergency! But with the right information in hand, finding the right pastor is an exciting pursuit. In bite-sized chapters, *Pastor Search 411* supports you to eliminate the guesswork. You won't be lost. You will have a map and compass to guide you on your journey. Follow the plan from beginning to end or simply start at your point of concern. You won't feel the need to dial 911." I had the immense enjoyment of assisting approximately 200 churches in their search for a new pastor.

Toward the end of my tenure with FEB Central, I proposed that an assessment of the ministry be conducted. To that end, an outside ministry organization was engaged. After a thorough study, it was recommended that the FEB Central focus on and pour its energy into three specific areas to strengthen the local churches: church planting, church health and leadership development. I determined that when the assessment was finalized, I would resign and leave the newly defined direction to a new leader. Bob Flemming, who was pastor of Springvale Baptist Church in Stouffville, was a most appropriate choice to succeed me. FEB Central continues to be vital to the strengthening of churches and pastors.

Upon leaving my role as regional director, from 2010 to 2015, I had the privilege of being on the pastoral staff at Emmanuel Baptist Church in Barrie, under the leadership of the lead pastor, Rick Buck. I was one of ten pastors, and I often referred to myself as Pastor Number 10! I started on staff as the pastor of seniors and spiritual care, replacing Paul Kerr who had served in that capacity in his transition from heading up the foreign missions ministry of the Fellowship to a fuller retirement. The plan was to eventually move me to a new role as the pastor of administration, to assist Emmanuel in "catching up" organizationally and administratively as the church had experienced a rapid growth from 750 to over 1,200 in its recent relocation.

Among my responsibilities as pastor of administration and leadership development was the task of leading the church in becoming incorporated. This provided the church with a significant opportunity to address its leadership structure to maximize the church's opportunity for growth and ministry efficiencies. Before I retired, the church had reached an attendance exceeding 1,500. I also had the joy of participating in the establishment of a new church plant in Orillia. It was a blessing to have served under Rick Buck's leadership.

In 2013, Emmanuel afforded me the time to teach a one-week course to a group of local church pastors and leaders in Volgograd, Russia, under the auspices of the Slavic Gospel Mission (SGM). The Russian pastors had asked the Mission to send someone to address how to resolve conflict in the local church. I was blessed to travel with Gary McNitt, pastor of Benton Baptist Church, Kitchener, as SGM never sent anyone alone into Russia. I was further blessed with an outstanding interpreter. The reception of the Russian church leaders was most warm and encouraging. One of my "souvenirs" is a copy of my notes translated into Russian.

Since late 2015, Marilyn and I have happily retired to Huntsville in a home on Fairy Lake. Faith Baptist Church is now our church home. I find it interesting to note when God's gracious hand transitioned me in all my ministry roles and opportunities. My first pastorate in Niagara Falls began when I was twenty-five years of age. I moved to Huron Park in Woodstock at age twenty-nine. I transitioned to the role of FEB Central regional director at age forty-nine and then moved into an associate pastoral role at Emmanuel Baptist Church in Barrie at age sixty-four. I was determined to "retire" on the last day of the month in which I turned seventy, which, in fact, I did. Some years ago I heard Dr. MacBain say that the time comes for a pastor to leave the Monday to Friday ministries to younger pastors and to enjoy being invited to preach on Sundays. That is good advice.

I'm happily busy being husband, dad, grandpa and great-grandpa, preaching fifteen to twenty times a year, mentoring younger pastors, assisting some churches in organizing their ministries to be fruitfully efficient and playing ice hockey throughout the year with a great group of new community friends who, like myself, are all over the age of seventy!

I conclude with some final comments:

Family: To Marilyn, I say, "You are the delight of my life, my constant encourager, and my inspiration as we continue to journey together until we see Jesus!" To my children, David, Darren and Sharon, I say, "Thank you. Thank you for being great pastor's kids. The swirl of expectations around you challenged you and you held in there with love and devotion, and you have all proven to be better for the experience."

Local church leaders: I have been blessed as a pastor and regional director to have worked with some excellent local church leaders over the years. I have often said to pastors that much of what can be accomplished in local church ministry is largely dependent on a pastor's relationship and partnership with godly, skilled men and women. I celebrate such leaders.

The Fellowship of Evangelical Baptist Churches in Canada: When I began as the regional director in 1995, the Fellowship was forty-two years old. When I finished my tenure with the FEB Central, the Fellowship was fifty-seven years old. I sensed that there was a feeling among other church groups outside the Fellowship that the Fellowship was dated and old. Not true! The Fellowship then and today attracts quality young men and women into our movement. When I attend conferences and conventions, I rejoice in all the young pastors who are present and participating in our movement. The Fellowship is not stale. We are in many ways a young movement—stable, active and growing! Today, in my retirement years, my heart is made glad! God is doing a great thing among the churches!

Grace: I started my story by sharing with you the entrance of God's grace into the Johnson family through my paternal grandmother, Minda Johnson. I end this writing with a further celebration of grace. As followers of Jesus, we believe and are empowered by the gospel of grace. We are what we are by the grace of God.

To my God, I humbly say, "To you and to you alone, belongs all the honour and glory." Great is the grace, love and faithfulness of my Lord.

Submitted by Rev. Lance C. Johnson

13 /

Rev. Steven F. Jones

"For the longest way round is the shortest way home." This insight from C.S. Lewis comes from his classic, *Mere Christianity*. My life has felt like a long journey home. Like Christian in John Bunyan's astonishing tale, there have been joys and sorrows, straight and crooked paths, virtues and flaws, along with victories and disappointments on the way home. However, my arrival home was made assured only on December 24, 1978—the most important day of my life.

I was raised in a nominal Christian home with two loving parents and two younger brothers, Greg and Chris. My parents, Bill and Joan Jones, had both come to Canada from England in the early 1950s on a one-year visa looking for adventure. They met each other while in Canada, got married in 1957 and established a new life. I was born on January 24

1960, in a hospital in the Notre-Dame-de-Grâce area on Montreal Island, and later christened as an infant. My brothers and I are first generation Canadians, with our entire extended family still living in the Liverpool area and Wales. My mum was a warm, extroverted, hard-working, affectionate, compassionate, strong, independent woman who was one of my best friends. I miss her.

My dad was quieter, but could tell a good yarn. He was a great provider, loyal friend, a man of few words and always dependable. He coached my soccer teams in my early years. He is the reason for my lifelong love of the Liverpool Football Club, a deep affection I have happily passed on to my son, Alec, who is also an avid LFC fan.

The most important day

My mum sought to expose my brothers and me to church as young boys. I recall going to St. Andrews and later St. Marks Anglican Church, from time to time, while growing up in Dorval, Quebec. The St. Andrews building later became the Fellowship's West Island Baptist Church, where I later served as a summer pastoral intern in the summer of 1983. Growing up, I recall a keen interest in spiritual things, but not the church. At thirteen I attended confirmation classes and recall on one occasion falling asleep during class and the minister lifting my head by my hair and chastening me for my lack of interest. I was confirmed and became a choir boy for a few months but quit as soon as I could. However, my interest in spiritual things remained. I remember describing myself throughout high school as a "Christian, but not a very good one."

We moved from Dorval to Brampton, Ontario, in 1976 and Mum never found us another church. My brothers and I were fine with that decision. My first high school friend was Bill Henderson, who later became a FEBC pastor and serves at Caledon Hills Fellowship Baptist Church. Bill, his mother and my friend Ian Lamont were used by the Lord to answer my questions and nurture my spiritual journey. After high school, I attended the Ontario College of Art & Design (OCAD) in Toronto to venture into life as an artist. My buddy Ian went off to Bible college in Florida. He had become a Christian in our last year of high school. After a semester of art college, I was ready to talk. Art school causes you to look at life and seek to interpret it with your choice of medium. I was seriously thinking about ultimate questions and during the Christmas break, Ian was back home from Bible school and sought to answer my questions.

I became convinced I could no longer sit on the fence about Jesus. I needed to accept or reject his claims as God. On Sunday, December 24, 1978, I attended Ian's church for a Christmas Eve service at St. Andrew's Presbyterian Church in Brampton, Ontario. Prior to the service, I bowed my head and quietly prayed to receive Christ as my Saviour. I was eighteen. My decision was not due to anything occurring in the church service itself. I had decided it would be good to receive Christ on his birthday and offer him a special gift—my life.

Three weeks after my conversion, Ian and I walked into Bramalea Baptist Church and while my adoption into God's family occurred on December 24, 1978, my adoption into the Fellowship family occurred on Sunday, January 14, 1979. Anything I have become in Christ today has largely been because of the fine people of Fellowship Baptist churches. I will be forever grateful for my Fellowship family.

I was baptized by immersion five months later in May 1979. I remember it being a defining moment in my early walk with Christ. I realized I really believed. I had decided to follow Jesus. I completed the Fellowship's discipleship course called SHARE, and Evangelism Explosion (EE) became a powerful tool for my continued understanding of the solid claims of Christianity. I recall sitting in the living room of one of our church member's homes with two of my EE colleagues. We shared Christ with a rebellious teen, while his Irish mother hid herself in the kitchen, praying and listening to every word. I passionately shared the Good News and we led this young man to Christ. This was my first occasion to lead someone to Christ, and I recall feeling euphoric. This happened week after week and was instrumental in changing my thinking about becoming an artist and filmmaker. Maybe God had another plan?

A change in trajectory

The Lord used many varied experiences to change the trajectory of my life, as the Spirit of God continued to whisper the wild idea of vocational ministry to my soul. I was enjoying the creative environment inherent in the two art colleges I had attended. I had quit OCAD to attend a film animation program at Sheridan College, Oakville, Ontario. I loved what I was doing and dreamed of working for Disney studios in California. However, a growing dissatisfaction was stirring in my soul.

Not long after, I quit and went to work as a shipper/receiver at a tool and die manufacturing plant. I also enrolled in a Prison Epistles evening class. I quickly discovered studying God's Word was my passion. The following September in 1980, I was attending Central Baptist Seminary in Toronto, Ontario. I had received confirmation of my calling. My mother and father, while not excited by my decision, were accepting of the idea, and I was passionate about training to become an evangelist.

Discovering my true identity

For my first day at Central Baptist Seminary, I drove up to the school in my muscle car, a British racing green 1968 Firebird with mag wheels. Dean Barton wondered what kind of student they were accepting into the student body. Four years later during my senior year, Dean Barton permitted me and two students to share the speaking time during the annual convocation gathering. Typically, a seasoned speaker was asked to address the students and constituency. This year it was three senior students. I was a novice preacher at best, whose only claim was receiving the seminary's Jack Scott Preaching Award. I preached my heart out for my allotted fifteen minutes. After the gathering, Mrs. Maime MacBain asked to speak to me. She was the wife of Dr. Hal MacBain, one of the esteemed founders of our Fellowship movement.

"Steve, that was some good preaching," she exclaimed. In my brief message she decided this young man needed a prayer partner. She told me, "I am committing to you tonight to pray daily for you for the rest of my life." I still get choked up recalling this moment over forty years ago. These were kind words shared to a young seminarian. Through the years, she kept her promise. At annual national conventions, she would sit down with me to receive a report and get prayer requests. The MacBains attended my in-laws' church and often asked for reports and prayer requests. At Maime MacBain's funeral, I quietly stood before her coffin to pay respects and felt Dr. MacBain put his arm around me and whisper, "Steve, she prayed for you every day. I know, I was there." I'm deeply grateful and likely eternally indebted to her for her intentional, faithful prayers for Marilyn and our family. I later established pastor and president prayer teams in all my ministry endeavours to ensure intentional and targeted prayer. Dear friends like Doug and Helene Kornwolf, whom I discipled while a young pastoral intern in Montreal, still pray for us every Sunday over forty years later. I desperately need prayer and I'm deeply grateful to those warriors who have committed themselves to the ministry of intercession.

I loved my time as a student at seminary. I discovered who I am in Christ, while studying and flourishing under professors like Dr. Stan Fowler and Dr. Michael Haykin. I remember competitive ping-pong games with fellow students, friendly theological banter in the cafeteria and the shock we all felt when we heard Keith Green had died in a plane crash.

The most important decision

While December 24, 1978, was the most important *day* of my life, February 14, 1985 was the most important *decision* of my life. It was Valentine's Day. We were the only tourists visiting the Falls, due to a blinding snow-storm, when I presented Marilyn a plastic ring from a gumball machine and asked her to marry me. Most importantly, she said, "Yes," and I later upgraded her fake ring to a diamond.

We were married on October 5, 1985, at Forward Baptist Church in Toronto. Both Rev. Stu Silvester and Dr. Paul Kerr were to be the officiating ministers. Paul was unable to officiate due to an emergency surgery, so Stu performed the entire ceremony. After a wonderful reception, Marilyn and I were ushered off on our honeymoon. We got in our car and my new bride informed me we were going to see Pastor Paul in hospital. Paul Kerr's first response was, "What are you two doing here?!"

Meeting my best friend

Forward Baptist Church is where I first met Marilyn. As a seminary student, I was serving with some Fellowship church planters who were planting a church in the Cabbagetown neighbourhood in Toronto. We couldn't get folks to come to morning worship services on Sunday, so we offered a worship service on Sunday evenings. We all attended our church of choice on Sunday mornings. My landlords were Henry (Bud) and Marg Wright who took in seminary students as boarders. I had lived with them for four years and called them "Mom and Dad Wright." Marilyn's parents, George and Madeline Wilson, were close friends of the Wrights. I asked the Wrights if I could join them on Sunday morning. After the service, we got into their car and I noticed Marilyn leaving the church. From the back seat I asked, "Who is that girl?" And I distinctly recalled Mom Wright turning around from the front seat, grinning ear to ear, and saying, "I can have her over for lunch next Sunday with her parents."

Pastoral internships and mentors

My first pastoral internship was at Bramalea Baptist Church in May 1981, under the supervision of Pastors Stu Silvester, Bill Huggins, Paul Richter and Eileen Morley. I was also serving with Rev. Phil Phillips, the senior Fellowship Chaplain at the Toronto Pearson Airport Chapel starting in September 1981. All of these leaders helped me to grow in my faith and my understanding of ministry. Stu's vision was unquenchable, Bill's counsel nourished my confidence, Paul's spiritual life was contagious and mysterious, Phil's faith was irrepressible and inspiring, while Eileen's care was ever present. I would later enjoy pastoral internships in Toronto at Forward Baptist Church, a church plant in Cabbagetown, summer 1983 at West Island Baptist Church in Montreal and summer 1984 at Parklawn Baptist Church in Etobicoke. The Lord blessed me with amazing people who were willing to answer my questions, let me fail falling forward while modelling for me genuine faith and effective ministry. I am incredibly grateful for the models and mentors God has allowed to intersect my life through the years. While not exhaustive, I'm grateful for the special care of men like Pastors Stu Silvester, Ian Bowie and Roy Lawson.

Stu's life was modelled before me and made an indelible impact on my foundational days as a believer and aspiring young pastor. I thought our growing church was the norm. People were coming to Christ regularly and Bramalea Baptist Church was thriving. My first church experience provided me with a tremendous sense of hope for kingdom advance in Canada.

Moving to the land of possibility

Ian Bowie offered me my first full-time vocational ministry position at Churchill Heights Baptist Church (CHBC) (1986–1989) in Scarborough, Ontario (now Morningstar Christian Fellowship). I began my ministry in June 1986, and two months later my father called me at my office and said four words that would change my life, "Your mother is gone." I was devastated. My mum, my best friend, had died in the early morning hours of August 22, 1986. Ian officiated the funeral and during her funeral wake one of her friends told me that in a recent conversation she had with my mum, she had mentioned she was going back to church. Not her church, but Steven's church, because she felt they "lived out the Bible more." Years earlier Mum had said she had made Jesus her "Saviour and Friend."

Ian Bowie was wonderful. Ian became "Uncle Ian" to my children. Ian was the "moving man" for me. Moving me to the land of possibility.

Convincing me never to allow our present circumstances to dictate our future reality. He was a visionary, but just as important he knew how to get us there. I learned a lot in my short time serving with Ian. He was a larger-than-life personality. When Ian entered the room, everyone knew the fun was about to begin. We laughed lots, but he led us on mission, and the congregation grew as we welcomed the multicultural community surrounding our church.

Steven & Marilyn Jones

Our Katelyn was born in 1989, only a few months before we were to leave CHBC. Marilyn was working as an registered nurse at Sick Kids hospital in Toronto in the pediatric intensive care unit—an incredible job caring for the sickest children. We accepted a call from Wortley Baptist Church in London, Ontario (1989–1994) as their youth pastor.

Our time in the Forest City

London was a thrilling experience, with a thriving youth ministry. I had the joy of serving with an amazing leadership team. The ministry grew with over 200 students being discipled in mid-week ministries and often over 300 students attending our weekend outreach events.

So significant was the leadership depth of our youth ministry that, a few years later, the elders asked me to lead other ministries and start preaching after our lead pastor, Murray Hicks, had left. I was beginning to make a shift from student ministry to lead pastoral duties. This was only possible because of the incredible leadership depth God had provided in our student ministries. We had the joy of seeing many teens and young adults come to Christ and others enter into vocational ministry.

It was in London that Marilyn and I welcomed Alec (1991) and Jessica (1994), as well as Joshua (1993) who was stillborn. We await the wonderful day of our reunion in glory. Our hearts were broken. So much is learned in times of grief and loss.

Landing in the Beautiful City

One Sunday afternoon I got a phone call from an unknown caller. "You don't know me, but I know you." Without my knowledge, the search team from Parkdale Baptist Church (PBC) in Belleville, Ontario, had been praying about me becoming their lead pastor. The Lord had been preparing us for this call, as other churches had been calling during the year. The Lord made his plans clear, and we left London for the beautiful city of Belleville. We recalled our hesitation of leaving the city of Toronto for London several years earlier because London seemed so small to us at that time. But now we were moving to Belleville and we bought a home on 2.5 acres in Foxboro. I laugh now when I recall my horror when two church members offered gun safety classes to help raise funds during our first building renovation. I had much to learn about living in the Quinte Region!

Living in the land of possibilities

I was thirty-four when I became lead pastor of this church family. Parkdale Baptist Church (1994–2000) was an example where pastor and people were knitted together on mission. We went on a journey together and grew from 225 to 451 in average weekly attendance. My mentor, Ian Bowie, had modelled how to move people to the "land of possibility." I was young, full of vision, hope, and serving with an incredible team of church leaders. Many of our deacons, and later elders, were small business owners who were used to navigating change, risk and innovation. My memories of Parkdale Baptist Church are warm and filled with joy.

Marilyn was nursing at the local Belleville General Hospital in her specialty, mother-baby care and also serving our church in the nursery. Our children were young and starting to go to school.

Leading Parkdale Baptist Church humbled me often. I realized I needed another mentor, and so I invited Dr. Roy Lawson to speak at our church. He thought his task was to conduct a Saturday leadership development workshop, but the real reason for my invitation was to ask him to prayerfully consider becoming my mentor. Dr. Roy was the general secretary of our Fellowship. He was loved, highly respected and greatly sought after. He was "Mr. Fellowship" back when most folks thought more highly of denominational life. I was a nobody; he was a larger-than-life leader. In my opinion, he was an Abrahamic character within our association of churches. Roy said he would pray about becoming my mentor and let me know. This began a close friendship of nineteen years where Roy and Joan adopted both Marilyn and me. I always encourage young pastors to look for a "Roy." He and Joan enriched our lives in so many ways. He listened and taught me so much by modelling ministry and sharing wisdom. I keep a list of what I call Royisms on the cork-board in my office: "If this doesn't light your fire, your wood is wet!" Roy encouraged me to accept solicitations to serve on the Fellowship National Council where I served as chair (2000–2002) during the days the Fellowship constituency discussed a women in ministry bylaw. He counselled me when invitations were offered to become the Fellowship National President both in 2004, when I said no, and later in 2011, when I accepted the call. He also counselled me while serving on the general council of the Evangelical Fellowship of Canada (EFC) in the late '90s. In 2024, once again I joined the EFC council and remain committed to help the FEBCC be an active partner in the larger evangelical commu-nity in Canada. These were opportunities used of the Lord to refine me. Roy has been gone ten years now. I miss him.

Leaving Parkdale Baptist Church was one of the most difficult decisions Marilyn and I have ever had to make. We loved the people at PBC and enjoyed the Quinte region. Many of our lifelong friendships were formed during our days in Belleville. However, God had other plans for Marilyn and me. We were called to a large church that was struggling. Before leav-ing, I spent a week asking the Lord for guidance. I wrote a vision plan for the next fifteen years. Sanctified dreams, aspirations and commitments in my personal, family and ministry life from forty to fifty-five years of age. I later itemized these objectives on multiple bookmarks and used them during reading to remind me to keep on mission. Fifteen years later, I discovered I had missed some of these objectives but accomplished many others. "If you aim at nothing, you will hit it every time."

A time of accelerated personal growth

On my sixtieth birthday, I was out with my family for dinner. One of my daughters mentioned that a question her friends asked at birthday parties was, "What is one helpful thought you learned or hoped to learn in the next year?" I told Jessica that I thought in my twenties I learned to manage my dreams while molding my identity, in my thirties I learned to manage my time as I shaped my life and ministry, in my forties I learned to manage my priorities to remain focused on the most important and in my fifties I learned to manage my energy, recognizing I was in a marathon and not a sprint. However, in my sixties, I believed I needed to learn to manage my expectations or suffer the consequences of dashed dreams, failed expectations and awful regret. In our sixties, we begin to realize we have run out of time or steam to land that dream ministry job or establish the type of lifelong friendships and family connections that nourish us deeply. We have much to regret if we poorly manage our expectations.

My forties were spent managing priorities in the midst of regular struggles. In the summer of 2000, we moved to Sarnia, Ontario, to be the lead pastor of Temple Baptist Church (2000–2011). Temple was a great church with a storied history, but had been struggling in recent years. Marilyn and I didn't want to leave Parkdale Baptist Church and Belleville. We loved it there among our friends. But God was very clear and persistent in our call to Temple. Marilyn has always known before me when a move was coming. Her spiritual gift of discernment has always been helpful in these difficult decisions—although she will tell you, I haven't always listened or agreed. Often to my detriment.

We moved to Sarnia and the Temple elders and I began to make some difficult decisions. Necessary, difficult decisions. Over 200 people left the church in the first twenty months. I did not go into ministry to upset people, but I was excelling at it. At each staff meeting I would ask: "Who left this week?" It was a difficult time for our church, and a devastating time for those who departed after calling Temple home for many years. I felt responsible, despite all the decisions being shared decisions by the elders and other leaders. Dr. Roy Lawson, who had been serving as the interim pastor, agreed to stay on after I took the lead pastor role. He agreed to three months and stayed ten years and was a bulwark in the storm, as the elders and I navigated Temple's missional refresh. We got through it a few years later, witnessing dozens of conversions and baptisms each year through our children summer camps, Alpha and Celebrate Recovery ministries.

At the same time, I was chairing the Fellowship's National Council through the women in ministry debate (2000–2004). In my opinion, it was not one of the Fellowship's finest hours. I was confident we had a strong national council, but I felt unprepared for the task, and was so grateful for Dr. Roy and my two national council vice-chairs, seasoned veterans, Gerry Kraft and Doug Harris, who counselled and supported my efforts in navigating this important conversation. After four years of constant struggle at Temple and serving our Fellowship family during the women in ministry debate, I was tired. Marilyn and I started to receive contacts, first from a large non-Fellowship church out West, then another denomination offered an executive position and finally the Fellowship National search team encouraged me to consider the newly vacated Fellowship National president's role. Dr Roy always counselled me that there was great power in an alternative. It often clarifies your commitment to remain planted where you are. I was tempted to escape the struggles, but Marilyn and I decided to stay planted in 2004. And we experienced some modest fruit over the next several years as a church family.

A big surprise

In November 2010, Marilyn and I attended the Fellowship National Conference in Banff, Alberta. The chair of the search team that was looking for our next national president quietly approached me to consider the role. Six years earlier I had said no, but Dr. Roy prophetically told me I should be prepared when they came back. Beside feeling no release to leave Temple in 2004, I also honestly struggled to understand how anyone could lead an organization with no clearly defined authority. However, years of learning to fashion a more nuanced leadership model in the midst of struggles prepared me for the unique servant-leadership approach necessary to serve, unite and help a group of Baptist churches thrive. I was also informed of another struggle. Our regions and national bodies were not getting along (to put it mildly). Accepting the role would necessitate clarifying Fellowship National's vision, our identity as a movement and healing among many National staff.

The Lord led us from Sarnia to Guelph during our daughter Jessica's last year of high school. For a man who doesn't generally live with regrets, this is one of the biggest regrets of my life. It was a brutal year for our daughter who left all her friends. However, I'll never forget her gracious words to me: "Dad, don't worry, if God called you here for some big reason, he must have a plan for me too." We moved to Elora (2011–2019) and later to Fergus (December 2019).

In Autumn 2014, we were visiting Fellowship International missionaries in Europe when Marilyn had a freak fall that fractured her ankle, leg and damaged her lower back. Her surgery was delayed in Athens and nerve damage was the result. Multiple surgeries and treatments, including an ankle replacement, resulted in significant chronic pain that changed Marilyn's life forever. My wife is an amazing woman who continues to trust Jesus despite suffering acute daily pain. She remains dependent on the Lord's providential care every day until her promised healing in this life or the next. I'm a firm believer in prayer and pills and I'm grateful for both in Marilyn's continued care. She remains one of my heroes.

Chasing our identity

At Fellowship National Convention (FNC) 2011, during my first presidential state of the union, I said, "The coffee break is over—we are going to become a church planting machine again!" Our history had been a movement of church multiplication. As early as the 1990s, we had planted 87 new churches in a decade. But that wasn't happening in the early 2000s. Now our churches, with the active support of our regions, began to enjoy a renewed movement of church planting. Between 2010–2024 our Fellowship planted 132 new churches. We still believe church multiplication is one of the best ways to see people come to faith in Christ. We must make church planting a priority in the years to come. I continue to be amazed by the depth of character, zeal and compassion we possess among our missionaries and church planters, establishing churches in Canada and around the world.

Another privilege has been the people I have had the honour to serve with for more than fourteen years—our Fellowship National staff, regional staff and especially the regional directors, and the faithful members of our national councils through the years, particularly our national council chairs, with a special appreciation for Doug Blair for his leadership among our churches and in my life.

We worked on better defining our identity as a fellowship of churches. All national departments got a refresh by creating direction documents identifying their mission, vision and values. We spent three years creating our Fellowship mission document entitled, *We Are the Fellowship* (2014), which identified our entire movement's (local, region and national) mission: *We are a movement of churches making passionate disciples of Jesus Christ*. This mission statement would accompany our *National Affirmation of Faith* (1953), clearly providing for our movement a definition of what we do and what we believe. We pursued clarifying our identity as a Fellowship of churches in our membership-baptism motion (2017) and later our marriage and human sexuality policy (2018).

At FNC2022, our churches approved a prescribed process to revise our Fellowship National *Affirmation of Faith*. This was a three-year process to improve an already excellent statement of faith that had served us well for seventy years but needed modifications and additions to prepare us for the realities of the twenty-first century. At the core, these were all attempts to clarify who Fellowship Baptists are, what they do and what they believe. It's difficult to be on mission when you're not clear on who you are.

God has blessed us as we sought to clarify identity and much fruit was enjoyed. While stewarding our Fellowship National ministry, as national president for fourteen years (2011–2025), we witnessed God's goodness. We grew from 500 churches in 2015 to 541 churches in 2025. Our churches planted 132 churches in Canada (2010–2024), along with 112 church plants internationally (2015–2025) through the ministry of our Fellowship International missionaries. Our Fellowship International missions family grew from 70 missionaries in 2011 to 100 in 2025. Our Fellowship chaplain appointments grew from 27 in 2012 to over 175 in 2025. Our FAIR ministry became a department in 2015 and their revenue more than doubled in ten years toward the holistic care of those suffering. In 2014, the Fellowship French Mission formally ended and a new model to support church planting in Quebec began in 2015. Close to 100 partnerships were established between Fellowship churches throughout Canada and ten new churches in Quebec in ten years. And lastly, the Fellowship Foundation was established in March 2015 and grew to over $31,000,000 in ten years. God is good.

The shortest way home

After forty-two years of ministry life, in the summer of 2022, I took my first sabbatical. I highly recommend it. I developed an obnoxious sabbatical schedule over the three months. I shaved my hair off as a "tip of the hat" to the apostle Paul, who shaved his head prior to commencing his spiritual pilgrimage into Europe. I planned to paint paintings, read a lot, go horseback riding and live outside for several days in the open. I did not accomplish half of what I planned. What I discovered as my most satisfying activity was being with my wife, family and our friends. This is the trick to life. Knowing and being known. To experience authentic nourishing community. To love your neighbour. To know the deep affection of a smile between two friends. To sit silently with those whom you love and never have to say a word. Their very presence is enough to fill your emotional reservoir.

I began my life in Christ in the late 1970s and realized early that anything of value I may be to God's kingdom would be because of the fine Fellowship folk who chose to invest in me, trust me and take a chance on me. Thank you. It has been an amazing journey "on the long way round" (C.S. Lewis) to eventually coming home.

Submitted by Rev. Steven F. Jones

14 /

Rev. Dr. Bob MacGregor

T he gospel message came to my childhood home in Scarborough in 1959 by way of a door-to-door evangelist/church planter. In those days people were not as suspicious of strangers appearing at the door selling things like brushes, vacuum cleaners or perfume. My father, who had abandoned his childhood decision for Christ in his native Scotland, was won over by a man he had met literally minutes before. In such a short time, the trajectory of his life and mine was changed forever—such is the power of the gospel. Door-to-door evangelism would become a lifelong passion and practice of my father well into his nineties.

At the same time, another church planter named Harry Strachan was planting a Baptist church in a nearby school—Churchill Heights Public School. Harry was a Bick's pickle salesman by day and winner of souls by night. One of the many kids in his Sunday school became best friends with my older sister. Her enthusiasm for her church was winsome and contagious. In 1962, the church announced the grand opening of their new building, an exciting event that my sister insisted we all attend. On a bright Sunday morning, with four kids in tow, Dad was introduced to Pastor Strachan and the people of Churchill Heights Baptist Church. This small congregation would become our spiritual family for the next generation. Mom was eventually persuaded to attend but had yet to receive Christ as her personal Saviour. Harry, as he was affectionately called, was a dynamic personality with a warm sense of humour. He was attending night classes at the Baptist seminary with many younger men, but his sales experience was a blessed advantage as he sought to persuade sinners to receive Christ.

There seemed to be an openness to the gospel in 1962, as the world tottered on the brink of nuclear war during the Cuban Missile Crisis. A young president John F. Kennedy stared down the Russian tyrant who blinked and thought better of his plan to install nuclear missiles just ninety miles from the American mainland. Shortly after this crisis, my little brother was born, the fifth of six MacGregor children. My mother's heart was prepared for the gospel by the faithful evangelistic preaching of Harry, and the kindness of his wife Hannah who gave her a gift for her baby boy. Such acts of kindness are beautiful adornments for the gospel and in just a few months, on November 25, 1963, as she and millions around the world watched the funeral of that courageous young president on television, mom quietly knelt before our black and white TV and prayed the sinner's prayer as best she knew how. Our entire family became immersed in church life, forming a worldview that anchored me in the gospel and the church of Jesus Christ. Four years later, I professed Christ as my own Lord and Saviour in the waters of baptism.

In the 1970s there was a spiritual stirring in North America, which was described in a recent movie called *The Jesus Revolution*. The Cold War and the threat of a nuclear nightmare were constant headlines as the doomsday clock crept closer to midnight. It seemed that once again people were desperate for hope. Such constant uncertainty led to fresh ears hearing the message of Jesus that was being preached worldwide on television and in massive crusades by evangelists like Billy Graham.

Our growing church had built a second building that was opened in 1967. The Jesus Revolution erupted in our church in a tragic but profound way on February 5, 1972. My younger sister Jayne and her best friend Marlene failed to return home from a tobogganing excursion in a ravine near our home. As evening approached and the police became involved, the frightening news of two missing girls spread rapidly through our church and neighbourhood as the story was picked up by local and city news outlets including CTV and the *Toronto Star*. Within a few hours, our home became ground zero in what was the largest manhunt to date in the history of Toronto. I recall a tall communications antenna that was quickly erected on our front lawn that allowed search coordinators to communicate with snowmobile operators, horseback riders, helicopter pilots and hundreds of volunteers. People I had never met were power napping on our living room floor or eating sandwiches dropped off by neighbours near and far. To this day, I meet strangers whose eyes well up as they tell me where they were during those awful hours.

After twenty-four hours of tireless searching, the girls' bodies were found buried under a blanket of snow. Police determined their deaths were caused when they stepped out onto a freak snowdrift that hung out over a twenty-foot precipice we called Bird's Cliff. It gave way under the weight of their eleven-year-old bodies, plunging them to their deaths and into the arms of Jesus. During those frantic hours, the news reporters picked up on something foreign to them. It was the unusual peace that sustained my parents and members of our church family during the search. Their questions and subsequent reporting drew attention to the hope of the gospel and the comfort of the Holy Spirit. It was a riveting story that reverberated across the country and in remote regions of the world. Our little church overflowed with seekers, in both morning and evening services. Christians were being revived and lost people were finding new life in Jesus—the hope of the world. It was during this time that I began to ponder how exciting it would be to serve the Lord as a pastor.

In those days, God added to our church youth group a young man who had just received Christ over the summer. John Mahaffey's faith in Jesus was new and dynamic, but like so many of the emerging Jesus People, it had yet to affect his coiffure or wardrobe. John's story appears elsewhere in this volume, but suffice to say that his appearance and that of his friends was a non-issue, as they were loved by our people whose lives were impacted by his great enthusiasm for Christ and evangelism. Each Sunday we sat joyfully in the front rows of our church while Pastor Martin Wedge explained the Scriptures from the original languages, and with the help of an overhead projector. Our youth group was led by two laymen who kept us focused on our lost friends and their need for salvation. For a few seasons, our youth meetings revolved around our drop-in ministry that attracted many of our high school friends. Each Friday night, we conducted prayer vigils while students in various stages of sobriety entered our church basement to hang out and hear the gospel. There were many nights when the sound of salvation echoed in the hallways. Our evangelistic fervour affected everything we did.

One night, my sister and a few others were cruising the streets of Scarborough in our 1966 Ford Meteor station wagon in search of hitchhikers to whom we could share our faith. We picked up two teenaged girls and began our conversation with a warning about the dangers of hitchhiking, which was followed by a passionate explanation of what Jesus meant for us and how real joy was found in him. The evening ended in a dimly lit school parking lot where they prayed to receive Christ.

I tell this story often because it was life altering for me. The two girls later showed up to our drop in with their friend, Eleanor. Her beautiful waist length hair and cool wire rimmed granny glasses quickly caught my eye and tied my tongue. I would be forever smitten. As it turned out, she was there under protest. Her newly converted girlfriends agreed to stop bugging her about Jesus if she would come to church with them. Eleanor, whose disappointment with God led her to atheism, was soon caught up in the infectious love she witnessed in our youth group.

She became an active participant in our gatherings, singing choruses, attending church and Sunday school, while she herself was still an unbeliever. The illogic of it all crashed in on her one night at a Jack Wyrtzen evangelistic crusade that our church organized. During the altar call, she decided to test God. "God if you're real" she said, "then save my mother." Her mother however, who was saved months later, was not God's focus at that moment. "It's not your mother I want, it's you," said the Holy Spirit in an audible voice. Her doubts and skepticism about God were replaced by a deep and lifelong faith in Jesus Christ that began that night—February 5, 1974—two years to the day after my sister's death. On May 6, 1977, with my tongue untied, I declared my vows to her as we were married and headed for a lifetime of ministry that included four precious children. I know that it is the love of Christ that should compel us to evangelize, but as I can attest, there are other factors to consider.

My interest in the pastorate became laser focused in my fourth year of high school. As I was selecting my courses for my fifth year (Grade 13), I realized that by adding a year to the degree program at Ontario Bible College, I could study courses that excited me and prepared me for ministry. So, in 1975, Eleanor and I enrolled at the college.

Ministry internships were not as common in those days as they are now. When our pastor intro-duced the concept to our church,

Bob & Eleanor MacGregor

which included a small stipend, they embraced it as a way to encourage the growing number of young people considering ministry. In the first year, three of us were approved and were quickly immersed into the life of our church. There was little structure to the program. We were basically assigned duties, the planning and implementation of which kept us fairly busy. If it appeared otherwise, our pastor would send us into the com-munity to knock on doors. My duties included the bus ministry, which had me on the streets each Saturday rounding up kids for Sunday pickup. I'm not a big fan of the flashy faith healers, but on those frosty Sunday mornings when our old bus wouldn't start, I was tempted at the very least to ask for the gift. Nevertheless, the Lord heard our groans, and with the help of some WD-40 we coaxed the engine to turn over and got on with our route, to the delight of the forty kids who were waiting for us.

Eleanor and I both helped lead our junior high youth ministry each Wednesday night. Over thirty of us packed into the small basement of the Robertson's home, a wonderful couple who provided a hot dinner for me as I was coming by city bus just minutes before the kids showed up. I also taught one of our adult Bible classes in our new and third building that was completed in 1977. I am grateful for the education I received at Ontario Bible College, but my internship made an indelible mark on my approach to ministry. I became comfortable with children, teens, adults, and occasionally the seniors in local nursing homes whose mental capac-ities were declining.

After graduation in 1979, Eleanor and I moved with our first daughter to Vancouver, British Columbia, where I served as pastor of youth and Christian education at Faith Baptist Church. My resume had caught the attention of Rev. Lester Laird, whose zeal and energy for ministry is legendary. He seemed unaware that few if any could keep pace with him. If I had any thoughts of easing back the throttle after graduation, they were soon dashed. Both Eleanor and I became convinced that such a frenetic pace was normal and that exhaustion was a badge of merit. In addition to overseeing three divisions of youth, I taught junior church on Sundays and a Bible class on Wednesday nights. Of course we also had to start a bus ministry, which had me out every week. Because few churches in the Lower Mainland had multiple staff, the ones that did were asked to send us youth pastors to lead interchurch events. I learned much from my older colleagues as we planned and ran various events in the Lower Mainland and throughout the province of British Columbia.

Sensing the need for more education, a recommendation from the council that ordained me in 1982, we resigned from the church and headed to London, Ontario, to enroll in the mastor of divinity program at the new London Baptist Seminary. It was a faith stretching time as there was no guarantee of an income in the London area and we had just increased our family size to three with the birth of our identical twin girls. We were very much loved by our church family, so much so that they sent us off with a generous love gift and the assurance of their continued prayer support. The president of the seminary, Dr. Gerry Benn, had given me solid counsel and encouraged me to prove the Lord's goodness by stepping out in faith. It was a powerful lesson for us as, in short order upon arriving in Ontario, I was called to be the pastor of the St. Marys Baptist Tabernacle, a small church within commuting distance of the school. The church gave us a small weekly stipend, in addition to housing, for the next four years. With the help of some fellow students, and by the grace of God, we saw the church double in size to about eighty each week. I theorized that sometimes pastors can exasperate their churches and actually hinder growth by too much tinkering. Because I was a full-time student, it was all I could do to fulfill the minimal but significant duties of a full-time pastor. To this day, I believe the church grew because I had no time to "get in the way" of its natural growth. Such was not the case for our own family, which increased by one more, a baby boy to be adored by his three sisters.

In 1986, we bid farewell to our beloved St. Marys family to lead one of our churches in crisis, which is what our Fellowship called churches that had become wards of the Fellowship. Calvary Baptist Church in Leamington was in the final year of its "crisis" which involved a rather toxic relationship with the New Testament Church from which it had split a few years prior. Shortly after I arrived, and to the credit of their pastor, Glen DeSota, the New Testament church initiated a reconciliation that led to the merger of the two churches. This did much to restore the reputation of both churches and of the gospel.

With the sale of the New Testament Church, Calvary Baptist's mortgage was paid off, which gave us some breathing room for ministry. The relative health of the church favourably disposed the deacons to accept my request for time off and funds to enroll in the doctor of ministry program at Central Baptist Seminary in Minneapolis. Churches that make such an investment to develop pastors, invariably reap great dividends for the church. For three years I would commute to the campus with the dean of London Baptist Bible College, who was also in the program. My area of focus was on leadership development, which had become a great interest of mine over the years. One of my assignments was to develop a lay preaching course, which gave me greater insight into a pastor's most important duty. I taught the material over ten weeks to fifteen lay leaders in our association of churches.

Dr. Arnold and May Dallimore were members of our church, having retired from a lifetime ministry at the nearby Cottam Baptist Church. I had known of his reputation as a pastor/historian from afar, but came to fully appreciate him as a mentor of sorts. I devoured his two-volume set on George Whitefield, a signed copy which he gifted to me. At his prompting I also read Iain Murray's biography of D. Martyn Lloyd-Jones. During those days, he challenged me to discover the Puritans and their Reformed thinking and approach to ministry, as opposed to some of the more contemporary seeker sensitive trends of the day. Sadly, I caught on too late and wearied the dear brother by adopting too quickly a worship style perhaps too contemporary. I have since become more sympathetic to his plight, but not before he felt compelled to leave us for the quiet reverence he found in another church. May assured us that it was not personal and that we remained on her prayer list for many years after. I have often wondered how many good church members were unsettled by the tinkering of pastors with too much time on their hands. Leading requires change, and great leaders know when and how to implement change. I had some learning to do.

In 1995—after nine years in Leamington—we accepted a call to Huron Park Baptist Church in Woodstock, Ontario, where Lance Johnson had just completed a very fruitful ministry to become our Ontario regional director. Our 350-seat auditorium was comfortably filled each Sunday, giving rise to either a building prospect or a second service. With the help of many dedicated lay people, we began a service in our full-sized gymnasium that ran concurrently with the one in the main auditorium. My sermons would be viewed in real time by way of a cable and the latest technology. There were awkward times when we had to pause our "sanctuary" service because the "gym" service was not quite ready for the live feed. The liturgical innovation, casual style and band led worship, made synchronization almost impossible. Nevertheless, newcomers appeared each week, not so much seeking salvation but rather a church that felt like home.

The lack of a live "in person" preacher was a fair price to pay. It was an exciting time of refreshing and rediscovery for many. The popularity of the service began to draw suspicion, especially regarding the feature of a prolonged time of meditation. Rumours began to spread that our church was caving to New Age theology and practice. Sadly, the rumours were disrupting our unity, so we closed down the gym service and continued together in the main auditorium with a more familiar liturgy and contemporary worship band. We still had a space problem that was resolved when we agreed to plant a new church, which seemed to draw mostly from the gymnasium group.

It was at Huron Park that I was introduced to the team at the Biblical Institute of Leadership Development (BILD) in Iowa, who had developed a church-based theological education (CBTE) training model that was being used by our Quebec seminary (SEMBEQ) to train pastors. For leaders who have no practical access to formal seminary, the BILD courses and in-service requirements intrigued me. I began teaching our first BILD cohort each Tuesday night for two hours over fifteen weeks. I was assisted by Dr. Hannibal Muhtar, one of our laymen whose business involved the non-formal training of farmers in the developing world. It was while tagging along on one of his training trips to Honduras that the Lord connected us to a church and a Baptist denomination whose formal theological school was closing. In the space of a year, we found ourselves working with their leadership in the implementation of a church-based theological education paradigm for over 300 churches in Honduras. This was the beginning of what would become an international pastoral training ministry, initially called LeadersFor until it was adopted by our Fellowship of Evangelical Baptist Churches in Canada and changed to Leaders Formation. To date, there have been leadership training cohorts led by Fellowship Baptist pastors in eight countries.

After nine years at Huron Park and with an empty nest, I found myself growing weary of my self-imposed ministry regimen. This was compounded by a growing anxiety over Eleanor's struggle with the unpredictable but downward spiral of her multiple sclerosis (MS). Sabbaticals were just emerging in our movement and I felt ill at ease to suggest one for myself, even though there was provision for it. Eleanor and I prayed about stepping out of pastoral ministry to consider other avenues of ministry. In the spring of 2005, we announced our resignation with no clear direction as to what was next, but we had a peace that was reminiscent of our move from Vancouver years earlier. When we applied for a car lease, the salesman wanted to know my vocation. For the first time in my life I heard myself utter the word, "Unemployed." "We'll put you down as retired," said the salesman, who seemed unconcerned that we had no income.

Eventually, the Lord opened up several doors of ministry that both refreshed me personally and kept us current with our mortgage payments. One day as we were contemplating our expenses, Eleanor became especially concerned as any thoughtful person might when there is no regular paycheque to count on. We began to calculate my various income streams and compared them to our expenses. My areas of service/employment included teaching courses at Tyndale University and Heritage College, pulpit supply, weekly meetings with a young pastoral mentee, coordinating LeadersFor for our Fellowship and the occasional wedding and funeral. We realized that although we had less take-home pay, our income was greater than our expenses. We again saw the faithfulness of God to those he has called. Having known only pastoral ministry, these other experiences gave me a greater appreciation for the kingdom of God beyond the local church.

The church where I served as pulpit supply was Morningstar Christian Fellowship, formerly Churchill Heights Baptist Church. I was back where I started, except the little church that cradled my faith was now a thriving multicultural congregation of over 1,000 people. It is generally held that interim preachers, such as I, should not candidate for the position they are filling. In fact, anyone who is formally registered as a Fellowship interim pastor must agree to such. This is generally good counsel, as it gives no advantage to one candidate over another. Besides, I was not interested in returning to the pastorate and I was happy to fill the pulpit each Sunday. But after a year of preaching in what had become the most multicultural church in Canada, my heart warmed to the prospect, even as the search committee had been praying about the same. We committed ourselves to the process as a sort of Gideon's fleece to help us determine God's will going forward. The fleece was wet with dew so with assurance and renewed passion for pastoral ministry, we returned to the pastorate in 2009.

While at Morningstar, I continued to participate in LeadersFor pastoral training projects around the world with a special focus on India with the help of staff member Jack Chen who was a native of Calcutta. Another staff member, Mario Villanueva, used his connections in the Philippines to initiate several training cohorts. God was leveraging his multicultural church in Toronto for the blessing of the nations and we were delighted to be part of it. With Eleanor's health challenges, I no longer travelled abroad, but continued to train the pastors who would lead the international cohorts. I would also seek out and train men with leadership potential in our church. One such leader was a software engineer named Oliver Ipwanshek who attended my BILD First Principles study each week for two years. The Lord has since led him and his wife Marie to plant a church in Ajax with our Fellowship. For the first few years at Morningstar, our local mission was focused on church planting and church revitalization in the multi-site model. There are many advantages to this model, such as shared resources, programs and administrative support. For these reasons, we adopted a struggling Fellowship church not too far from us with the hope to revitalize it. After several years however it has closed. I wonder if things might have been different if we simply sought to restore the church and recommission it as an autonomous Baptist church with a pickle sales-man pastor.

After nine years at Morningstar, we began to ask the Lord to lead us to the Kitchener area where three of our four children had settled. Anyone with grandchildren can relate to this prayer. In addition, we also realized that proximity to our adult children meant more family care for Eleanor. In 2017, a letter came to my desk from Grandview Baptist Church in Kitchener. Unlike most of my mail, this one was unopened, keeping secret from my staff what God was about to do.

Grandview's search for a lead pastor was triggered by the sudden death of Steve Baxter, a friend of mine and a much-loved pastor with whom I would inevitably be compared. Pastoral transitions can be very hard on a church, but by God's grace we were able to settle into what would be our last pastorate. One of the things that interested me about Grandview was that it was on track to plant a church. Church planting has been part of my ministry strategy since the founding conference of FEB Central in 1986. Our first regional director was George Bell, who gave an impassioned plea that hammered church planting into my young head. Our planting efforts at Grandview seemed stalled by the inability of FEB Central to find a planter for us.

Meanwhile, a young firefighter who was leading one of our small groups and participating in our leadership training volunteered for the job. Sensing that such an unusual prospect might be of God, even as was the son of Jesse, we sent him to be assessed by FEB Central. The result is that Heritage Grace was started at the beginning of the COVID pandemic lockdowns, under the leadership of Aaron and Mariah Roeck. Aaron is enrolled at Heritage while serving full time as the pastor of Heritage Grace Church in Kitchener.

Like most of Kitchener, Grandview was a visibly European congregation. But with the spike in immigration and flood of international students in our region, it has become a beautiful multicultural church family of 900 and a powerful testimony of the power of the gospel to transcend racial barriers. Grandview also worked toward launching an Arabic speaking ministry—something that was realized after my retirement. Arabic has surpassed German as the second most common language in the Tri-City area. Our time at Morningstar gave us a clear vision of what an international church could accomplish for God's glory.

In June 2024, at the age of sixty-seven, after forty-seven years of ministry and in our seventh year at Grandview, we retired from full-time service. While driving my eleven-year-old granddaughter to her dance studio recently, she asked me what I planned to do in retirement. "Important things," I said, "like driving you to dance." The ministry is like that, God's people doing small but important things that adorn and prove the gospel. For all of the grand initiatives in pastoral work, it comes down to the church as a family of families, caring for its own while seeking to add to its number those who are being saved to the praise and Glory of God.

Submitted by Rev. Dr. Bob MacGregor

15 /

Rev. John Mahaffey

I was born in 1956, but the story of my conversion to Christ began in 1946. It started when my uncle and aunt, Gordon and Mary Lean, were converted to Christ through the influence of their landlords, an elderly couple who were connected to the Moriah Street Mission in Toronto. During training with the Royal Canadian Air Force in 1945, Gordon was introduced to the gospel while stationed in Quebec. With the end of hostilities in Europe, Gordon returned to his wife and within the year, after many discussions, they both knelt by their beds and surrendered their lives to Christ.

As a child, I remember being with my parents on a few occasions when we visited in the Lean's home, first in Gladstone and then in Boston, Ontario. There was something wholesome about my aunt and uncle that attracted me to them. Gordon had an incredible sense of humour and a winsome personality. They were filled with joy, and I sensed their love for me. It was their godly influence that led me when I was about seven years old to ask my mother if I could go to Sunday school. I distinctly remember having a strong desire to know God at that time, and this was certainly not because of my parents' influence. They were non-practicing Anglicans who had me baptized as an infant, but they never darkened the door of a church after this, except for funerals, weddings and maybe at Christmas. My Aunt Mary had witnessed to my mother Margaret on several occasions both before and after she married my father, John, but my father discouraged any interest my mother had in the gospel.

We lived in the Caledonia-Fairbank neighbourhood of West Toronto, and my mother quickly made arrangements for me to attend Sunday school at the closest local church, Earlscourt United. I attended faithfully for one year, but after I received a Bible on the occasion of my promotion from the primary to the junior department of the Sunday school, I never returned. The desire to know God had evaporated. Years later, after I had come to faith in Christ, I realized I never heard the gospel there as I was fed the unbelief of the New Curriculum which saturated the teaching and preaching of the United Church in the late 1950s and early 1960s.

When I was ten, our family moved to Scarborough, and I attended Churchill Heights Public School. This neighbourhood of Woburn was so different from where we had lived before. I remember how happy my mother was to live in a modern bungalow built in the late 1950s. At this time, the eastern section of Scarborough was filled with wide-open spaces and a number of prosperous farms. I enjoyed making new friends and riding our bicycles carefree along newly-paved roads void of traffic congestion.

When I entered high school in 1970, the hippie subculture and world-view of the sexual revolution was well underway. The pressure to fit in was strong, and it wasn't long before I felt like I was living just to party on the weekends. Getting drunk on cheap wine, stoned on marijuana and behaving promiscuously became my sole focus. My life was out of control. I felt trapped and I hated what I was becoming. But God was at work in my life. I had several encounters with Christians.

There was a Christian girl in my grade 10 biology class who tried to share the gospel with me, but I mocked and humiliated her in front of the class for her "stupid" beliefs. When I was hitchhiking to my girlfriend's place, the man who gave me a ride talked to me about Christ and gave me a gospel tract to read. Somehow I attended a Youth for Christ Rally at Castle Frank High School in downtown Toronto. At the conclusion of the meeting, I remember feeling an inner pressure to take Christ as my Saviour, but I resisted. It was shortly after this that my uncle and aunt came back into my life. On a visit to our Scarborough home my uncle shared with me that there was an opportunity to get a summer job in Boston, Ontario, and they invited me to live with them for the summer.

In late June 1972, I arrived at their home and started my first summer job working at a livestock auction house chasing pigs and cows in and out of the auction ring. Almost every evening for the next eight weeks, my aunt and uncle engaged me in conversation about evolution, creation, atheism, faith, God, Christ and the Bible. These conversations grew with seriousness and intensity as the summer dragged on. On Sundays, without any pressure from them, I went with them to worship and attended the young people's class where I met and became friends with Dan Shurr, who also shared his faith with me. My hair length was well below my shoulders and I later learned my presence in this very rural conservative farming community had caused a stir in Boston Baptist Church as people frequently discussed the "long-haired hippie" nephew of the pastor. But a greater stir occurred every Sunday over lunch in the parsonage, as I discussed my uncle's sermons with him.

By mid-August I was struggling deeply with the things I was learning and with the state of my life. I remember one evening lying on my bed looking at the ceiling, wrestling with a whirlwind of thoughts and feelings, when I started to pray for my friends in Scarborough. I expressed to God my heartache for the way they were destroying their lives and then suddenly I stopped and asked myself, "What are you doing? You're praying!" At that moment, I realized that I believed. I spent the next day on the farm of the Bowen family, who were members of Boston Baptist Church. All day long as I picked cucumbers in the field, I was constantly wiping the tears from my face as I felt wave upon wave of God's love touch me. At the end of the day at the Lean's home, I shared what had happened to me and made arrangements to return home to share Christ with my friends. It was then that I learned that Gordon and Mary had prayed for my salvation every day for the last sixteen years.

When I came through the door of our Scarborough home, my mother knew immediately what had happened to me. Within two weeks she came to Christ. Within two years she was in heaven at forty years of age. My father was disgruntled, and on a number of occasions informed me that he didn't want me talking and pushing religion in his home. I began attending Churchill Heights Baptist Church where I was greeted and welcomed warmly by Bob MacGregor who would soon become a dear lifelong friend.

I began sharing my faith with many of my fellow students in Woburn Collegiate and within two months, two of my friends came to Christ. The three of us were baptized together in early November 1972, by Pastor Martin Wedge. This was the start of an explosion of witness for Christ, and the beginning of an awakening within our high school and in parts of Scarborough. Like the people in Boston, the people of Churchill Heights didn't quite know what to make of all these "long-haired freaky people" who sat every Sunday in the front seats of the auditorium. By the time I graduated from high school in June 1976, over 200 of our peers had professed faith in Christ. These fruitful experiences of sharing Christ with others, and the preaching of Pastor Wedge, placed within my heart the sole focus of preparing myself for a life of evangelism and Bible teaching.

At Churchill Heights, I met Andrea Karram. In Grade 13 we began serving the Lord together as leaders in the college and career ministry. It wasn't long before this beautiful Lebanese girl from Kingston, Jamaica, laid aside her misgivings about me and we began dating.

Central Baptist Seminary—preparing for ministry

The next four years were momentous in preparing me for ministry. In the fall of 1976, I entered Central Baptist Seminary. I was accompanied by five friends, including Andrea, who were part of that move of the Spirit during our high school years. One of these was my best-friend Don Greedy, who I led to Christ in February 1974. During the next four years we were inseparable, as we often studied and prayed together about God's call on our lives and missionary service. Don and I were introduced to the ministry of George Verwer of Operation Mobilization (OM) through Brenda Taylor who had recently returned from serving with OM in India. George's passion to reach the lost galvanized our commitment to world missions.

My four years at "the Sem" were life changing. It was exciting to be surrounded every day by other young men and women who were committed to doing the will of God. Time in the classroom with men like Jack Scott, Denzill Raymer, Les Tarr, George Bell, Hal MacBain, Jack Hannah,

Robert Mitchell and Roy Lawson shaped my thinking and inspired vision. In my second year, I became a weekend youth pastor at Meadowcrest Baptist Church working with Pastor Don Foley in Brooklin, Ontario. In my last two years, I became a ministry intern with Bob MacGregor at Churchill Heights serving under Pastor Wedge.

In July 1978, Andrea and I were married. Together we earnestly sought the Lord as to how and where we would serve him. Having already experienced the upheaval that came from immigrating from Jamaica to Canada, the thought of serving Christ overseas was not appealing to her. But the Lord was at work in ways we had not imagined.

Dr. Russell and Betty Honeywell moved from Minneapolis to Toronto to open the Canadian Office of The Far Eastern Gospel Crusade (now SEND International). Russell was a seasoned missionary and educator who established the famous FEBIAS College of the Bible, the largest interdenominational Bible college in the Philippines. The Honeywells became members of Churchill Heights and their influence among the college age students in our church was far-reaching. In early 1979, Russell brought Chuck Hufstetler to Toronto to preach at our church and at a chapel service at the seminary. My personal meeting with Chuck set in motion the trajectory of the next forty years of ministry.

Chuck was a veteran church planting evangelist who excelled in training and mentoring young men. After meeting with our pastor, he met with me and asked if I would come to the Philippines and be part of his church planting team reaching young professionals in Makati, the business district of Manila. This was not the conventional way of recruiting missionaries, but the prospect of working with an evangelist as part of a large church planting team was appealing. After struggling in prayer and seeking the godly counsel of my father-in-law, Stan Karram, Andrea and I became missionary appointees and began raising our monthly support.

The Philippine years

On February 4, 1980, we arrived in Manila and were greeted by Mario Villanueva, a member of Chuck's team and a recent graduate of FEBIAS. Mario was a gifted evangelist and we became good friends.

Our first year was spent in language study at the Overseas Missionary Fellowship's language school in Batangas City. Almost every weekend we would travel to Manila to join Chuck's team for door-to-door evangelism, evangelistic Bible studies with people who expressed an interest in the gospel and in worship with the team and a growing number of the newly converted. With the basics of the Tagalog language, we moved to Manila, next door to the Hufstetlers, and dove full-time into evangelizing Roman Catholic Filipinos. All of our team of Americans, Australians, Canadians and Filipinos were trained by Chuck and his wife Joanne in the Evangelism Explosion method and this training was then extended to the new converts.

The 1970s and 1980s were a watershed moment in the history of the Philippines. The imposition of martial law by Ferdinand Marcos in 1972 created a social climate and political unrest that shook Philippine society. This created an openness to the gospel, and before long the Roman Catholic Church struggled to maintain its influence on the people. This socio-political unrest was used by the Spirit to produce a spiritual awakening and explosive church growth. Every week, through door-to-door evangelism and Bible studies in people's homes, we saw people coming to Christ. Soon the Hufstetler's home was overcrowded with up to 100 people every Sunday coming to worship. The Lord then provided space at a school for the deaf. After four years of ministry, there were 300 worshipping every week. The Makati Bible Christian Fellowship was now established and became an official local church of The Alliance of Bible Christian Communities of the Philippines. In 1983, Chuck and Joanne returned to the USA for a year of home service, and I became the leader of our international church planting team. During this time, I was assisted greatly by Mario Villanueva who continued to mentor me in all things Filipino.

Of the hundreds of Filipinos we saw come to Christ in our first term, there was one young married couple who became very special to us. When Andrea was eight months pregnant with Katherine, our first child, she knocked on the door of Pabi and Emy Fajiculay's home. She was warmly received and both of them gave their lives to Christ. On the second visit to their home I accompanied Andrea and we began to disciple them. They were hungry for God's Word and their spiritual growth was incredible. Today Pabi is the pastor of Hope Advance Church in Paranaque, South Manila. They have become the spiritual parents of hundreds of Filipinos.

In 1984 we returned to Canada with our two children Katherine and John David, for one year of home service. I became the "missionary in residence" at Churchill Heights and had the joy of serving under Pastor Art Larson, who for many years was the radio preacher on Canada's National

Bible Hour. This was a wonderful year of reconnecting with old friends and supporters of our ministry, as well as introducing our children to their family in Canada. We travelled home via Europe and in Paris, France, spent time with our dear friends, Don and Brenda (née Taylor) Greedy who had just completed a year of French language study and were soon to go to Fez, Morrocco, with Arab World Ministries.

After a year of home service, we returned to the Philippines and within days learned that my friend Don had contracted Hepatitis B in Morrocco. He had been wrongly diagnosed and his condition worsened. He was airlifted to the south of France but suffered a heart attack and died at twenty-nine years of age, leaving behind his wife Brenda and a six-month-old daughter, Natalie. News of Don's death shook us, and deepened us in our commitment to the cause of world evangelization.

SEND International leaders saw a great need and an open door in Baliwag, Bulacan, a growing city one hour north of Manila. As we grieved Don's death, we were assigned to lead a church planting team there. Unlike Makati, with its young professionals who were fluent and comfortable in speaking in English, Baliwag was marked by its pride in using pure Tagalog. This required several months of upgrading my language study. Baliwag was also a stronghold of Roman Catholic idolatry and devotion to the Santo Niño (the baby Jesus). There was little evangelical presence in Baliwag, and the few Protestant churches that were there were cultic in their approach and attitude. There was an incredible need to reach the 300,000 people who resided there. By God's grace we built another team of international missionaries—Germans, Americans, Canadians and Filipinos and within a short time we had a worshipping body of sixty believers.

We started home Bible studies among interested people throughout Baliwag. One of them was the Cruz family. After going to their home for several months, eight of them were converted. I remember the joy and excitement when they gathered to destroy their idols and be baptized in a public pool. Other members of our team also experienced household conversions and baptisms.

In 1987 the Philippines was engulfed in the People's Power Revolution and Baliwag was cut off from Manila for several days as protestors and conflict raged on the streets. Miraculously, the dictator President Marcos and his infamous wife, Imelda, were ousted from Malacañang Palace with little violence and life returned to normal. Two more children, Mary-Lue and Peter, were added to our family while in Baliwag. The Baliwag Bible

Christian Church grew to about 200 people and Mario Villanueva and his new wife Raquel joined us there in our last year; the leadership of the team was transferred to him when we returned to Canada. Under Mario's leadership, the church purchased land and built a centrally located worship and ministry centre. One of the young people converted when Mario led the team and the church is now the pastor. Today the Baliwag Church has started several other churches and is a leading church in Luzon.

SEND International began work in Mindanao among the unreached Maguindanaoan Muslims. While leading the church planting team in Baliwag, I was assigned to oversee our missionaries there and this required several trips to the region. The work here was difficult and dangerous. One of our missionaries, a good friend, John Speers, was martyred during this time, gunned down by a Muslim extremist in the local marketplace.

In May 1989, we returned home to Canada with our four children. We were uncertain about the future as we sensed that God was redirecting us.

The Churchill Heights—Morningstar years

Within a month of our arrival in Toronto and our reunion with our home church, Pastor Ian Bowie resigned his ministry at Churchill Heights to pastor a church in British Columbia. The elders approached us about the possibility of assisting, which I did for several months and, in June 1990, I was appointed as the lead pastor.

During the 1980s, the church struggled with the changing demographics of its surrounding community. Ian Bowie saw this new reality and laid the foundation for a refocused outreach to the increasing West Indian and Asian populations. With the vision of a multicultural church in mind, we developed Vision 1000 by 2000—a ministry plan to become an international worshipping community of 1,000 people by the year 2000. Dr. Sidney Kerr was the first to join my team. This eighty-year-old veteran increased significantly the median age of our pastoral team. We nicknamed our church East Scarborough's International Worship Centre. Within a year, Kim Bauer became my first associate pastor. SEND International missionary Cathleen Miles was seconded to us to help us develop ministries to reach the needs of immigrants and new Canadians. Later Jack Chen from Calcutta, India, Dennis Campbell from St. Vincent, Dave Hunt who had grown up at Churchill Heights and my good friend, Mario Villanueva from the Philippines, joined the team.

In 1991 there was a steady stream of conversions and baptisms. One of them was a Sudanese Muslim named Salah Adam. Salah was an outstanding athlete who trained with the Canadian Track and Field Team. Through Shaline Booher, one of our members, he was invited to church and attended regularly. One Sunday when I was preaching through Galatians, he fell to the floor of the auditorium, was immediately surrounded by people who prayed silently and when he stood up he was soundly converted. When he was baptized, he gave his testimony in

John Mahaffey

English and shouted in Arabic "Jesus is Lord!" as he came up out of the water. Later he and Shaline married, and through Arab World Ministries began evangelizing Arabic-speaking Muslims in Toronto. On October 31, 1999, they were on EgyptAir Flight 990 on their way to visit Salah's family in the Sudan, when they and their two children Joshua (four years) and Rebecca (22 months) perished when the terrorist pilot crashed the plane into the North Atlantic killing all 217 people on board.

The Adams' funeral brought the attention of the national media to our church, and I had the privilege of preaching the gospel to over 1,200 people, including Salah's parents who had come from Sudan, along with other Muslims who had been influenced by Salah and Shaline's witness. I later worked closely with Arab World Ministries to establish Adam House, a ministry to refugees in downtown Toronto.

During Holy Week 1994, we held a week of evangelistic services with Canadian evangelist, Dr. Barry Moore. For each service the church was packed and we saw 140 people make decisions for Christ. This was a significant turning point, and it was not long before we began two morning services to accommodate the growing number of worshippers. We also expanded our facilities to provide additional office, educational and foyer space as well as a gymnasium, which we named after Salah Adam. In 2005 Churchill Heights became Morningstar Christian Fellowship, a needed change to reflect the expansion of the ministry well beyond the original community in which it started in 1958. In our eighteen years of ministry there, the church grew from a predominantly white, anglo community of 400 each Sunday to over 1,200 people from seventy-seven different nations.

In 2005 I was invited by D.A. Carson to take part in a pastors colloquium at the Trinity Evangelical Divinity School in Deerfield, Illinois. Carson was the speaker at the Fellowship Convention in Toronto in 2003, and I had arranged to have him preach at Churchill Heights the Sunday before. This "connection" was the reason for this kind invitation. I soon discovered I was the only pastor at the colloquium who was pastoring a church in Canada. This colloquium was the beginning of what would become The Gospel Coalition (TGC). I was privileged to meet with these theological giants, and it was incredibly edifying to work together with the council members to produce TGC's foundation documents: "The Confessional Statement" and "Theological Vision of Ministry." All of this grew out of the deep concern of evangelicalism being defined by its fringes and losing the centrality of the historic gospel. TGC soon became a theological home for "churches deeply committed to renewing our faith in the gospel of Christ and to reforming our ministry practices to conform fully to the Scriptures."[1]

I had always envisioned that, Lord willing, I would pastor for more than thirty years at Morningstar before I retired. But this was not to be. A series of circumstances and unique phone calls from the chair of the search committee at West Highland Baptist Church in Hamilton, Ontario, led Andrea and me to seek the Lord for the better part of a year. While on a brief sabbatical, the Lord made it clear to me that our ministry at Morningstar was coming to an end, and I should accept the call to move to Hamilton.

The West Highland years and beyond

After a teary farewell to our Morningstar family, I became lead pastor of West Highland on January 1, 2008. West Highland had grown during the three years it was without a pastor. The capable church board and pastoral team maintained well the church's ministries and outreaches. There was widespread agreement of the need to expand the church's facilities but an overall vision and direction for the church was needed.

On our first Sunday I preached from Colossians 1:24–29 and stressed that I wanted my ministry there to be one of "making the Word of God

---

1   "The Gospel for All of Life: Preamble," in *The Gospel Coalition: Foundational Documents: English*, 4.

fully known and the people of God fully mature." This phrase soon became a motto for the church.

After a year of getting to know the staff and the people, I was requested by the board to write a vision paper which would serve as a map for the development of ministry for the next decade. Drawing from my observations of the church's strengths and weaknesses, as well as its growing community, Vision 2020 was developed and after prayerful discussion was fine-tuned to share with the church. This led to significant changes. A hard decision was made to move the church offices out of the building to provide needed room for the children's ministries. The church had a deacon's board which had managed ministry since its beginning in 1972, and we transitioned to elders who governed the work and placed the management of ministry into the hands of the pastoral team.

West Highland had a strong children's ministry, but the number of adult converts was very low. We made the conversion of adults, particularly the heads of households, a priority, and over time we saw the number of adult conversions and baptisms increase significantly. In cooperation with Operation Mobilization we began Hamilton Challenge, a yearly summer outreach of door-to-door evangelism in high density communities of immigrants. A well-staffed and well-attended Alpha program, held twice a year, became a comfortable place for the people to bring their friends to hear the gospel. An emphasis on small group ministry incorporated more people into weekly gatherings in people's homes for fellowship, prayer, sermon discussion and application.

Before we came to West Highland, the church family of over 700 people filled the church's auditorium each Sunday. Vision 2020 included two morning services which began in 2009 and this enabled me and the other pastors to have two opportunities to connect with more people after the services. The decision to expand the church's facilities was postponed for eight years, and we focused our energies on disciple-making, ministry development and building the administrative and ministry staff.

In addition to leading the West Highland pastoral team, I developed with the help of Dwayne Cline, pastor of Hughson St. Baptist Church, the Ontario Regional chapter of The Gospel Coalition. Our first meeting was held at West Highland in April 2010, with D.A Carson and Mike Bullmore of Crossway Community Church in Wisconsin as our two speakers. Then in 2016, I gathered several key pastors from across Canada for a meeting in Ottawa at Church of the Messiah to begin the work of TGC Canada.

West Highland agreed to house the new TGC Canada office and Wyatt Graham was appointed as our executive director. He quickly established our website, which provides quality gospel-centred articles geared to Canadian pastors and church leaders.

As part of a new missions focus we became involved in two LeadersFor projects, first in India and later in the Philippines. Teaching Bengali pastors alongside Jack Chen, who had returned to Kolkata to pastor the famous Carey Baptist Church, was a life changing experience. Returning to the Philippines after twenty-five years gave opportunity to visit old friends and teach young Cebuano pastors in the Visayas and Mindanao.

In 2015 the decision was finally made to expand our facilities, with an over 98 per cent vote of the members. Nevertheless, during the three-year project, over 200 people expressed their disapproval and left West Highland. This was a major blow, but throughout those three years the financial giving did not wane and our attendance remained steady. We were able to double the footprint of the church, repatriate our off-site offices and provide space for growing ministries and outreaches. Today, two years since my retirement in June 2023, 1,000 people regularly worship each Sunday and are ably led by Pastor Jamie Strickland who served as my associate for the last four years of our ministry there.

As I look back over forty-five years in missionary and pastoral ministry, I can see how God wonderfully prepared us in one place for ministry in another. Our cross-cultural experience in the Philippines prepared us to minister fruitfully in a multicultural community in Toronto. The things I learned from Chuck Hufstetler's leadership of a large team of international missionaries prepared me to lead a diverse team of pastors and elders in establishing a remarkable international church. And these two "missionary journeys" equipped me with the maturity needed for our third "missionary journey," to help an established church in Hamilton transition through needed changes for its next period of gospel-centred ministry. To God be the glory!

Since retirement it has been a privilege to serve with our Fellowship president, Steve Jones, as part of the Affirmation of Faith committee, to continue serving as a council member of TGC Canada and to lead an interdenominational ministerial called the Steeltown Fellowship, comprised of fifty evangelical pastors serving in the Greater Hamilton Area.

Submitted by Rev. John Mahaffey

16 /

Dr. Mark and Karen Naylor

I n 1977, two young students arrived at Northwest Baptist Theological College, fresh out of high school. Mark Naylor, raised in a British Columbia church-planting family, and Karen Braunberger (from Calgary and then Ottawa), were about to begin a journey that would impact many lives across continents. What started as Mark's one-year Bible school commitment and Karen's four-year bachelor of religious education program would evolve into a lifelong mission of translation, teaching and cross-cultural influence.

The call to Pakistan

During our time at Northwest, Professor Vern Middleton issued a challenge to bring the gospel to the Muslim world. His call resonated with us.

So after our wedding in 1981, and Mark's completion of both a bachelor of science at UBC and a master of divinity at Northwest, we were accepted as missionaries with Fellowship International. In 1985, with our eighteen-month-old daughter Becky, we embarked on our journey to Pakistan.

We spent the next fourteen years in the southern province of Sindh, home to 8 million Muslims. During that time, we raised our three children—Becky, Matthew and Philip—while immersing ourselves in a culture vastly different from our Canadian home. Mark focused on meeting with Sindhi men, sharing the gospel, and working to plant churches, while Karen devoted countless hours visiting local women and homeschooling the children.

Our early years were spent learning the Sindhi language and trying to understand the values, priorities and customs that were so different from what we were comfortable with. Our goal was to communicate the gospel in a way that would resonate with the people of Sindh and make its relevance as God's good news clear. As we grew in understanding and ability, we also faced numerous cultural dilemmas and made our share of mistakes. Yet, through these challenges, we continued to learn and press forward in our mission to share Christ's love in this unique and complex context.

The clash of cultures—nuances matter!

Early on in my efforts to learn Sindhi, I (Mark) tried out a newly discovered word for "dying." It had a meaning similar to the English idiom "to pass away." I used the new word with my friend and he reacted to my comment with amused disgust, explaining, "That idiom is never used when speaking of yourself, only of others. When you referred to your own death in that way, it implied that you considered yourself an important person." Rather than being a casual reference to my death, I had communicated an arrogant and self-important attitude.

Confronting demons and the spirit world

One day when visiting a friend, I noticed a man sitting alone in the corner of the courtyard, so I asked who he was. "That's my uncle," my friend replied. "But don't talk to him. He has a demon." I was somewhat taken aback by this and rehearsed in my mind any teaching or training I had received at seminary that would have equipped me to deal with a demon. I was chagrined to realize that I did not know how to respond to such situations.

We were learning that the life experiences of Sindhis in their world and culture had shaped how they responded to the stories of the Bible. We could see that the accounts of Jesus' authority over demons was resonating differently with Sindhis than with us, as Canadians. While Sindhis welcome the possibility of overcoming a very real fear in their lives by calling on the name of Jesus, Canadians tend to be puzzled about the presence of demons in the world and wonder how that should be understood and handled.

From language learning to Bible translation

What began as a focus on evangelism and church planting took on a new and significant dimension when I (Mark) joined a Pakistan Bible Society translation team in 1989. This initiative quickly became a cornerstone of our ministry, one that would continue even after we returned to Canada. But why Bible translation? Why devote decades to creating a new translation when an existing translation was already available?

The answer lies in the heart of our calling: to make God's Word accessible and transformative for the people we served. While the existing translation was functional, it was written using high level and difficult Sindhi, which did not communicate well with Sindhi speakers. We wanted a translation that was accurate and felt personal, natural and compelling—a translation that spoke directly to the hearts of Sindhi readers, enabling them to encounter the gospel in a way that was truly their own.

In 1990, while working on the Sindhi Old Testament translation, I was shocked to hear an evangelist to Sindhi speaking Hindus say, "We don't use that New Testament translation in our work." The Sindhi New Testament, published in 1985 after years of effort by a dedicated team, had been written in common Sindhi and distributed by the Pakistan Bible Society to reach the predominantly Muslim Sindhi population. I had assumed it would also serve Hindu-background believers in the Sindh, where churches were growing among tribal Hindus, but this assumption proved incorrect.

The evangelist explained, "It's full of Islamic names and terms, and Hindus find this offensive." His honesty made me realize that producing a clear and understandable translation wasn't enough. A translation also had to resonate with the audience's cultural and religious context. Terminology carries emotional, political and intellectual baggage, and the Islamic terms in the Sindhi New Testament alienated Hindu-background readers. For these marginalized groups, the language of the text reinforced their sense of being disrespected outsiders.

When I asked how they shared the gospel with Hindus, the evangelist replied, "We read to them from the Urdu Bible and then explain what it means." This answer troubled me. Urdu, often a third language for tribal Hindus, was difficult for them to understand, especially for the illiterate. I realized the urgent need for a Bible translation that Hindu Sindhi speakers could connect with.

As a result, I pursued a new initiative to create two parallel Sindhi New Testament versions: one for Muslims and another for Hindus. The Hindu Sindhi version was designed to serve both tribal Hindu-background believers and mother-tongue Hindu Sindhis. Our translation team brought together a diverse group: a Muslim Sindhi translator, a Hindu mother-tongue Sindhi speaker and a tribal Hindu-background evangelist fluent in Sindhi. My role as the supervisor and primary exegete was to ensure the accuracy of the translation.

The goal was to produce culturally appropriate translations that addressed the distinct terminology needs of each audience based on the same translated text: the same Sindhi translation but with dialectical differences. This experience taught me that Bible translation isn't just about linguistic accuracy but also about overcoming cultural and emotional barriers to ensure the message truly resonates with its audience.

Translation seeks communication

Bible translators are not as much concerned with formal definitions of words as they are with how the translation is understood by the receptor audience. The need to implement this principle became clear during revisions of the verse, "Rejoice and be glad, because great is your reward in heaven" (Matthew 5:12 NIV).

The Sindhi word for "heaven" first suggested for Muslim Sindhi reflected a concept of paradise tied to Islamic beliefs—an eternal reward earned by good deeds. However, this interpretation did not appropriately reflect Jesus' intent, which was a reference to heaven as God's dwelling, not as a transactional reward system in a future paradise. So the translation was corrected to speak of a great reward "in God's throne room," referring to the *presence* of God. For Hindu Sindhi, where no equivalent term for "heaven as God's dwelling" exists, the translation reads, "With God is a great reward for you." This rendering ensures clarity and avoids any unintended doctrinal implications.

Both changes represent a theological shift, moving readers away from the idea of earning rewards, and redirecting them toward seeking God as the ultimate focus. Through careful revision, the translation now reflects a deeper, God-centred understanding, bridging biblical theology with cultural spirituality and opening new paths for meaningful communication.

Translation goes beyond finding the right *words*. It's about ensuring the audience grasps the intended *meaning*. It serves as a bridge connecting biblical truth to cultural

Karen & Mark Naylor

understanding. In Sindhi, translating religious terms such as prophet, salvation, sin or faith involves carefully choosing terms rooted in the audience's theological understanding, as no neutral option exists. Effective translation builds on existing terminology within the language while remaining faithful to the original text and embracing cultural parallels. When Sindhi readers encounter familiar concepts in the New Testament, it not only affirms the Bible's message but also fosters deeper trust in God's Word.

How translators get the job done

The journey to create the new Hindu Sindhi and revised Muslim Sindhi New Testaments was a blend of tradition and innovation. Unlike previous translations painstakingly completed without computers, these updated translations harnessed the latest Bible software and scholarly expertise, including consultation input from Northwest's Dr. Larry Perkins. To prepare an initial Hindu Sindhi New Testament draft copy, and so that cultural gaps could be bridged, chapters of the 1980 New Testament were shared with Hindu Sindhis, who proposed alternatives to Islamic terms for concepts like God, grace and love.

As the supervisor and primary exegete, I worked alongside a team of Muslim and Hindu translators to refine drafts, adjusting grammar and style, to resonate with the intended audiences. Rigorous exegetical checks ensured the translations were not only clear and accurate, but also meaningful for their readers. This collaborative effort resulted in several landmark achievements. In 2007, we completed the Old Testament in Sindhi for a Muslim audience as companion to the 1980 Sindhi New Testament. In 2024, the New Testament in Sindhi for a Hindu audience was finished along with a revision of the New Testament for a Muslim audience. Most recently, in 2025, the New Testament in Sindhi for a Hindu audience, the revised New Testament for a Muslim audience and the complete Sindhi Bible for a Muslim audience were all published. A Study New Testament with extended notes for a Muslim audience is currently a work in progress.

Learning the hard way

Our years in Pakistan were marked by what we often describe as learning "the hard way" about several crucial aspects of ministry: the grace of God, the needs of the Muslim world, the limitations of our own efforts, the centrality of prayer and the wisdom of involving others in the work. As young, idealistic "wannabe world changers," we discovered that our initial self-confidence needed to be tempered with humility and a deeper dependence on God.

The challenges were particularly acute for Karen: As a western woman, I found setting up a home and living in the very limiting culture of a traditional Muslim country hard. Really hard. During our final term, I (Karen) faced a crisis of faith, wrestling with feelings of abandonment in what I perceived as a "God-forsaken place." This struggle ultimately led us to return to Canada in 1999, where we settled in Victoria, British Columbia. Over time and by God's grace I found spiritual healing and restoration that has allowed me to continue supporting Mark in his ongoing efforts to serve Sindhis in the name of Christ.

A new chapter in ministry—open doors for Mark

Upon returning to Canada, our ministry expanded in new directions. In 2002, I (Mark) joined the faculty of Northwest Baptist Seminary in a joint venture with Fellowship International as coordinator of international leadership development.

I went on to earn both an MTh and a DTh in missiology through UNISA (University of South Africa), focusing my research on how Sindhi men's understanding of God changed when reading the Bible in their heart language. This academic work has enhanced my ability to train others in cross-cultural ministry. It has also allowed me to leverage my cross-cultural experience to mentor and develop new missionaries and cross-cultural workers, equipping them to navigate the same challenges we once faced.

Current ministry impact

Today, our ministry is evolving and expanding. Because of existing relationships in Pakistan, I (Mark) am able to continue supervising, training, mentoring and encouraging our Pakistani colleagues from a distance.

As part of overseeing the Sindhi Bible translation project, I supervise typesetting and printing, ensuring accuracy and quality in every detail. I am also involved in preparing study materials tailored to various audiences, equipping them to engage Scripture in their heart language.

My continued disciple-making efforts focus on weekly mentoring men from Sindh, building on a foundation of mutual respect and longstanding friendships. Some became believers during our ministry while living in Pakistan, while the others were members of the Bible translation team. Through online connections, I invest in their spiritual growth and leadership development, as they disciple others in the way of Christ. These men create opportunities for disciple-making through relief and development initiatives, as well as by initiating discovery Bible studies in the homes of neighbours and family members who live in villages around the Sindh. Together, we strategize on ways to ensure their local initiatives have a multiplying effect, fostering sustainable movements that empower communities to continue spreading the message of Christ.

Since 2002, I have been teaching at Northwest Baptist Seminary, equipping students to discover how cultures influence the way people think, respond, act and communicate. The emphasis is on how the gospel—presented, understood and lived out—is shaped by such cultural contexts, how communication occurs across cultural boundaries, and how cultural perspectives shape theological understandings. Courses include Dynamics of Cross-Cultural Ministry, World Faiths and Ways of Religion, Global and Cross-Cultural Dimensions of Christian Leadership, Intercultural Theology, Contextualized Communication of the Cross, and Cross-Cultural Conflict. Through these courses, students gain the tools and insights needed for effective cross-cultural ministry and leadership.

At Fellowship International, we are committed to exploring and implementing better ways to be effective change agents, striving to identify and remove unnecessary obstacles in our understanding and practices that hinder our impact. It's not simply about having good intentions or trying harder; true effectiveness comes from proper training and the application of sound methods. As part of my responsibilities, I play a role in training and equipping missionaries with the skills and perspectives they need to serve with greater understanding and effectiveness in cross-cultural contexts.

Spiritual fruit

For decades, missionaries in Pakistan have been praying and looking for ways to overcome barriers to the gospel. Around the world, missionaries driven by "spiritual discontent" have sought to address unfruitfulness among those resistant to the gospel. Through embracing an emphasis on catalyzing movements, Fellowship International has accepted the challenge to discover and focus on ministry practices that are aligned with what God is doing to draw people to himself. By reflecting on Scripture, missionaries are learning how to identify and embrace disciple-making practices that God is blessing with fruitfulness. Those working in catalyzing movements continually ask, "What practices produce spiritual fruit, and how can we encourage multiplication?"

Sensitively applying principles of productivity and fruitfulness leads to greater kingdom growth, by bringing people to Christ and involving them in his mission. This approach challenges unfruitful practices and encourages aligning ministry efforts with how God works through people. These principles do not promise easy or quick results. Instead, they demand dedication, hard work and contextualization. These principles require rigorous commitment to spread the gospel effectively, engage with spiritual hunger and multiply movements.

Spiritual fruit is ultimately the work of the Holy Spirit. Fruitfulness in ministry comes from aligning our efforts with God's design, much like farmers enhance conditions to maximize yield while relying on natural growth processes. As disciple makers conform their practices to conform to the work of God's Spirit, the transformative message of the gospel finds its impact in people's hearts and lives. We praise God that the faithful seed-sowing and teaching done in previous decades is now resulting in more and more people coming to faith.

Sindhi believers who were discipled and trained in years past are now training and discipling others who in turn reach their families and neighbours for Christ. The Bible translations continue to reach new readers, and training programs equip new generations of cross-cultural workers. After years of many missionaries and their supporters faithfully working on behalf of Pakistan, a movement of catalyzing disciple makers is emerging.

Looking back and to the future

Our journey from young Bible college students to veteran missionaries and trainers spans over four decades of service. Our story demonstrates how God can use those willing to persist, so that multiple generations, cultures and communities are impacted. Through our experiences—both the successes and the failures—we have learned to rely on God's grace and leading.

As we look to the future, our focus remains on multiplying our impact through training others and ensuring God's Word continues to reach new audiences. Our story serves as a testament to the importance of long-term commitment in ministry, investing time and effort in learning and training, always with reliance on God's Spirit to draw people to salvation in Christ.

Submitted by Dr. Mark and Karen Naylor

17 /

Rev. Bob Parks

My lifelong interest in genealogy has led me to many interesting discoveries about my family history. One of those is that, although I was born in the United States, I have Canadian ancestry leading back to two sets of great-grandparents on my mother's side. One set hailed from Wentworth County, Ontario, and the other from the Eastern Townships of Quebec. Both immigrated to Michigan in the 1800s. I mention that because it must be that it was my "Canadian blood" that drew me back across the border at strategic points in my life.

I was born in Caledonia, Michigan (not Caledonia, Ontario), a small town just south of the city of Grand Rapids, on September 22, 1943. I arrived as the seventh child in what would end up as a family of nine children. My mother, Ella Belle Roelofson Parks, who had come to faith in Christ a year after her marriage to my father, would be the primary spiritual influence not only in my life, but in the lives of each of her nine children. My father, Hosmer Dewey Parks, who was not a believer for most of his life, largely because of his overly-strict religious upbringing, struggled not only spiritually, but with alcoholism. His influence on his family, unlike that of my mother, was largely a negative one, until the final years of his life brought a better end to his story, as I will later reflect.

My earliest and most lasting memories are of my church experiences in Sunday morning and evening services, Sunday school, Wednesday night prayer meetings, home Bible studies and youth group meetings. I loved music, congregational singing and preaching. I would sit in the very first row of the little church we attended, just to be close to what was happening on the platform. That earned me the title of "the little deacon" before I turned five years old. I came to faith in Christ at age seven through the ministry of our church, and the influence of my mother, and was baptized at age ten. It seems I knew even in those early years of my life that God had a plan for me that involved service in ministry to his church.

My childhood years went quickly as I entered kindergarten at age four, took two grades together in one year in a country one-room schoolhouse, and entered high school in a new community of Wayland, Michigan, at the age of twelve. My interests in music, drama and public speaking grew during my teen years and much of my time was spent in high school choirs, marching band, school plays and concerts, church services and youth activities.

The first time I crossed the border from the USA into Canada came in my mid-teens when my older brother, Monty Parks, took me with him to Dorion Bible Camp, a Canadian Sunday school camp north of what was then Fort William and Port Arthur (these two cities amalgamated to form Thunder Bay, Ontario, in 1970). I served as a junior staff member and gained a good deal of experience washing dishes and doing other camp chores. Monty was ten years older than I and had a strong commitment to Christ and a desire to be a mentor and spiritual model for his younger siblings. He would later serve with Youth for Christ in Belleville, Ontario, in camping and church ministries, and with people who had intellectual disabilities in Thunder Bay.

A major event occurred during one of those summers when I and another junior staff member took what we thought would be a day-long rowboat trip that turned into a harrowing experience. We were caught in a flash storm and blown across Black Bay. We spent a cold night in a forest preserve until being rescued by a local pontoon plane pilot who spotted us and ferried us back to a relieved camp staff who had spent the night before praying for our safe return. The camp director emphasized to me that God had spared our lives for a purpose—something I would later more fully understand and appreciate.

Following graduation from high school at age sixteen, I enrolled at the Grand Rapids School of the Bible and Music (GRSBM), a Bible institute my brother Monty had attended years earlier. There I trained in both Bible and music, with the goal of serving the Lord in churches or on the mission field, wherever he might choose. My involvement with travelling choirs and male quartets would give me a great deal of practical experience for the next chapters of my life.

My next experience in Canada came in 1963, just after I graduated from Bible school at age nineteen. I was asked to serve with a pastor in Moncton, New Brunswick, as youth and music director at Lewisville United Baptist Church. There I directed the youth program, played the organ, led the adult choir, preached at a nearby church plant and formed a young men's gospel group—the Fellowship Quartet. The quartet sang at YouthTime rallies and local churches, travelled throughout the New England states and recorded a gospel album, all within a short twelve-month period. I returned to Michigan in the fall of 1964, having received a notice from the American government to report for a physical for the military. There I spent another year taking additional Bible courses at GRSBM and working as a part-time staff member in the music department of the school.

In June 1965, I was married to Clarice Ruth Jackson, whom I had met and dated when we were both students at the school. Our first year of marriage was spent in St. Joseph, Michigan, in youth and music ministries at the First Baptist Church. I was then asked to return to teach at GRSBM, where I spent the next eight years teaching music, training travelling music groups and travelling and recording gospel albums with a men's quartet I had formed—the Evangelaires. I was ordained to the ministry at my home church in Wayland, Michigan, in 1966 and my daughter, Jennifer, was born in 1969. Those years in Grand Rapids were years of growth and development.

In the fall of 1974, I was called by Calvary Baptist Church of Santa Barbara, California, to serve as assistant pastor and worship director, a position I held for the next ten years. In the summer of 1979, I had another significant experience in Canada when I was given a three-month leave to take a summer language course at Regent College in Vancouver, British Columbia. Not only did I learn Greek that summer, but God taught me so much more as he did a deep work in my life and marriage. It would prove to be another major life experience in a Canadian context.

Returning to Santa Barbara that September, my wife and I learned that we were expecting a second child. It was somewhat of a surprise, as it had been nearly eleven years since our daughter had been born, and we had thought that we might not be able to have any more children. Our joy over this good news was soon tempered by the sobering discovery in the seventh month of my wife's pregnancy that she had breast cancer and would have to undergo surgery and follow-up chemotherapy. Our little son, still in the womb, went through the surgery with his mother, and was born full-term and in good health in May 1980. His name, Jonathan—from the Hebrew for "gift of God"—reflected our deep gratitude to God for his protection and safe arrival.

In the fall of 1985, I was called to serve at Mission Hills Baptist Church in Littleton, Colorado, as associate pastor of worship and singles ministries. Life in Colorado not only revolved around church ministry and family life, but also around medical appointments and treatments for my wife, whose cancer had returned and had grown more life-threatening. Little did I know when I took on ministry to single adults that I would join their ranks during those years. My wife, Clarice, died in February 1988, and I became both a single parent and a single pastor at the same time. While my daughter was at an out-of-state university, I was challenged with the task of raising a young son, while serving in two ministry areas that each presented full-time demands. I was finally led to the decision to resign my ministry position to allow me to concentrate on parenting my son, while completing work I had begun at nearby Denver Seminary in a masters of Old Testament program. Toward the end of my seminary training, I began working part-time with another Denver area church, Foothills Bible Church in Littleton, and after graduation from seminary, I was asked to come on full-time staff at the church as associate pastor of worship and singles, where I served for the next five years.

During my time of ministry at Foothills Bible Church, I was introduced to Judy Mininger Fehsenfeld, a widow and mother of five children, whose husband, Del Fehsenfeld Jr., was the founder of a revival ministry based in Buchanan, Michigan, called Life Action, and who had died of a malignant brain tumor at age forty-two. After our first meeting at the Navigators headquarters in Colorado Springs, we began a long-distance relationship that involved many phone conversations and short-term visits between Colorado and Michigan over the next two years. We were married in August 1992, and began the daunting task of blending both our lives and families. We lived and ministered in Colorado

Bob Parks

for two years after our marriage until Canada came into the picture once again.

In September 1994, I was called to Benton Street Baptist Church in Kitchener to serve as associate pastor, alongside senior pastor Jim Reese, a fellow Michigander who, as he often said, also became a Canada goose! While still adjusting to married life and working to blend our families, my wife Judy and I were tasked with adapting to a new homeland and a new church ministry. With those challenges facing us, God gave us sufficient grace to serve both the church and our family for what would be the next thirty years.

After three years of serving together as fellow pastors at Benton, Jim Reese and I traded roles. I became the church's senior pastor and Jim Reese became associate pastor. That arrangement helped the church handle the transition well, and Jim and I served together for the next five years in those roles. When Jim left the Benton pastoral team to pursue interim ministry, he had served at Benton Street Baptist Church for twenty-five years, the longest serving pastor in the church's history.

My ministry years at Benton began and ended as associate pastor, with twelve years service as senior pastor in between. Gary McNitt came to serve as associate pastor at Benton in 2005, and after five years, he and I did the same kind of transition that Jim Reese and I had done years before. After a total of nineteen years of serving at Benton Street Baptist Church, I left staff to follow my predecessor's lead and enter a time of interim pastoral ministry, which included service at several Fellowship Baptist churches. I began at South Zorra Baptist Church in Woodstock, then served at Stoney Creek Baptist Church in London and Calvary Baptist Church in Guelph. Other churches followed, including Northside Community Church (AGC) in Kitchener, and Pineland Baptist Church in Burlington (NAB). In addition to interim ministry, I was afforded opportunities at Heritage Seminary in Cambridge to serve as adjunct professor, seminary chaplain and director of the graduate certificate in biblical preaching. My years of service at Heritage were very fulfilling, especially working alongside then-president Rick Reed, and were a good conclusion to my years of active ministry. Turning eighty in September 2023 seemed to be the right time to round out my ministry in the place where it had started sixty years earlier—in Canada.

As I reflect on the many years of ministry opportunities that were afforded me, I think of one highlight that I alluded to earlier. It has to do with my own father, who after many years of resisting the gospel, finally yielded his heart to Christ at the age of sixty-eight. What a privilege it was for me to baptize him at a lakeside family gathering in Michigan on June 28, 1975. Since that time, I have had the honour of baptizing a number of our children and grandchildren. My wife and I are happy that we now have a legacy of twenty-eight grandchildren and four great-grandchildren who are being raised to know and follow the same Lord and Saviour, Jesus Christ, whom we have known throughout our lives.

I think of myself as a "Canadian-improved" American whose life has been enriched by my experiences in God's country of Canada.

Submitted by Rev. Bob Parks

18 /

Dr. Larry James Perkins

J udy, my lifelong ministry partner, and our children, along with godly mentors, friends and colleagues, empower my story. I am indebted to each one who has shaped my identity, enabled my vocation, and held me accountable to my Christian confession. Whatever contribution I may have made only reflects their generous contribution of time, wisdom and resources.

My mom and dad, Verna and Jay Perkins, gave birth to me in Vancouver, British Columbia, shortly after the end of World War II (March 25, 1948). Donna, my sister, is three years older than I am. Jay and Verna modelled devotion to Jesus coupled with deep wisdom, entrepreneurial competence and courage, generosity of spirit and a diligent work ethic. Although neither graduated from high school due to various circumstances, they became lifelong learners as they pursued their own self-designed educational pathway. Dad's experience in the forest industry enabled him to develop, in partnership with David Methven, companies that manufactured various wood products. This is where I experienced my first taste of work—at the grand pay of 25 cents an hour. Twice his factories were seriously damaged by fire, and I saw firsthand how their faith in Jesus carried them through.

During these growing years, our family life revolved around our church community at Ruth Morton Memorial Baptist Church, one of the historic Vancouver churches. Dad served as chair of the deacons board and Sunday school superintendent (600 children were registered at its peak) and Mom enjoyed leading in women's ministries, the primary department and Pioneer Girls. They were both also instrumental in developing the Point Roberts Bible Camp that served Regular Baptist churches in the Vancouver area. My sister and I were constantly involved in church activities and influenced by so many godly men and women, including pastoral leaders like Howard Philips, William Sloan, Grahame Reeve (professor at Northwest Baptist Theological College), Dr. Sam Mikolaski and Doug Harris, as well as committed church leaders, especially Will Blackaby.

When a young boy, I made my initial commitment to Jesus through the guidance of my mother and following the example of my older sister. Pastor Doug Harris baptized me when I was twelve. However, a deeper commitment to Christ occurred years later when I was at Oxford University and had to decide whether I was "all in" in terms of the gospel. Fortunately, God's Spirit was working in me at that point. High school years were fairly calm. I enjoyed learning and excelled.

Our family formed deep friendships within the Ruth Morton Church community. One of these families was the Hansells. Herb was the choir director and organist, and Margaret supported him and led in the Sunday school. Music was part of our lives, including piano lessons—the bane of any boy's life—and elementary school choir. In my later teens, Herb Hansell taught me how to play the pipe organ—a rather unique instrument in Regular Baptist churches in British Columbia in those years. Herb and Margaret had three children, one of whom was Judy. We knew each other as friends throughout our pre-adult years. When I was partway through my first university degree, we began dating and were married August 26, 1972. God gave us four children (Patricia, Laura, Sarah and Andrew). We now enjoy twelve grandchildren and one great-grandchild.

My sister trained as a nurse. When she graduated, she married Gordon Reeve, her high school sweetheart. He was a son of Norma and Grahame Reeve. He later became a pastor and led churches in Edson, Alberta, and Barrie, Ontario, and in several cities in British Columbia (Campbell River, Parksville and Vernon), as well as serving as the regional director for Fellowship Baptist churches in British Columbia.

Larry Perkins

In my Christian understanding, every believer has the same calling, that is to live for Jesus 24/7. God's Spirit, however, guides believers to live out that calling in many different ways. Because I did well in high school, it became clear that I would attend university. Because of my sister's involvement with Gordon Reeve, I had opportunity to interact with Professor Grahame Reeve and I found his knowledge of Greek and Hebrew intriguing. As a result, although I had some interest in a possible medical career, I took courses in classical Greek and Hebrew during the initial years of my bachelor of arts program at the University of British Columbia (UBC). I eventually graduated with an honours degree in Classics (1968). As I was concluding this undergraduate degree program, Grahame Reeve challenged me to consider further education that might enable me to make some contribution to evangelical scholarship. Dr. Mikolaski (then professor of systematic theology at New Orleans Theological Seminary), visited our home at this time and showed interest in my future plans. He insisted that if a vocation in evangelical scholarship was my intention, the next step was a degree program at Oxford University. He held a DPhil in theology from Oxford. He offered to write a letter of reference for me, if I should decide to apply. This was a huge step for me. I had never lived away from home, the financial challenges seemed insurmountable and the transition into a very different mode of higher education seemed daunting. However, my mom and dad were very supportive, offering to look after my living costs if I paid for all other costs. So, I applied to Mansfield College, linked with the Congregational Church in England, for a BA in theology and, when I learned I had been accepted, my parents and I took it as God's leading. This required me to live in Oxford, England, from 1970 to 1972.

Around this time, Judy and I began to date more seriously. Nurturing a romantic relationship when we were separated by such distance taught us some very valuable lessons. Although this predated computers, cell phones and the internet, we managed to maintain and deepen the relationship thorough snail mail, and my occasional visits home. During the months of July and August 1971, I returned to Vancouver and we became engaged. Marriage followed on August 26, 1972, after my graduation from Oxford.

I cannot say that my studies at Oxford were easy. Adjusting to British culture as well as the Oxford educational method was challenging for me. Writing a paper a week on a topic presented by my tutor, Dr. G.B. Caird, principal of Mansfield College, and then writing a week of exams at the end of two years based upon what I had learned, generated considerable anxiety. It was during these times that I had to discern whether the wisdom of Jesus was true and the Christian worldview offered the best way for humans to live their lives—following the design of the Creator. God was gracious and his Spirit helped me to settle that matter during some reflective walks in the Oxford countryside. The weekly Oxford Christian Union (CU) Bible studies became a wonderful, supportive Christian environment.

My tutor, Dr. Caird, was trained both as a classicist and as a biblical scholar. In his research, he contributed to the study of the Greek translation of the Old Testament, commonly known as the Septuagint. He introduced me to this area of biblical studies and encouraged me to apply for the Junior Septuagint Prize offered by Oxford University, a small scholarship that required applicants to write an exam. The year I sat for it, there were only two of us writing. As soon as I saw the exam, I knew something was wrong, because the text set was not from those we had been advised to study. I later learned that they had given us the wrong exam. The evaluators awarded the prize to both of us. I used to the money to fund a four-week bus tour through Holland, France, Germany and Northern Italy during the spring break.

As my Oxford studies were concluding, Dr. Caird urged me to consider doing doctoral work in Septuagint Studies. I lacked the resources to continue studying in Europe and so I applied to the only institution in North America that offered a PhD program in Septuagint studies, the University of Toronto. A week after our wedding, officiated by Doug Harris, we drove from Vancouver to Toronto so I could begin studies. The university required me to complete a masters in Near Eastern studies to qualify for PhD studies. I completed that in 1974 and began doctoral studies that fall. My doctoral advisor was Dr. John Wevers, the premier Septuagint scholar in North America at that time. I had little awareness of his academic status when I applied to the program. God was certainly guiding my steps in these matters.

We truly were blessed during our five years in Toronto (1972–1977). We lived in the university apartments located at Yonge and Bloor in downtown Toronto. Being completely new to the city, we took the advice of a friend in Vancouver and checked out Jarvis Street Baptist Church. Unbeknownst to us, when she learned we were moving to Toronto, she contacted Dr. Slade, pastor of Jarvis Street Baptist Church to let him know we were coming. So, a few weeks after we arrived, Dr. Slade showed up at our apartment door. We only had one chair and he graciously accepted what little hospitality we could offer. To our amazement, he invited Judy to apply for a position in the Jarvis Street Church office. She eventually became his assistant. This employment cared for all our living expenses. My tuition and fees were covered by a series of Ontario Graduate Fellowships.

We made many wonderful friends at Jarvis Street. The organist was J.C. Penny. At that point he was in his nineties and coming to the end of a remarkable ministry as organist. The choir director was seeking someone to replace him and when asked, I jumped at the opportunity. For four years I served as organist. I had inquired at Central Baptist Seminary about part-time teaching, but nothing was available. Dr. Geoff Adams, principal of Toronto Baptist Seminary (TBS), invited me to become an adjunct faculty member, teaching courses in New Testament Greek and biblical Hebrew. These experiences taught me a great deal about seminary teaching and engagement with colleagues and students. Pastor Harold Duckworth, who also was adjunct at TBS, became a good friend and mentor. Through Judy's work, the scholarships and the part-time teaching, we were able to complete five years of graduate study at the University of Toronto without any debt.

Without question, the most important event that happened while we were in Toronto was the birth of our first child in 1976, Patricia Ann

Perkins. Grandma Hansell, who had never flown in her life, courageously flew by herself from Vancouver to help with her new grandchild!

Through my experience in Toronto, I became convinced that God was opening a way for me to be involved in seminary teaching. I perceived that if I was to have opportunity to influence the church in Canada, training future leaders would be the most productive way to accomplish that mission. In early 1977, Dr. Howard Anderson, principal of Northwest Baptist Theological College in Vancouver, encouraged me to consider relocating to Vancouver to work as an adjunct faculty member while gaining pastoral experience. Although my dissertation was not yet finished, we believed this was the right time to make this move. Judy's mom and dad flew to Toronto to help us. Judy flew back with her mom and Patricia, and Dad Hansell and I drove our car back with a U-Haul trailer in tow. Don Merrett, the pastor at Ruth Morton Baptist Church, invited me to join him as assistant pastor in a half-time role. Don was a great evangelist and a caring shepherd. His mentoring gave me significant insight into what makes a good pastor. This was important learning as I began a ministry of training Christian leaders in seminary. With various changes happening at Northwest Baptist Theological College in 1977/78, the opportunity came to teach full time. So, in August 1978, I accepted a position as assistant professor in Biblical studies. Our second daughter, Laura Lynne, was born that November.

My dissertation needed to be completed and so, during the summers of 1977, 1978 and 1979, I concentrated on that project, realizing that earning a PhD was key to continuing my development as a seminary professor. I was able to submit the dissertation for examination in late 1979 and defended it in spring 1980, with graduation that summer. After eight years, it was wonderful to finally complete my doctoral studies. My research focused on the Greek translation of Deuteronomy. In the sixth century AD, just before Islamic forces swept across North Africa, Paul of Tella translated into Syriac the edition of Greek Deuteronomy edited by Origen. My dissertation worked with a new manuscript of the so-called Syro-Hexapla of Deuteronomy, evaluating the degree to which it could be used to inform our knowledge of the original Greek text of Deuteronomy. As abstruse as this topic might seem, it gave me competence in textual criticism of the Hebrew Bible, the Septuagint and the Greek New Testament, as well increased skill in exegeting these biblical texts in their original languages. However, it was not until the late nineties that I was able once again to pursue serious research in Septuagint studies. The demands of my teaching and my administrative leadership responsibilities at Northwest consumed my time and energies. Our third daughter, Sarah Mae, joined our family in 1980.

In 1980, Doug Harris became Northwest's president, and in 1981, he invited me to fill the role of academic dean. This was not an easy time in Northwest's history. Being both the youngest and newest faculty member, as well as academic dean, generated considerable stress. Needless to say, it was a significant period for learning the ins and outs of academic leadership. During a partial sabbatical in 1985, I completed an MA in academic leadership at UBC in order to deepen my understanding about the role of academic dean. Surprisingly, at that time there were few resources available to help individuals understand this role in higher education. I managed to become part of the network of evangelical deans that met annually in Phoenix for professional development and mutual encouragement. The members were exceedingly generous in sharing their wisdom. Jim Sweeney, dean of Western Seminary, Portland, Oregon, became a wonderful colleague, as did Joseph Wong, dean of Multnomah Biblical Seminary.

As part of my vision to advance Northwest's mission, from 1983 to 1985 I led the faculty and administration in gaining accreditation with the American Association of Bible Colleges (AABC, now the Association of Biblical Higher Education, with which Northwest currently is accredited) for the undergraduate division. At this time Dr. Ken Davis, dean of Trinity Western University (TWU), and I developed the master of ministry degree to assist pastors in their professional development. This became a very successful program, and we ran it until the mid-90s until our accreditation with the Association of Theological Schools (ATS) required us to stop offering this degree. It was our first official academic relationship with TWU, which laid the groundwork for the development of the consortium that came to be known as the Association of Canadian Theological Schools (ACTS). Andrew James, our fourth child, came along in 1983.

In the mid-80s, the leadership of Northwest became conscious that the future of undergraduate biblical education in Canada was bleak. There was growing pressure within evangelical churches for lead pastors to possess an MDiv credential. Along with this, many began questioning the relevance of a Bible college degree for Christians who did not perceive pastoral work as their chosen vocation. Within the world of

AABC, many institutions were moving away from BTh and BRE degrees and were offering BA degrees instead. Northwest's charter did not have the scope for us to offer general bachelor of arts degrees. At the same time, supporting an independent, denominational seminary (graduate level) was becoming less and less viable. We could not generate enough enrolment to sustain the mounting costs. All of these challenges led President Harris, the Northwest board and me to begin discussions with TWU about the possibility of becoming an affiliated college, a Canadian method of enabling small colleges with very focused academic missions to enhance their academic credibility and offerings by coming under the academic umbrella of recognized universities. After much discussion, this became a reality in 1987. The result was the creation of ACTS, the decision to relocate Northwest to the campus of TWU and major changes in the way Northwest operated.

Such major changes were controversial. Many in the church constituency were skeptical about the wisdom of this plan. They feared Northwest would lose its theological values and no longer control its educational mission. However, financial realities and assurances from the leadership of TWU, particularly Dr. Neil Snider, the president, Dr. Guy Saffold, the vice-president and Dr. Ken Davis, the dean, generated sufficient confidence, and the plan was approved by the churches. Northwest then sold its campus, located in southeast Vancouver, and used the funds to build a new facility on land purchased from TWU. Despite realizing a significant amount of money from the sale of the Vancouver property, Northwest needed to raise several millions of dollars to make the plan work. Unfortunately, despite several years of hard work, the leadership of Northwest was unable to achieve its fundraising targets, resulting in significant debt that needed servicing over the coming years.

ACTS became a resounding success, achieving enrolments of 500 students within ten years of its creation, the third largest "seminary" (a consortium of seminaries) in Canada. Along with Ken Davis, Guy Saffold and Barrie Palfreyman (dean of Canadian Baptist Seminary), I provided academic leadership for ACTS. We "built the bridge as we walked on it." Although seminary consortia existed elsewhere in Canada (for example, the Toronto School of Theology), evangelical seminaries had never ventured to do anything of this nature in Canada (or the United States). Since Northwest had the only operating seminary among the three seminaries that initially formed ACTS, its faculty, academic programs and library served as the resources for ACTS in the initial years. The ACTS leadership appointed me as dean, and I served in that capacity for ten years (1995–2005), while remaining dean of Northwest College (until 2000) and Northwest Seminary (2005). Major developments in this period included accreditation of ACTS with the Association of the Theological Schools (ATS), even though they struggled to understand our structure. We also established the John W. Wevers Institute for Septuagint Studies, implemented a doctor of ministry degree program, and initiated work for a chaplaincy program. Moreover, the consortium grew from three to five seminaries.

Negotiating the academic relationship between the ACTS consortium and TWU was always a bit tricky. Some interests in TWU did not appreciate what ACTS was doing academically, as developing programs at TWU (eg. MA Counselling, MAL and MA in biblical studies and Christian thought) competed directly with ACTS programs, affecting enrollment.

These were busy years for me as I provided academic leadership for ACTS and Northwest, taught at least two courses each semester, and began to revive a research program in the Septuagint. Around 2000, the opportunity came to participate in a project that would prepare a new English translation of the Greek Old Testament. The person originally assigned the book of Exodus in this project was unable to fulfill it, so Dr. Al Pietersma invited me to participate. Oxford University Press published *A New English Translation of the Septuagint* (NETS) in 2007. This has become the standard translation of the Septuagint used in the English-speaking academic circles. Several years into this translation work the supervising committee announced their intention to launch a series of commentaries based on the Septuagint and developed under the auspices of the Society of Biblical Literature. The translators involved in NETS were given first opportunity to develop the commentary related to the Septuagint document they translated. I was "all in" and since then the research and writing of a commentary on Septuagint Exodus has become my research priority. I invited a colleague, Joel Korytko (one of the my MTS students who later earned a DPhil at Oxford based on his research in Greek translation of Exodus 21–23), to collaborate with me and we hope to complete the commentary in its essentials by the end of 2025, Lord willing. Because of the research invested in this project on Greek Exodus, I have published more than twenty peer-reviewed articles on various questions related to this text.

Through my teaching I developed a particular interest in the Gospel of Mark. This research enabled the publication of ten articles exploring the meaning of various concepts and texts in this gospel. All of this work brought the opportunity to write *The Pastoral Epistles: A Handbook on the Greek Text* published by Baylor University Press in 2017. My interest in Greek terms and constructions encountered in the New Testament led me to write 190 blogs on various texts and these are accessible on the Northwest website (nbseminary.ca) under the tabs about/research/ Nimer/internet moments with God's Word (moments.nbseminary.com).

Although the leadership at Northwest worked valiantly to improve the financial health of the institution, things came to a head in 1998/99, as deficits grew and presidential decisions were questioned. As a result, the Northwest board took a very difficult decision to close the undergraduate division. As you can imagine, this was traumatic for employees, students, alumni and supporters. During these events, the president's contract was not renewed. Following a search process, the board invited me to serve as president. My initial years in this role were not pleasant, as the board mandated the closure of the undergraduate division. Giving notice to faithful faculty and other employees was gut-wrenching. Negotiating the sale of the building and property to TWU was quite difficult, placing tremendous stress on long-standing relationships. I am indebted to Alan Elander, the board chair, who was a stabilizing force, wise negotiator and constant encouragement. Largely due to his efforts, Northwest eventually achieved stability with a substantial endowment and became a viable seminary operation. The analysis of these events related to Northwest, TWU and ACTS reflects my perceptions and opinions. Others undoubtedly will hold different views.

The last five years of my presidential term saw growth in new initiatives, particularly in the development of Korean language programs, including ATS-accredited Korean language DMin, MDiv and MA programs, a unique contribution to graduate theological education in Canada. Larry Nelson served as board chair and we developed a deep friendship and effective working relationship. Judy and I also had several opportunities to teach in a seminary located in North Sulawesi, Indonesia, under the leadership of Dr. Karwur. This gave us insight into the experience of Christians who live in cultures dominated by other religions.

In 2001, Judy and I were blessed with the first of twelve grandchildren. This opened an entirely new chapter in our marriage and parenting experience, as we now have opportunity to pray for, encourage and mentor a new generation in our family circle. In 2023, the first great-grandchild came along.

Because of the presidential workload, I finished my work as Northwest and ACTS dean in 2005. Dr. Kent Anderson, a Northwest faculty member, took on that role. When I completed my second term as president in 2010, I resigned and returned to full-time teaching until my retirement in 2015. Dr. Anderson became president in 2010. During the ten years following my retirement, I have continued my teaching and research. It has been a wonderful experience finally to teach courses in Septuagint studies during this period as part of the ACTS curriculum. As far as I know, ACTS/NBS is the only seminary in Canada where Septuagint studies are a formal part of the curriculum.

During my term as president, I discerned a personal need to understand more fully the nature of board work, particularly in relationship to non-profit board governance and institutional health. I developed a connection with an agency named InTrust, that assists seminary boards to learn how to govern well. Northwest and eventually ACTS became members, and I was invited to serve on their advisory board. This proved very helpful, and for five years I was privileged to interact with seasoned seminary leaders who understood the principles that facilitate excellence in non-profit board governance. It soon became clear that many of the principles that produced good governance in seminaries could also generate good governance in local congregational churches (legally non-profit charities in Canada).

For many years I served as deacon or elder in the Baptist churches our family attended. This included ten years (2005–2015) as an elder at Southridge Fellowship Baptist Church, Langley, BC, and six years as the board chair, during a time when the church built a multi-million dollar facility. This became a wonderful adventure, seeing God provide in remarkable ways for the completion of this project. It did not take long to discover that many pastors and most deacons/elders have limited understanding and training for serving as non-profit board members. And in the case of some, there is little interest in developing such competence. Regrettably, this results in much unnecessary conflict within boards and congregations, as well as frustration among pastoral leaders.

With this developing awareness, I teamed up with a Northwest colleague, Dr. Lyle Schrag, and Northwest's board chair, Larry Nelson, to develop a series of seminars called Best Board Practices, and offered this for interested church boards. More than sixty church boards in Western Canada participated in these seminars between 2005 and 2015. From this experience came a book called *The Art of Kubernesis (1 Corinthians 12:28): Leading as the Church Board Chairperson*, published in 2019. In this publication, I attempt to provide a biblically based framework to help church board leaders provide effective leadership for their board and congregation. Simultaneously, I wrote a series of blogs related to church board work (now accessible at churchboard.ca; 333 blogs are available on the Northwest website under the tabs about/research/NIMER).

As I indicated at the beginning of this chapter, all these experiences were only possible because of the constant support of my wife, Judy, and through the growing network of colleagues and mentors God has graciously provided. I cannot claim every decision I made was right or implemented in the best way, but such matters are my responsibility, and I am thankful for God's forgiveness. Entrepreneurial energy abounded, but considerable amounts of wisdom—academic, institutional, relational, cultural and spiritual—were needed to direct that energy appropriately. What a privilege to spend fifty years teaching God's Word and interacting with the original texts. It taught me that worship occurs in all aspects of our lives, particularly our ability to worship through the engagement of our minds with God's revelation, God's thoughts and God's purposes. Year after year, the opportunity to mentor a new group of emerging leaders proved to be humbling and inspiring. I am more convinced than I was fifty years ago that the biblical worldview provides us with the best pattern for human *being* and *living*. Secular philosophies and ideologies are bankrupt and offer little in the way of solutions for the deep problems that plague human societies.

The journey continues with the loving support of Judy and our growing family—the source of my constant joy. God has provided us with opportunities to travel and together we enjoy opportunities to explore our world. The writing and research continue. Thoughts turn these days to finishing this chapter of life well, in service of our Lord Jesus, and reflecting on what the next chapter will be like in heaven. What is in store, only God knows, but I am fully confident that whatever he has planned will be for his glory and our good. My life text is Jeremiah 9:23–24:

"Let not the wise boast of their wisdom or the strong boast of their strength or the rich boast of their riches, but let the one who boasts boast about this: that they have the understanding to know me, that I am the Lord, who exercises kindness, justice and righteousness on earth, for in these I delight," declares the LORD (NIV).

Submitted by Dr. Larry James Perkins

19 /

Dr. Rick Maynor Reed

Rick Maynor Reed is always serving others. He simply said, "I can't write about myself."

That is the story of his life. But I, who have had the up-close and personal privilege of sharing his life for forty-two years, think you may wish to know this exemplary man.

Rick was born in Everett, Washington, on July 6 around the time of mid-century modern furniture and hippies in Haight-Ashbury. His father, Maynor Otto Reed, was the son of Norwegian immigrants; Maynor being the only child not born in Norway. Maynor met Joanie (who is officially Marjorie Joan Reed) at Multnomah School of the Bible, where he was class president and she the valedictorian. During those years, they pledged their lives to one another and to serve Jesus together.

Maynor, with Joanie, pastored four churches, and during the first little Ricky was born (she said she "named him what she would call him" because her own two names were often mixed up). Ricky remains on some key documents. His parents soon moved to San Jose, California, then Grass Valley, Oregon, and later settled in Napa, California (for twenty-one years). Maynor's final ministry was as the district superintendent for eighty or more Baptist churches in California.

Like Timothy's mother, Rick learned the books of the Bible on his mother's knees by the time he was two years old. He was taught the Scriptures thoroughly and his parents modelled those virtues in daily life. Rick wrote of his father, "The man up in the pulpit matched the man down on my street."[1] This would be the same of his son, Rick.

Rick's life was spared by God on several occasions. In one case, he nearly drowned in a resort pool, only spared due to his father's intervention. At other moments, he was slammed into by other vehicles. If you'd like a wild story, ask him about the day he and his sisters, as teenagers, summited Half Dome from the back side. God protected this young man for his purposes.

At a church vacation Bible school program, Rick clearly understood the claims of the gospel for his own personal life. With a few friends, he solemnly entered his father's office to receive the Lord Jesus into his life. But a wave of embarrassment in doing this in front of his friends came on him, and he chuckled softly. To such a sincere heart, this caused great wondering if he had truly meant it, for which he often sought the Lord.

For Joan Reed, nothing was more desirous than a table set for guests. Her scalloped potatoes, pies of every flavour and soft potato rolls are legendary. Rick knew he was loved every time he came home from college—there were few hugs but heaping sandwiches.

During his junior high and high school years, Rick began to play the guitar and write music. Many Christmas Eve services were nearly begun as Rick and his friend Charlie put the finishing touches on that year's Christmas song. Rick went on to write numerous other songs, and many are recorded on cassette tapes. Like the era in which he lived, his hair touched his collar and his bell-bottom jeans had hand-sewed-on braid.

Rick attended Vintage High School and began to perform in various ways at school as well. A strong memory has always been his gift, and he

---

1 Song written for his father's retirement, "The man that we called Dad."

had leading roles in many a school play. For *Camelot*, he did not feel free in his spirit to play the shenanigan lead role of Lancelot, choosing instead to play Pellinore, repeating lines that lent laughter to the audience.

During these same years, the Jesus Movement impacted many youth. In his church, the Galatians 2:20 Singers toured by bus to neighbouring states. From this group, Rick formed a small band. The picture of these young men in Estes Park, Colorado, is priceless. You'll need to check out the shades!

As Rick began to consider Christian colleges, his initial choice was Seattle Pacific University. Through a last-minute Cal-State scholarship, he was able to attend Biola University, starting as a music major. Often found in the practice room alongside all the other music majors, he noticed he did not love it. Instead, he loved ministry through music and transitioned into Christian education. During one of his years at Biola, Rick was a resident assistant. Concerned about his grades when he took the role, God enabled him to have a perfect GPA while still serving students who interrupted his study.

One thing you must know about this time in his life: Rick was a prankster. He and a friend posted "school photos" on Biola bulletin boards taken by smashing their faces into the photocopy machine. On other occasions, Rick and a friend created "singing telegrams" to be delivered to fellow students in the dining hall or in class.

Rick's sister Rosi attended the same college, and Rick, always a kind and considerate brother, could be seen eating with her. On another occasion, Rick was seen tackling his friend, Rick Epperly, which made Rick E. laugh. It should be noted that Rick E. was blind, and Rick had whispered to him of his presence. Rick was kind to all.

Rick sang in the Biola Chorale and as president, often made introductions to songs. In them, Rick quoted sections from J.I. Packer's book, *Knowing God*:

There is unspeakable comfort—the sort of comfort that energizes, be it said, not enervates—in knowing that God is constantly taking knowledge of me in love and watching over me for my good. There is tremendous relief in knowing that his love to me is utterly realistic, based at every point on prior knowledge of the worst about me, so that no discovery now can disillusion him about me, in the way I am so often disillusioned about myself, and quench his determination to bless me.[2]

In this same chorale, Rick somehow noticed a young brunette, Linda Honcoop. Linda's intimidation led her to cross-stitch, unable to comprehend that such a godly man would take an interest in her, let alone have romantic interests.

Between his final college years, Rick spent a full summer in Kamata, Tokyo, Japan. His delight in the nations and understanding of world religions expanded during this time.

Graduating from Biola with highest honours, Rick spent a year working as a substitute teacher in a junior high school. Rick loves junior highers and developed a church program for "Josiah's Junior Highas." Rick used his art skills to draw graphics for the group.

The pivotal call of God upon his life occurred at Urbana. Sensing God's presence under a starry sky in Illinois, he sensed God say, "You will be a pastor, but you don't have to do this in the States."

Rick chose Dallas Seminary for its world-famous professors: John Walvoord, Dwight Pentecost, Charles Ryrie and Howard Hendricks. Bill McRae came to Dallas for a chapel series, and Rick remembered those outlines until the day he met him in person in Canada!

Rick's Dallas years were filled with academics and activity. No one would know, but Rick graduated with the highest GPA from Dallas in his graduation year. His friends were shocked, they simply said, "But you were such a nice guy!" Again, this humble servant was not about to mention it—instead, he played weekly on a basketball team named The Idiot and the Oddities with these friends.

Rick could be found each Saturday with the poor. He served "in the projects" of Dallas when it wasn't that safe. He loved, cared and shepherded those who were destitute.

On our first date, Rick had no real sum of money. But I recall him stopping the car he had borrowed, taking a homeless person into a convenience store, buying him some food, and we going without that evening. This was to be a pattern in our lives.

---

2 J.I. Packer, *Knowing God*, as cited by Justin Taylor, The Gospel Coalition blog, https://www.thegospelcoalition.org/blogs/justin-taylor/jip/, accessed May 13, 2025.

Rick's friendships have remained for a lifetime. There is no recollection of conflict. To be his friend is to be a friend for life. He will remember your name or do his best to recall it. He learned well from his father's, "Just ask other people questions," and don't speak about yourself.

Rick and I married between this third and fourth years at Dallas Seminary. Rick's thesis was on the concept of sin and Theravada Buddhism, due in part of our shared ministry with teenage Laotian refugees. Ask him sometime about the memorable day he taught on Genesis 3 with a sign from the ceiling, "Do not look under this cup." (It was an upside-down glass full of water!) Both our master's theses were typed on first generation computers.

Following Dallas, we moved to California, which, for the record, has many large and influential churches. We lived across from Apple Computer and served college and career students at Valley Church in Cupertino, California. During these years, he became a father, a role he loved. The camaraderie of the other eight pastoral staff members was tremendous, but times of turmoil between these gatherings opened our eyes to the real world of behind-the-scenes church ministry, and we quietly left, seeking missions in Brazil.

Rick began to preach for various churches while on missionary deputation. You guessed it—people began to request he become their pastor or guest speaker. After years of waiting on a visa that did not materialize, Rick had a choice of two church opportunities:

1. Being on staff at a large church in the Northwest.
2. Being the sole pastor of a small church in the central coast of California.

Rick was keen to put his hand to the plow, choosing the small church and he never looked back. He began as an interim pastor as we waited on visas, and then became the senior pastor. When we thought we'd be going to Brazil, he again became the interim pastor, and then again, the pastor. The final decision to stay was reached through Abraham offering Isaac as a willing sacrifice, but not one that God required.

The church then began to grow quickly. Taking down some walls, the sanctuary was L-shaped. Those on one side could not see attendees on the other side. Rick gained valuable—and some painful—small church experience, including a critical letter which he took to a park, spread out on a picnic table and prayed over, much as Hezekiah in Isaiah 37. Rick remained faithful, and in time, all appreciated his leadership.

As Rick's fortieth birthday approached, he expressed an interest in a possible change. The church was now healthy and about 400 people. A new Christian education facility was being built by the men of the church. We learned how involved this method was.

In August 1997, we received a call from John Gowling in Ottawa, Canada, to consider coming to pastor Metropolitan Bible Church in Ottawa, Canada. Unsure of this location, Barnes & Noble provided guides to the location and the weather (the coldest and possibly snowiest capital in the world). Gary Stubblefield assured us that this was a church that "had a heart for the Word of God and a heart for the world for God."

We did move. It was dramatic. While painful to leave close friends and colleagues, it was even harder to say goodbye to wonderful grandparents. We regularly put on this Steven Curtis Chapman's song:

Saddle up your horses
We've got a trail to blaze
Through the yonder of God's Amazing grace
Let's follow our leader into the Glorious unknown
This is the life like no other whoa whoa
This is The Great Adventure

Our first trip to Ottawa was during the ice storm of 1998. The electrical towers bent over, trees cracked in the night and hotels offered free housing. It was a storm unlike any other. Rick had brought sermon notes along, and as he paced the platform of the historic downtown Met preaching on "God's Power Perfected in Hard Times" it seemed a perfect fit.

From 1998 to 2012, God worked in powerful ways at the Met. Highlights for Rick were times on Parliament Hill, many of which were private stories, not spoken to others. He loved Senators' hockey games with friends and his sons. Preaching and singing with Randy Jost and musical numbers with his whole family on Christmas Eve were highlights. We watched God work in evangelism through the Billy Graham Crusade (when again the power went out in the city, and the rain poured so hard attendees outside wore black garbage bags). At the Met, salvation stories were celebrated weekly, and the entire church was challenged toward outreach.

Privately, Rick is a man of prayer. Quietly, behind the scenes over the years, he slips away for days of prayer. During this time, his regular work was often left undone. It did not take long to observe in days following hasty answers to prayer, the strength of his soul in God, and supernatural "coincidences." Often, Rick may be observed at home with eyes closed, wiggling his head a little bit, his manner of earnest prayer. George Müller, through books, has been a mentor to our whole family.

Rick Reed

Also behind the scenes, Rick kept working quietly on the doctor of ministry degree he had begun in California. Trinity Evangelical Divinity School in Deerfield, Illinois, played a part in strengthening his leadership. In addition to this, we made trips to encourage national pastors and missionaries in places such as Papua, New Guinea, Tanzania, Kenya, Singapore, Lebanon and Indonesia. Rick wrote weekly for an "Ask the Religion Experts" column in the *Ottawa Citizen*, which was read, and sometimes discussed, in our own neighbourhood.

The old Met was a beautiful structure just blocks from Parliament, with stately dark wood. On one of Rick's first Sundays, the front row of pews was being removed to enlarge the platform. I mentioned quietly, "You are going to need these pews," and soon this was the case. Another building program was begun.

Faithful to his promises, God provided millions for the new Met at the very visible intersection of Prince of Wales and Hunt Club. This time, no access was given to Rick (just a symbolic hard hat). At the grand opening, a parade was planned, passing an old Bible from one generation to the next until the walk was completed at the new building. The church grew by 500 people in a month.

Following these events, Rick began to note health challenges. His father had had cancer, leaving us concerned. The biopsy results brought the fateful words: "You have cancer." From that moment on, life blurred. God provided in amazing ways for two surgeries, and nearly forty rounds of radiation. God was sovereign, kind and testing our faith.

When he began to preach again, life had somehow shifted. He agreed to meet with the leadership team of Heritage College and Seminary to consider the role of president. Through much prayer and a powerful weekend at another Christian college, God led him to accept the role. He started in January 2013.

The transition to Heritage began with an induction service limited greatly by a snowstorm. Due to this, Kent and Karen Anderson and the Barkers had a simple celebration at the Reeds—with mom's potato rolls.

Rick assumed the role of president seemingly unaware of a 3.7 million dollar debt. George Müller's persistent prayer was again his example, and God's provision legendary. Rick loved leading the staff, particularly in prayer, and teaching homiletics and pastoral theology. Behind the scenes, his connections to donors were often "God coincidences" and his friendships genuine. We will always remember the burning of the mortgage!

The worldwide pandemic in 2020 shifted the college and seminary to online platforms. There were tremendous challenges and changes for students, faculty and staff. The recent movement to MyHeritage preserved all records online. Rick will always be grateful for the hard work that so many did to transition during this pivotal time.

The pandemic also gave space and time to dream of a new seminary building. The amazing stories of those who gave will remain in his heart. Behind the scenes, Rick carried the weight of this responsibility. We had several key moments of testing and of blessing. As in Ephesians 3:20, God did immeasurably more than we could dream or imagine, and "to him be the glory in Christ Jesus."

In January 2023, after significant challenges behind the scenes, Rick contracted pneumonia, perhaps COVID pneumonia. The hospital advised staying home, and college students circled our home to sing and pray. Rick again turned to new music, Scripture and prayer. In August 2023, it was agreed another president would carry Heritage forward.

Early that fall, servant-hearted Rick, with a trolley in hand, brought his books to his car, and quietly headed home. We said goodbye, and began to say hello more often to our families—both on the West Coast (our moms) and on the East Coast (our children).

Since that time, Rick has spoken at many conferences and has served as the interim preaching pastor at Grandview Church in Kitchener, Ontario. We are able to join others and sing: "All my life You have been faithful."

His heart remains concerned and passionate for pastoral leaders and for a lost world. His writing resources carry on his legacy. Recently *The Heart of the Preacher* was given to all attendees at the 2025 Shepherds Conference in California. It has been his delight to faithfully open God's Word to people from around the world.

In our wedding rings is inscribed Psalm 18:30, which states:

As for God, his way is perfect
The Word of the LORD is tried
He is a shield to those who take refuge in him.

This man knows God and his perfect ways. He has found the Word of God tried and true. He has taken refuge in the Lord.

During his cancer journey, I prayed daily: "With a long life I will satisfy him and let him see my salvation" (Psalm 91:16 NASB1995). May it be.

Submitted by Dr. Linda Marie Reed

20 /

Dr. Linda Marie Reed

On a hot July day, while my dad was making hay, I was born in Bellingham, Washington. Little did I know that my future husband was thirteen days old and living nearby in Everett, just sixty miles away. I joined my sister, born with spina bifida, in a home where both Dutch and Frisian were spoken, and World War II was discussed firsthand.

Life was idyllic with the beautiful northwest Washington landscape. Tall Douglas Fir trees, the smell of the ocean, the taste of tender salmon and local dairy ice cream were delights. Sweet fresh-picked blackberry pie and the August NW Fair were childhood highlights.

But my life was not to be in the West. Mrs. Bame, my Sunday school teacher, passed to each of us a little black baby doll, and in all our family photos, I am holding little Moko. I prayed for his family and sent my toys to Africa. Missionary guests intrigued me with their rolled-up snakeskins and handmade baskets.

One morning, while still a toddler in a highchair, a radio broadcast shared the gospel, and I gave my heart to Jesus. From that moment on, I would run out to the rare visitor in our country laneway and ask: "Do you know Jesus?" My life became about sharing Jesus. At school, I'd put my feet up to block the playground tunnel and share the hope of Jesus. A little leader, I organized my grade one class to present the Christmas story with carols, somehow outfitting everyone with white Christmas collars. (I cried when a blizzard cancelled the day.) Life was an adventure. All except the farm chores.

Along the way, I began to read. Or take the lead in biology in dissecting animals. And in memorizing all the countries in the world. Learning was a delight, and Scripture memory through our church required 100 verses each year to go free to camp.

In my small town of Lynden, Washington, God blessed my life with five solid Christian friends, and we moved through the primary grades to graduation together. This provided great accountability and blessing in my life. (We're having a reunion in 2025).

After graduation, I left my little town and hit the big city of Los Angeles. The contrast of lifestyles couldn't have been greater, and I began to doubt my faith once I realized the big world thought variously on world religions. This began a search that deepened as I went away from the conservative Christian life I had known.

One star-filled night, after falling into depression and a spiritual wilderness, I cried out to God: "God, if you are there, please show yourself to me." A peace came over me and I knew I needed to seek God. Josh McDowell's resource, *Evidence that Demands a Verdict*, was intellectually helpful to me, and the living example of a fellow student changed my life.

To make a fresh start, I transferred to Biola University in La Mirada, California, and, by chance, tried out for the Biola Chorale. I thought everyone made the school choir, but the first rehearsal revealed that most students were music majors. It was either quit or embark on a steep learning curve. The director, Dr. Loren Wiebe, had Canadian relatives near Abbotsford, British Columbia. I will always be grateful for his deep piety and worship. While conducting the hymn, "I see Thy cross there, teach my heart to cling," tears flowed down his face. It was an unforgettable experience, deepening my drawing near to God.

As God would have it, Rick Reed gave the spiritual introductions for the songs before we sang. I was still spiritually recovering, so when Rick sat next to me on the tour bus, I focused on cross stitching (framed in our home). He gave me a book, *The Fight*, and expected that I would know this was a romantic gesture! We discussed the book. That's all.

When I completed Biola as a sociology major with a psychology minor, I thought I might attend Rosemead graduate school. Instead, I headed home to make money working at a bank. But this did not satisfy. In time, I yielded to that internal whisper since childhood, "Where he leads me, I will follow." My missions adventure took me to the rice terraces of northern Luzon, Philippines, with its stilt houses and a bursting church of new believers. Wycliffe Bible Translator, Joanne Shetler, whose story is told in *And the Word Came with Power* and at Urbana, became my friend and mentor. In her, God gave me a living example of a linguist, a practicing medical practitioner and someone who loves to laugh.

Somehow, over the many miles of that summer, I enrolled in the Summer Institute of Linguistics in south Dallas, Texas. The school was accredited by the University of Texas at Arlington, and I began my master's with trepidation. Linguistics is the process of putting together foreign grammar puzzles, and linguists are the interesting people who play dulcimers, wood flutes and barefoot volleyball. They were often left-handed. Kenneth Pike's tagmemic grammar allowed these amazing students to untangle yet undecoded language in patterns that would help anyone trying to learn high school Spanish.

Just three weeks into that fall semester, I walked into Chapel in the Woods, a small country church near Duncanville, Texas, and astonishingly Rick Reed walked toward me. A little voice, perhaps my own, said, "I bet I'm going to marry this man." But the words that came out were: "What are you doing here?" Both of us had worked for a year, travelled globally and were now both graduate students in Dallas.

What I didn't know was that Rick faced a challenge: he had no car and no money. So, every other month we had coffee. We spoke of old friends and he asked about my future. It was during this time that Rick wrote a song we would sing together for the rest of our lives:

Where are all the Daniels?
Where are the men and the women who will stand alone?

Though I'm told there's only a handful,
Still I want to be faithful to the One who made me His own.

Since we were both musicians in the Jesus music era, I joined my alto to his tenor.

God blessed this time academically, and the privilege of being a teaching assistant in articulatory phonetics was presented. From this experience, an opportunity was given to teach English as a Second Language (ESL) at the University of Texas. A teaching career, never imagined before, had begun.

The tale is beyond this word count, but one day I saw Rick with another gal on the Dallas Seminary campus, and I put it together: he had a girlfriend and I was the old friend! Not wishing to ask questions, this misunderstanding took weeks to clarify. Shortly after a confirming conversation at White Rock Lake, we set off to meet his parents in Napa, California. We married, both completing coursework at Dallas, and typed both our master's theses on the first prototype computers!

From Dallas, we accepted a position at Valley Church in the Silicon Valley of California. One of nine staff pastors, we lived opposite Apple Computer. A missions-minded church, they offered financial support for Rick to teach in a Brazilian seminary. Hesitantly, I began to say, "You should be a preacher." Everyone already had our prayer card on their refrigerator and so we pressed on until all hope of receiving visas to Brazil was lost (who doesn't get into Brazil?).

Our delay was the Lord's destiny, and Rick became the solo pastor at a Berean Bible Church in Atascadero, California. On his first Sunday, I counted thirty-seven adults in the sanctuary—with likely sixty children upstairs. As the church grew, we faced strong headwinds; learning valuable leadership lessons for small church pastors.

During these years, I began to lose myself in three children, laundry and small town pastors wives' expectations. Criticism, rejection and loneliness stung, to which many pastor's wives can relate. Still young, I was overtaken by a virus that led to pneumonia and the hospital, and a doctor leaning in to say: "She needs to fight!"

I sometimes did not care. It was all too much.

Truth be told, I had a relative who struggled with severe mental illness, and I had been told that this could be my future. God changed the course of my life through a Precept Ministry Conference. As I read and reread

Paul's ministry challenges in 2 Timothy, I realized ministry is difficult! God changed the course of my life through three words: "Fulfill your ministry" (2 Timothy 4:5).

God led a tiny, older woman—a former pastor's wife—to "walk with me." We walked around Atascadero Lake (means "mudhole") and she taught me to "take every thought captive and make it obedient to Christ" (2 Corinthians 10:5). I began to study God's Word seriously, and to memorize it as I had as a child. I filled my mind with the things of God, and as Psalm 1 promised, Rick noticed a steady strength.

Our two churches had been hard, and our mission plans had not materialized. As sung well by Twila Paris: "In a hidden valley, God writes a life song." Our pastoral plans for greatness dimmed as we humbly served within the reality of a small town. A mission's trip to Indonesia impressed upon us that we were not world changers. We became just faithful—week in and week out. Faithful as we led worship together. Faithful as we set up Christmas Eve decor, then performed and put it all away. Faithful.

One day, near his fortieth birthday, we sat at a kids' park, and Rick shared he was "restless." Within a few days, he received a phone call from a friend who had just been in Ottawa, Canada, revealing he had put Rick's name in at a church in Ottawa.

We made the flight toward Ottawa, only to be told in Chicago that all the flights to Ottawa were cancelled for an ice storm. Arriving in Ottawa at the start of the infamous ice Storm of 1998 was an unforgettable experience. We borrowed boots and Rick whispered, "Just smile at the people, and we'll pretend this never happened." By March we were living in Ottawa with our three children.

A close friend, knowing our backstory, wrote a note as we were packing, "May the Lord make up the years the locusts have eaten" (Joel 2:25). Our years at the Met were truly incredible years. All time is a gift from God, but these years were kissed by him. We loved gathering all the nations together for worship. We both loved the people, the embassies and the Ottawa cityscape. During these years, having children now in high school, I began to teach women's Bible studies.

In 2004, an American embassy friend, Ruth Rivera, asked me to join her in creating a Bible study for women who had never studied the Bible before. We rented the Laurentian Centre, and women came to study and accept Christ night after night. Met attendees brought neighbours, friends and family, and we watched God work in women's lives as new believers and as servant leaders.

We soon learned there isn't Bible study curriculum for those who are not Bible people, so I began to write materials. With the kindness of the Met and Lou Ranahan, I took a curriculum writing course through The Women's Centre for Ministry at Western Seminary in Portland, Oregon. While Rick visited his parents, several masters level courses were completed. God brought into my life then what would later begin the Heritage Graduate Certificate for Women in Ministry.

No one can ever prepare you for the day in a doctor's office you hear the words: "You have cancer." During 2011, we walked often into Ottawa General Hospital for Rick's two surgeries, and nearly forty rounds of radiation. Rick and I have always been close, but this drew us together as we prayed and walked daily together through this trial.

When completed, our lives had changed. The church had also changed to accommodate his absence from the pulpit. In mid-2012, the phone rang with the request, "We'd like you to be the president of Heritage College and Seminary." This move would check off the last of Jesus' list: we'd now left houses, brothers, sisters, fathers, mothers, farms and children, for his names' sake (Matthew 19:29).

Once at Heritage, Rick suggested I take courses (this was now my third seminary, but not the last). Dr. David Barker approved a proposal to begin The Women's Centre for Ministry and the grad certificate previously mentioned. Dr. Barker also encouraged me to pursue doctoral work. Without children nearby, and a busy husband, this was a delight. The kindness of Southern Seminary was matched by the sovereignty of God: all educational requirements for admission had been previously met without any of my plans.

The first DMin course I took had sixteen men and just me. Soon after, I received a call to start again in the doctor of education program with a cohort with five other women already teaching at complementarian colleges or seminaries. This began one of the richest seasons of my life. We read voraciously (which I love). I recall one day requiring two books! Posts were written carefully and wildly, one posted frantically on Christmas Eve was a hit.

God used Southern Seminary, a place I never would have dreamed I'd be, to change my life. In a course on social change and education, I presented the statistical plight of refugees and immigrants who make the transition to Canada only to be unaccepted in local churches. When I finished, the professor simply said, "Is this your life calling?"

Linda Reed

At Heritage, God allowed my life to experience the convergence written about by J. Robert Clinton.[1] My office wall plaque said it all in two words: "God Can." And he did. The courses were rich with conversations around resources and academics, but the hallway conversations brought out deep hurts that God knew I would need to understand by experience. The gospel went out through students in the TESOL course, and God wove together linguistics and love for my ESL students that continues to the present time. An ESL lesson with grammar from Psalm 23 (simple present) or Psalms 40a (past tense) integrates a passion for language, culture and Jesus. Heritage students have taught overseas, become certified or found local church ministry.

God has always given visionary passion, and during the pandemic a small folding table was set up to sketch dreams of a seminary building. The behind-the-scenes footage, with its painful setbacks and dramatic donations, may someday be shown in heaven. Suffice it to say, "God Can."

Recently, a *Christianity Today* article captured in a beautiful way the life of Katharine Barnwell. The article shares the story of this unsung hero who created training resources for all Bible translators of our time. She survived a coup and intends to serve Jesus for the rest of her life, currently on a Zoom screen from England.[2] I do not know God's plans for me, but I pray that I, too, will be faithful. And still dream big. And pray hard. And serve those who like Jesus, come to their own, and their own do not receive them" (John 1:12). My passion for serving women remains,

---

1 J. Robert Clinton, *The Making of a Leader: Recognizing the Lessons and Stages of Leadership Development* (Colorado Springs, CO: NavPress, 2012).

2 Jordan K. Monson, "The Woman Who Gave the World a Thousand Names for God: How a British linguist and a failed Nigerian coup changed everything about Bible translation," *Christianity Today*, October 2022, https://www.christianitytoday.com/2022/10/linguist-katharine-barnwell-bible-translation-jesus-film/; accessed June 4, 2025.

including women who arrive at Pearson airport, and that evening are homeless, without language or sponsor.

There have been memorable moments in these final years. Just a few years ago, while at an academic conference in Dallas, Texas, a female professor from Nigeria was not immediately welcomed to sit among our academic friends. Reminiscent of Moko and my childhood, I joined her. As others headed to the buses after our meal served with jousting at Medieval Times, she quietly asked our waiter, "Do you enjoy your job?" I could see that her goal was "Do you know Jesus?"

In a matter of moments, the young waiter was led to Jesus. Meanwhile, all had gone. With cell phone coverage in Africa and Canada, finding a ride to the hotel was complicated. In time, we slid into a taxi, only to hear my new friend say: "Do you like your job?" I knew that soon we'd be asking this "chariot driver," who happened to be from Ethiopia, about Jesus. (This is the only time I asked someone on earth if they were from heaven.)

The next day, I entered the sanctuary where Dr. Charles Swindoll preached. In his powerful sermon, tucked between "The Plot to Kill Jesus" and "Judas' Bargain" (Matthew 26), he praised that woman who poured out for the Master her vial of alabaster. Fresh memories of that weekend rose within me, and I wept. In his grace, I see the image of God so beautifully displayed in all nations, and deeply long for the day we will all worship together (Revelation 7).

By his grace, he forgave me and set his affections on me. He sovereignly purposed as Rick and I sang together at our wedding: "We'll illumine the darkness where his light has not shown." All praise to him for using us to share the gospel on our streets and in our churches.

It's more than a little girl on a farm could ever imagine. To him must be the glory.

Submitted by Dr. Linda Marie Reed

21 /

Lynda Schultz

I f I had taken seriously those who, over the years, have said that I couldn't, or shouldn't, do what God has made part of my journey, this story might be quite different.

My parents moved to Timmins, Ontario, from the Ottawa Valley several years after their wedding in the 1940s. My dad worked a farm for one of my uncles in those early days and then took a job as a mechanic, a position he held for the rest of his working life. Dad came from a Lutheran background, mom from what was then known as the Evangelical United Brethren. When they moved to Timmins, they began to attend First Baptist Church whose beginnings predate the Fellowship, but whose roots are strongly connected to Fellowship history.

My parents had married late in life and were surprised when my brother was born in 1946, then even more surprised when I came along in 1949.

My first pastor was E.C. Wood. His wife taught me in the primary department of the Sunday school, one of the many teachers who had a spiritual impact on me during those early years. I came to faith when I was eleven after a Friday night children's meeting at the church. Then pastor R.D. Holliday suggested that on the following Sunday I come forward when he gave the invitation after the service. I went home and told my parents about my decision.

When the invitation was given on Sunday, I went forward. I did not notice until I got to the front of the church that my mother had followed me. We were baptized together by Pastor Holliday.

Oddly enough, my sense of call to ministry predated that decision. First Baptist had always been a strongly missionary-minded church and has, especially during the 1960s and 1970s, sent out many of their youth into ministry at home and overseas. When I was in grade 5, I wrote an essay for a public speaking contest. The subject was on what I wanted to be when I grew up: I wanted to be a missionary. The essay was a good one, but the teacher took me aside and told me that he believed that a nine-year-old could not possibly have written it!

I was active in First Baptist. I graduated from attending Sunday school to teaching when I was fourteen. I later served in choir, Sky Force and youth group. I also was active in my high school's Christian fellowship group. All during those years, my end goal was to serve the Lord overseas. Our Timmins youth had the privilege of travelling over the May long weekends to Quebec. Here we participated in street meetings on Sunday evenings alongside Murray Heron and were exposed to just a taste of the persecution that pioneers in Quebec had long suffered. It was something I would recall when we faced it again in doing ministry in Colombia years later.

Just prior to graduating from high school, we were individually called into the guidance counsellor's office to discuss our futures. I was asked what I was planning to do after graduation. I told the counsellor that I was planning to go to seminary. He emphatically told me that I didn't have the intellect for seminary studies and that I should consider something else. I was just an average student at the time, but since I never had much interest in most of the subjects we studied—and really hadn't put much effort into many of them with the exception of English and history—I was not deterred.

I was accepted as a student at Central Baptist Seminary (CBS) in Toronto in 1967. But there was a little matter of money to pay for school and for room and board. I had none. A couple from First Baptist regularly spent a couple of weeks each summer at Canadian Keswick, a high-class retreat centre in the Muskokas. They learned of an opening in housekeeping, and I was given the job at the munificent sum of 11 cents an hour. In the fall I went to Toronto with just enough to pay for the first semester. When I returned to Timmins for Christmas break, I had no money to pay for the second. But when I arrived home, I discovered that the members of the congregation had foregone buying Christmas cards and stamps and had saved that money to give to me so that I could go back to school. Again, it was just enough.

CBS was a missionary school and missionaries were frequent speakers at chapel. I was excited about every place they spoke about, and every ministry opportunity they described. But there was no specific place or ministry that stood out more than any of the others. I wondered if perhaps overseas was not where God wanted me.

When I moved to Toronto, I began attending Oakwood Baptist Church. The pastor, George McAlpine, along with his wife, had been missionaries in Chad. The church embraced me—literally, and I was able to serve with this wonderful congregation during seminary years and later, both as a volunteer and as a part of its staff.

Some students were privileged to have summer placements as interns. After my first year at seminary, I was invited back to my home church to serve for the summer. The pastor then was Ron Baxter. He and his wife, Glenys, were great mentors. When the pastor spoke to the congregation about my coming to spend the summer in Timmins, one of the dear ladies of the church whispered to her husband quite loudly, "What does he think a girl can do?" I happened to be sitting within earshot at the time.

Pastor Baxter always said that he taught me everything I knew. He did teach me a lot—even though that summer he was away working on his doctorate, and I was basically on my own. It was sometimes "trial by fire" but it was a wonderful learning experience. I visited hundreds of homes door-to-door, did hospital visitation, prepared and ran special summer ministries for children, handled office responsibilities and narrowly avoided doing a funeral service at the age of eighteen (something I would later do in Caracas).

My second summer I went back to Timmins but worked in retail. In my third year, just before summer break, I was interviewed for a couple of internships: one in Sudbury and one in Peterborough. A close friend was also interviewed for the Sudbury position. Typically, Dr. Boyd, the pastor of Berean Baptist Church and known widely as "the Bishop of the North," would hire a male and a female student to work alongside him during the summers. I heard nothing about the position for some time—until my friend reluctantly told me that she had been accepted for the job. She had been afraid to tell me because she thought I'd be disappointed. In fact, I was happy for her—principally because I was terrified of Dr. Boyd.

But the Lord always puts us where we need to be. Though I would have learned a lot from an experience in Sudbury, I needed to be in Peterborough. I spent the summer there and returned on weekends to continue ministry while I completed my final year at Central. Through those years were countless examples of the God's provision for me, often in miraculous ways.

I graduated from CBS in 1971 as valedictorian of my class—this, I learned, had caused a bit of a problem for some of the seminary board who felt that a woman should not represent the school in this way. Just before graduation, I was interviewed for a position in a church north of Toronto. The position was as office secretary—something I was not qualified for, nor did I have any interest in. There were other factors that sent up red flags so I turned the position down, a risky thing to do when positions for women in ministry were rare.

So, I waited, and God led the church in Peterborough to issue an invitation to me to return there as the church's director of Christian education. Though I had worked in the church as a student, returning as a permanent staff was not without its challenges. The elder who picked me up at the bus station when I first arrived was honest and blunt. His first words when I got into the car were: "I didn't want you here. What can a girl do?" This was getting a little tedious! It took a while to make a "believer" out of him.

The situation in Peterborough was unique. It was a church plant. We met in a school for some time before the congregation was able to get land and put up a building. But my role there was even more unique.

The pastor, Everett Wicks, was a mechanical engineer and worked full time for General Electric. He carried out his pastoral duties on weekends and evenings. That left me basically on my own to carry on my work independently and to use my own initiative. It was here that my interest in curriculum development, research and writing began to develop. But as time passed, I realized that this situation was not ideal for the church. The church needed a full-time pastor and would not

Lynda Schultz

have one while I was still there. But what would be my next steps if I left Peterborough?

One Sunday evening, a missionary serving with the Fellowship foreign mission board in Colombia came to the church to speak. The speaker was describing a new initiative that had been launched in Medellín: a Bible institute for the training of national pastors and workers. I had put overseas service behind me, believing that it was not part of God's plan for my life, but his message to me could not have been clearer than if he had chosen to write it with a divine finger on the wall behind the platform. I literally trembled in the pew where I was sitting. I knew that this was the place and that this was, finally, the time.

I told Pastor Wicks. At the time, I could not complete the application as a photograph was required, and I didn't have one with me. However, I was heading to Timmins for vacation and knew I had one at home. The first thing I did was put the photo in the envelope and mail the application. It was now out of my hands.

The morning after posting the application, I got a phone call from Dr. Jack Watt, general secretary of the Fellowship. To this day I do not know why he called me, why he thought I might be looking for a new position or why this position should be of interest to me. At that time, the Fellowship national office operated a bookstore next to its main office on Shepherd Avenue in Toronto. They were looking for someone to work in the bookstore. Dr. Watt called me.

I explained to him what had happened in Peterborough and my con-viction that the Lord was directing me overseas. Why would I want to go work in a bookstore? He asked if I would at least pray about it during my two weeks up north. I agreed to do that.

When the two weeks were up, I called Dr. Watt back and told him that, though I had no idea what God was up to, I had become convinced that I should take the job. Of course, one of the first people I ran into when I started the job was Dr. Hal MacBain, then director of the mission. I told him that though I couldn't explain the detour, I wanted him to hang onto my application.

I worked in the bookstore for more than a year. It was a valuable expe-rience, both in terms of what I learned about books (which was valuable to me when I was tasked with setting up the library at the Bible Institute in Medellín) and the networking I was able to do with pastors and church leaders. Then I asked Dr. MacBain to reactivate my application for service in Colombia. In early 1975 I was formally accepted and in January 1976 headed to Costa Rica for language study. Dr. MacBain had warned me that it might be hard for me, as a single woman, to raise support (there was that "What can a girl do?" thing again). But it only took a few months for that to fall into place—probably a surprise for both of us.

I felt that I had "arrived." That sense of "arrival" almost became my undoing.

There was one small glitch. While I was in Costa Rica, I learned that my visa (along with the visas of others heading to Colombia) was being held up. When I finally bought my ticket to fly to Medellín, I had to go in on a three-month tourist visa.

My arrival was discouraging. I learned via the grapevine that the "What use is she?" had crossed borders and lodged in a least a few of my new colleagues. However, the biggest obstacle to any chance of "success" in Colombia was *me*. The feeling of finally *arriving* had planted in me a seed that, because of conflicts among the missionaries at the time, blossomed into spiritual pride and a judgemental spirit. When the three months were complete, I returned to Canada pretty much determined to turn in my resignation. How could God expect me to work with *these* people—the other missionaries!

I returned to Timmins. Miserable hardly describes my feelings during those weeks. I had not had a chance to speak with Dr. MacBain alone, but he travelled north on a speaking tour and stopped at the church. Here I met with him and poured out my story. Dr. MacBain was a wise man. He let me pour out my anger, frustration, criticisms and said nothing until the very end of the interview. Then he said: "I am heading to Kapuskasing for a meeting and will be back here in a couple of days. When I come back we'll meet again and I want you to answer one question: 'Do you still feel called by God to serve in Colombia?'"

I went home, threw myself on my bed to pray. What triggered the revelation that followed can only be described as a "God-thing." The answer to Dr. MacBain's question was, "Yes, I still feel called to Colombia." That was why the thought of resigning had made me so miserable for all those weeks. So, what was the problem? In those moments, the Lord showed me what I had done. I had set myself up as judge, jury and executioner because of the situation among my colleagues in Medellín at the time. It was my sin that had almost caused me to throw away what I knew God wanted from me from the time I was nine years old.

When Dr. MacBain returned to Timmins, I walked into the pastor's office to meet with him. Before any words were said, he looked at my face and said: "Now that's the Lynda we know and love!"

I wrote a letter of apology to my co-workers in Medellín for the bad attitude I surely had shown during those first three months. But the miracles weren't done. Days after these events, the long-awaited visa came through. God knew that I needed to come home and get myself back on track before I would be any use to him in Medellín.

For the following eight years, I taught in the Bible Institute, trained teachers in the churches, worked with the students doing children's ministry and supported a church plant in Machado, the village just below the Bible Institute. Those were challenging years for many reasons, but God worked through them. I had the privilege of returning to Medellín more than thirty years later to find wonderful blessings, including a flourishing congregation in Machado pastored by one of my former students.

Then the blow fell. I called home just before Christmas and discovered that a serious health crisis had developed. My parents would never ask for help, or ask that I come home, but I knew I had to make a decision. I had waited all my life to get here. Was God about to close the door on a lifelong dream? I promised the Lord that if I was to stay, I would trust him to look after the needs of my parents. But if I was to go, I needed to know without a doubt that it was his will. In the weeks that followed, he gave me very specific indications that he was closing the door to Colombia.

I struggled after I came home, despite what I had recorded of how God had led me to this decision. I had not realized that without being Lynda Schultz the missionary, I didn't know who I was. Gradually the Spirit of God helped me realize that my identity was not to be found in a job description, but in who I was and who I needed to be—simply obedient. I stayed up north for a couple of years. During that period, God did a miracle in my family and restored my mother's health to the point where it became time for me to move on.

Now what?

Though phone calls are normally quite passé today, back in the '80s they were usually the normal way of communication. One morning I got a phone call from Paul Kerr, who had succeeded Dr. MacBain as director of the mission. Like Dr. Watt, he would not have had any indication, except by the working of God, to know that I was thinking about next steps. This was another "God thing." Paul informed me that the mission was wanting to develop a communications component for their staff. He offered me the position. I was speechless (a rare thing for me!). The Lord was giving me the opportunity to return to the mission, to write and to be close enough to family to respond to any needs without being underfoot.

So it was back to Toronto, back to Oakwood Baptist Church to serve there again, and back to a much broader involvement in the Fellowship's overseas program, including trips to Pakistan and Japan. It was another learning curve as the role developed, but these years were of great encouragement and blessing to me.

Then, Fellowship National made the decision to move to Guelph. I had grandiose plans—convince my parents to sell their home and move with me being the most ambitious of them. I went so far as to visit a couple of homes for sale in Guelph. But the closer the moving date came, the more uncomfortable I was feeling. Finally, I went into Paul's office and told him that I couldn't make the move. I resigned again, took a part-time position as director of Christian education at Oakwood and did writing and graphic design to augment my income.

In 1989, while I was still on staff, the missionaries currently in Colombia had been forced to evacuate and the mission began to look for an alternate field of service in Latin America. The Lord led them to choose Venezuela as that additional field. In 1990, some of the Colombian missionaries began ministry in Caracas. Their task was to plant a church among the middle and upper classes in the Boyera/Hatillo area of the city. In 1991, they asked to have a team come and do children's ministry and outreach among the contacts they had made—and they asked that I lead the team. In August 1991, I arrived in Caracas. As soon as I got off the plane, I felt right at home. It was a weird sensation since I had never been in Venezuela before. The feeling never left during the month we were there. Bevin Wray, with whom I had worked in Medellín, was the team leader and I remember him telling me that I was welcome to join the team permanently if the Lord should open the way.

At the end of September 1991, the Lord took my father home. Less than three months later, just before Christmas, he took my mother home. There has never been any question in my mind that the Lord gave me that month in Caracas to serve as a reminder that when the world falls apart, there is still hope. He knew what I did not, and opened a door before I knew that one needed to be opened.

Paul Kerr phoned over Christmas to offer his condolences and to, gently, tell me that the door was open. By 1994, I was in Caracas where I would stay as part of the church planting team until 2010. Those were challenging years of political turmoil, of gains and losses, of flourishing and floundering—including conducting my first funeral!

During those years in Venezuela, I had the opportunity to turn several years' worth of journal notes based on my devotional times into a book. A member of our congregation, fluent in English and Spanish, translated it for me, and one of our Colombian colleagues, Diego Cardona, arranged to have it printed in Colombia. Copies of the book have been to many parts of the world, been broadcast in Latin America and later republished in English. That project started me on a path that has become increasingly important, and since that first book I have published several of the Bible studies and materials that I have developed over my years in ministry. I have also had the privilege of writing for the Fellowship national publication and being its managing editor for several years.

In 2010, I returned home to accept a part-time position at my home church in Timmins. It was the third time and the third pastor of First Baptist who had asked me to come back during my fifteen years in Caracas. This time seemed the right time. It was, although these were perhaps some of the most challenging years of all of those I had given to ministry.

During my years in Canada between overseas assignments I have had the privilege of serving briefly on the Christian education board of the

Fellowship and the board of directors of Central Baptist Seminary. I have also been privileged to fill in for Dr. MacBain as lecturer on missions at CBS and in teaching some Christian education classes there.

I "retired" in 2016 and oddly enough moved to Guelph, making the journey there that the Lord had prevented me from making years earlier. I am now a member of Calvary Baptist Church, have served on Calvary's global missions team, continue to teach the Bible to an amazing group of seniors, serve in women's ministry and advance the prayer ministry. As well, I am doing contract work with the Fellowship in setting up their archives, which are to be housed at Heritage Seminary in Cambridge so that students and researchers will have access to information about the people, the churches and the events that have made the Fellowship what it is. My ministry with Fellowship International (FI) continues as part of the coaching team, working with missionaries serving with FI. And I continue to write.

I realize that I am finally coming back to those things that reflect the passions that have been my life and my journey with the Lord. Studying, teaching and writing about the Scriptures is primary. The hope of the world is Jesus and I try to make much of him, who he is, what he did and what he wants to do in all of us. Fellowship history is *my* history, and it has much to teach us about ourselves. And the women of this generation, and the next, need to know that the answer to the question: "What can a girl do?" is "Everything God asks of her."

Submitted by Lynda Schultz

22 /

Rev. Dr. G. Leslie Somers

"The Lord says, 'I will guide you along the best pathway for your life. I will advise you and watch over you'" (Psalm 32:8 NLT). Mine has been a privileged life. Not the privilege of status and wealth but rather the privilege of being guided by God along the best pathway for me for each season of my life so far. By the providence of the Lord, I have passed beyond the "three-score and ten" and have, in that span of time, genuinely enjoyed fifty years of full-time gospel ministry.

I was born into a large family of boys on April 14, 1952. I have seven brothers, five older and two younger. My birthplace was at the Miramichi Hospital in Miramichi in northeastern New Brunswick. I had a rural upbringing with a loving and at times overly active family, as you can imagine, with eight boys experiencing whatever life had to offer. My mother Blanche was a deeply spiritual woman who ensured we were weekly regulars in Sunday school and church. We lived just two houses away from the local Baptist church. My father Dintz was a hard-working believer who was a lumberman in my younger years and transitioned into being the local government highway foreman for the area during my teen years.

From very early in life, I had a sense that God had his hand on me for his service—a calling to the work of the ministry, which rooted itself in the church. In 1961, I invited Jesus into my life at the vacation Bible school that was being held at my church. Little Southwest Baptist Church was to become a key part of my life in ways that I initially could not have foreseen when I was saved that day at nine years of age.

For the most part, when the church doors were open, I was there in my growing-up years. I was happy to be a part of this local assembly of believers, many of whom modelled my life Godward. My pastors influenced my developing walk with God. Rev. Dr. Ivor Bennett led me to Christ. Rev. David Linden placed within me a hunger to study the Scriptures. He had a weekly Bible study for teens. Rev. Paul Legge opened up for me the opportunities of hands-on ministry. He involved me in leadership among my peers, a ministry which grew substantially under his mentorship. Rev. Legge also got me involved in Christian camping, including being a counsellor at Truth for Youth Bible Camp in Cape Blomidon, Nova Scotia. It was here that I tasted the joy of leading others to Christ. My passion for dedicated church-related service was growing. It was at a missions conference at church that I more fully surrendered my life to Christ. Several missionaries were home on furlough at the time and were presenting what God was doing through them in Africa, India and northern Canada. Through tears of surrender, this young teen gave all to the One who had saved me. From that time forward, it was to be Jesus and only his will for my future. Such missionaries as Gene and Nita Tozer, Wilbur and Leona Matthews and Percy and Jean Tozer helped to fan the flame of Christian service in my heart. My mother and father were always supportive.

As my high school years were drawing to a close, I began to research the possibilities for training related to the Bible and Christian ministry. Through an annual listing of Canadian and American colleges in the Moody Bible Institute magazine, I requested by mail that several colleges send me their latest admissions materials. Soon, a stack of school calendars arrived at our house. Two of the colleges caught my attention, one of which was Columbia Bible College (Columbia International University) in Columbia, South Carolina. At eighteen years old, I became a student there in the deep south. From northeastern rural Canada to southeastern urban America, this experience stretched me in many life-changing ways. Over time, God has blessed me with earned degrees through Columbia International University, Liberty University of Lynchburg, Virginia, and a doctor of ministry degree at Acadia University (Acadia Divinity College) of Wolfville, Nova Scotia. Lifelong learning has been a passion of mine. Many professors and administrators have poured themselves and their knowledge into my life. Whatever usefulness I have been to the advancement of the kingdom of God rests to a large degree on those dedicated Christian educators.

Just prior to completing my studies at Columbia Bible College, I was given the opportunity to experience pastoral ministry at Calvary Baptist Church in Newcastle, New Brunswick. There, as a student minister, God reassured me in his calling on my life as I learned to do some of the important things that pastors do. This church family was so very encouraging toward this fledgling apprentice in ministry.

Graduation from Columbia Bible College came in June 1974. Seeking guidance for my next steps, I arrived back home, where during the summer months, I was asked to fill in the pastorate as a student pastor while the church, my home church, was in the process of searching for their next pastor. Little did they know that it was me! God laid it upon their hearts to ask if I would step into this role. With a favourable vote, God enabled me to embark upon nearly thirteen years of blessed work. I remember one visitor "from away" saying to me, "This church is like a city church in the country!" The hand of the Lord was upon us as we witnessed him leading us through two significant building programs, one in 1976 and the other in 1983.

Many came to Christ, and over 130 souls were baptized. Jesus once said to his hometown folk that "no prophet is accepted in his own hometown" (Luke 4:24). I'm glad that I was sent back home as a pastor who, in this capacity, was more than well-accepted on home turf. After all, the leadership of New Testament churches were more often than not those of their own communities.

After four years of living a bachelor pastor's life in the church parsonage, I began to grow thin—literally, weighing just 138 pounds. My thick "bottle-bottomed" glasses added to my skinny frame. God had mercy on me. A young parishioner by the name of Ardith Hamilton came into my life. On an unusually warm and sunny October day in 1978, we were married. For forty years, she was my love, my friend and my companion in the gospel ministry. Two precious children were born to us, Tamara Caroline and then Adam Lewis. They enriched our lives in innumerable ways as they expanded our hearts with five grandchildren.

Taking on our second church as senior pastor ushered us into the world of the Fellowship of Evangelical Churches of Canada. It was 1987 when I became the pastor of the eleven-year-old Temple Baptist Church of Lower Sackville, Nova Scotia. Over the span of twenty-seven years, the Lord enabled this church to grow to become one of the largest in Atlantic Canada. Growth necessitated a major building program on the original site, and later a relocation to a fifty-four-acre property bordering Lower Sackville and Bedford, Nova Scotia. With this new initiative, the name of the church was changed to StoneRidge Fellowship Baptist Church. This chapter opened in 2009 as the congregation entered a new facility offering a home base of ministry throughout the Halifax Regional Municipality.

Affiliation with the Fellowship opened up many opportunities for personal growth and corporate partnership. It was a privilege for almost three decades to represent the Atlantic Fellowship churches at the national council level, including being elected national chair for the three years of 1997, 1998 and 2006. What a joy it was to serve alongside the then president of the Fellowship, Rev. Terry Cuthbert. Terry was always high-energy and deeply committed to Christ, with an obvious love for the Fellowship of churches nationally and internationally. Bottom line, it was fun serving our Lord and others with Terry Cuthbert. Even at times when he would pick me up at an airport, he would check the gauges on the vehicle he was driving, as if we were about to enter the skies in a fighter jet to get the job done! One always received more than one contributed when serving the Fellowship National, Fellowship International or Fellowship French ministries. Relationships made with brothers and sisters in Christ still warm my heart.

For the years 2015 to 2017, I was lead pastor of NorthLife Fellowship Baptist Church of Fort McMurray, Alberta. My wife and I immersed ourselves in this unique northern city. The multi-ethnic nature of the city and church thrilled both of us. It was a personal joy to serve alongside Pastor Mark Usher and other members of the staff at that period in the church's history. We were made so welcome by so many dedicated believers. Both homes and hearts were open to our ministry. I also loved being a part of the city's clergy ministerial, enabling us to appreciate what God was doing in the city across denominational lines.

It was in 2016, while we were serving NorthLife, that the massive wildfire broke out, causing the evacuation of the entire city in a matter of hours. What a frightening event that was! I remember looking out from the fourth floor of our downtown

Leslie Somers

apartment building and watching the flames leaping across the southern highway of the city. I said to Ardith, that we must leave very soon or we will be cut off from getting out of the city. She was packing our suitcases for our exit. As it so happened, it was too late to exit to the south, so we made our escape to the north. We ran out of gas in Fort McKay, where we stayed for a couple of hours before catching a bus north to the oilsands camp of Firebag. After four days there, we were able to head down to Fort McKay, get our vehicle refuelled and then be escorted by helicopter and police cruiser through Fort McMurray along with many others who had been stranded in various northern accommodations. We lived with relatives in Bruderheim, Alberta, for a month prior to being allowed to return to Fort McMurray.

The darkest valley of my life began while we were ministering at NorthLife. In 2016, my wife Ardith became ill, and it was discovered that a cancerous neuroendocrine tumour had to be removed within days, or she would not survive. Back to Halifax, Nova Scotia, we flew—leaving one emergency room and arriving at the other. The operation was partially successful. The Lord was gracious to give us over two more years together before he called her home to heaven in May 2019. Further complications of a cardiac arrest and severe reactions to needed treatments had taken their toll. For me, life went on, even while time seemed to stop. The "ache" in heartache became very real to me. The legacy of her love continues to reverberate in the lives of the many she impacted for Christ.

During our lengthy pastorate in Nova Scotia from 1987 to 2014, a couple of our parishioners became key to a broader international ministry for me. Dr. Manfred Kohl and his wife, Dr. Barbara Kohl, had for many years served with World Vision. I became their pastor by virtue of my being the lead pastor of Temple Baptist Church of Lower Sackville, Nova Scotia. Manfred was affiliated with the Overseas Council, an organization whose emphasis was to develop effective Christian leaders globally, especially throughout the developing world. On many occasions, I was invited to participate in training sessions and leadership enhancement events in the Middle East, Eastern Europe, Asia, Africa and South America. At times, I taught leadership concepts, and at other times, I became the in-house pastoral chaplain for some top Christian educators and leaders. We gathered in chosen cities for multi-day institutes of indepth pastoral, theological and administrative training. Needless to say, these commitments opened my eyes to develop a global view of the amazing work that God was doing among those of many countries and ethnicities. In cities as diverse as Beirut, Lebanon; Kiev, Ukraine; Manila, Philippines; Nairobi, Kenya; Allahabad, India; Lima, Peru; Quito, Ecuador; and others, we were able to interact with key leaders who were dedicated to the building up of the kingdom of Christ.

With an increased exposure to many Christian leaders across denominational lines, a desire for the well-being of pastors was growing within my soul. From time to time, I would hear individuals share their leading of God to minister to athletes, the homeless, the underprivileged, the addicted, children, youth, men or women—all of which are commendable and often produce genuine life change. I have never been athletic, nor particularly drawn to those living on the fringe of life. Yet, for me, God was birthing in my heart a burden for the clergy of whatever stripe or title. So many pastors I encountered were struggling with a variety of concerns: loneliness, weariness, lack of focus and people issues, while at the same time feeling a calling to be faithful to the Lord in their specific churches. It was the oft-repeated cliché, "Who shepherds the shepherds?" With this desire to encourage fellow pastors of congregations, I once asked a brother of a denomination different than mine, "How might I be of assistance to clergy in a broader sense than I have been?" His answer moved my heart and set me on a path wherein God began to open doors to mutual spiritual and ministerial growth. He said that if you desire to touch other clergy in a proper way, "You must ask God to give you the same heart for them as God the Father has for them." Heart touches hearts! From that time forward, I have attempted to become more intentionally a friend to those in vocational ministry. My heart has been enlarged with mutual friendships along the way, which sometimes developed into mentorships.

In this latter season of life and ministry, I see the Lord guiding me along the best pathway for my life. Walking through the initial months of the loss of my wife was very difficult. Waves of sadness often swept over my spirit. Yet, God is too kind to be unloving and too wise to ever make a mistake. He brought into my life a lady who had also walked through her dark valley with the loss of her husband. Gay Bryenton caught my eye and began to capture my heart. I later learned that she, too, was considering if there might be a future for the both of us to be together. We had both been praying, "If this attraction is foolish, please take it away!" Well, nothing was taken away, and so in June 2020, we were married! It is like a dream that we have already had several years together in life and ministry. We have embraced the world of step-children and step-grandchildren. Now, we have an expanded family of five children and eight grandchildren. God continues to weave the tapestry of our lives.

Upon a shelf in my church office rest two beautiful marble bookends, one in the shape of a cross and the other in the shape of a globe. The bookends seem so appropriate to my life. In recent years, God has brought me back home to the place and church of my origins. I accepted, for the second time, the call to pastor my home church. God is blessing us with his presence and power. The message of the gospel of Jesus Christ continues to be the power of God unto salvation to everyone who believes (Romans 1:16). With a renewed vision, Miramichi River Baptist Church is thriving to the glory of God. With this name change, we are now known simply as the River Church here in northeastern New Brunswick. A short while ago, an elderly pastor friend of mine said to me, "Pastor Les, I pray that these later years of ministry will be like the frosting on the cake." Seems like his prayer might be coming true.

As a boy, I remember my grandfather, John Somers, sitting in the church pew (same pew every Sunday). He was a long-time deacon of the church, a man of consistent faith in Christ. Although I was only fifteen years old when he went on to his reward, I do remember his favourite hymn entitled, "All the Way My Saviour Leads Me." Periodically along life's journey, the words of this Fanny Crosby song have brought to my mind a sense of divine presence, daily guidance and eternal hope:

> All the way my Saviour leads me; What have I to ask beside?
> Can I doubt His tender mercy, Who thru life has been my guide?
> Heav'nly peace, divinest comfort, Here by faith in Him to dwell!
> For I know, whate'er befall me, Jesus doeth all things well;
> For I know, whate'er befall me, Jesus doeth all things well.
>
> All the way my Saviour leads me; cheers each winding path I tread;
> Gives me grace for every trial, feeds me with the living bread;
> Though my weary steps may falter, and my soul a-thirst may be,
> Gushing from the rock before me, Lo! a spring of joy I see,
> Gushing from the rock before me, Lo! a spring of joy I see.
>
> All the way my Saviour leads me; O the fullness of His love!
> Perfect rest to me is promised in my Father's house above;
> When my spirit, clothed immortal, wings its flight to realms of day,
> This my song thru endless ages, Jesus led me all the way.
> This my song thru endless ages, Jesus led me all the way.

After a decade, a beautiful handcrafted desk has come back into my possession. I saw it advertised for sale by its original craftsman. The desk had travelled many kilometres from one province to another. It had been restored and looked like new again. Now I sit once more at this desk doing what I do, filled with great memories and future possibilities. God continues to refurbish each one of us, putting us back into circulation, for his glory!

Submitted by Rev. Dr. G. Leslie Somers

23 /

Carol Stewart, CPA

I am an unlikely candidate for a book called *Fellowship Baptist Trailblazers*. I'm a woman, and I did not grow up in an evangelical tradition. I'm the second of four children born to Andrew and Marion Watson. I was born September 20, 1962, in the hospital in Trenton, Ontario. My parents lived nearby in Brighton and attended the Presbyterian Church. In 1968, we relocated to Chatham, Ontario, where my parents joined St. Andrew's United Church.

We moved to a small acreage just outside Chatham when I was nine. There was a tiny Anglican church and community hall across the highway. Each Sunday, our kind neighbours would pick up us kids, and the local farm ladies taught us stories from the Bible. To me, God and Jesus were like characters in a book. When I was fourteen and began to attend high school, I joined my older sister at the Joy Unlimited youth group at St. Andrew's United Church. The minister was Dr. Allen Churchill, a scholar and an evangelical. While under his leadership, I attended a youth retreat at the church and was confronted with fundamental questions like, "Where did I come from?" "Where will I go when I die?" and "Where am I in my walk with Jesus?" I recall Dr. Churchill saying, 'Perhaps you don't even know what a walk with Jesus is." That was true for me! The retreat caused me to think deeply about Jesus in new and challenging ways. I asked lots of questions. Some nights later, I could not sleep; I felt pursued by the love of God. I finally spoke out loud, "Okay, okay. I believe you. I believe Jesus is the Son of God." It only made sense to me that I should then follow Jesus.

Dr. Churchill departed within a few years, and my growth as a disciple of Jesus was stunted. High school at Tecumseh Secondary (1976–1980) and university at Wilfrid Laurier (1980–1984) in Waterloo, where I studied business to become an accountant, were rocky years. I lived with one foot in the kingdom and one foot in the world. I was deeply involved in the Youth Parliament movement, which provided many leadership development opportunities. After graduation, I worked for KPMG (then Thorne Riddell) in North York. I still had never stepped into an evangelical church. I attended Lansing United, where a friend invited me to a Bible study. There, I met a young man named Brian Stewart. He invited me to the Peoples Church. It sounded radical! I stood him up on the first night, but he asked again, so I attended. Wow, such teaching from the Bible! I was mesmerized and kept going back. It turned out we met at a time when we both wanted to grow deeper in our Christian walk and serve the Lord.

Brian attended Eglington Baptist until age five, then Willowdale Baptist. His home was close to the Peoples Church, which he often visited as a teenager. His mother, Rosalie Elizabeth (Blackburn) Stewart, graduated from Ontario Bible College (OBC, now Tyndale University) and was a faithful follower of Jesus her whole life. His father, Doug, an immigrant from the UK, came forward at a Billy Graham Crusade in Toronto in 1955, but drifted away from the church, preferring to stay home with their small children. Brian attended York University, graduating with a degree in economics. Sensing a desire to know God more, Brian completed a one-year program at OBC in 1985 to 1986. He then accepted a position with InterVarsity Christian Fellowship (IVCF), assisting with finance and administration in their Canadian national office.

We married on my twenty-fourth birthday, September 20, 1986. When I returned to work at KPMG (then known as Thorne, Ernst & Whinney) after our wedding and honeymoon to Calgary and Vancouver, the client I expected to visit was not ready. I was then redirected to help with the audit of a new client, The Fellowship of Evangelical Baptist Churches in Canada. There, I met Dave Findlay. After the audit, Dave called and asked if I would consider leaving KPMG to work for The Fellowship. I was just a kid who knew a lot about accounting and almost nothing about Baptists, but I said, "Yes," and dove into the deep end of the Fellowship Baptist group.

Lynda Schultz, communications coordinator for the foreign mission board, and I, were the first women appointed to the executive team at the national ministry centre. I thought I was proceeding slowly and gently with the many changes necessary to improve documentation, efficiency, internal control and financial reporting. But I can still recall Dr. Paul Kerr storming into the accounting office and telling me why they would not go along with the new system I had designed for monthly disbursements to international missionaries. With a bit of intervention from the general secretary, Dr. Roy Lawson, Paul agreed to try it. Before long, the new system was rolling along just fine. Paul became a caring friend and role model.

I was privileged to help the Fellowship Baptist leaders and members better understand their precarious financial position through the late 1980s. I recall sitting in Dr. Lawson's office and explaining how we did not have enough cash and investments to cover our externally restricted funds. That level of clarity was not happy news, but he received this revelation with grace and responded with prayer. From a financial perspective, the Fellowship survived those years under the steam of international missionaries and the support they secured from churches and other donors. Dave Chapman was a fruitful fundraiser. Home missions struggled financially, and the French Missions were the most challenging corner of the Fellowship to untangle. I have fond memories of my colleagues in the accounting department, Theresa Flat and Joyce Findlay. Our monstrous custom-coded bookkeeping system operated on a computer about the size of a refrigerator. Elmore Millar, retired from IBM, was our technology angel. He kept that old system running and made changes as requested. George Layzell, a retired chartered accountant who served on the finance committee, would show up once a month and spend hours labouring over our no-tech bank reconciliations.

Ted Flemming, father of Rodger, Bob and Richard, played a significant role in relocating the national office from Bayview Avenue in North York to Guelph, Ontario, in 1990. Around this time, Central Baptist Seminary (now Heritage College and Seminary) was facing a financial crisis. Our accounting team leaned in to assist. During the final months of 1990, I worked part-time at Central Baptist Seminary and part-time at the new Fellowship office in Guelph, commuting with Elmore Millar. It was my honour to co-labour with such gifted, seasoned leaders. I learned much from Dr. Roy Lawson, Dr. Paul Kerr, Ted Flemming and many others.

During my years at the national Fellowship office, my husband, Brian, completed his master of divinity at Tyndale Seminary. Brian encouraged me to take a course at Tyndale. I was reluctant. During my undergraduate studies, I avoided courses requiring research in the library or writing papers. But I finally agreed. I took my first course on Jeremiah with Dr. Don Leggett. The question of the biblical role of women in marriage, ministry and church leadership was growing more significant for me and Baptist churches. I was pleased to enroll in the inaugural Women in Ministry course at Tyndale to explore these questions more fully. Although I was raised in a family with a traditional structure—dad worked, mom stayed home—my dad always made his three daughters and one son believe we could do anything. As a business student and young professional accountant, I was comfortable in a world with many men in charge. Quite naively, I thought those old-fashioned ideas about traditional roles for women died back in the sixties. Everything was changing. Right? Wrong! I could see where the biblical arguments for male leadership came from, but I firmly believed the biblical arguments for leadership based on giftedness were stronger. Little did I know this would become quite the battleground in the Fellowship in the coming years, and I would end up on the front lines.

As Brian finished his MDiv, we discerned a calling to Alta Vista Baptist Church in Ottawa, where Brian served as associate pastor from 1990 to 1998. Our two children, Mark (1991) and Rachel (1993), were born in Ottawa. These were busy years of parenting and involvement in church and neighbourhood ministry. I partnered with Brian to lead the young adult ministry. I also rekindled my connection to Dr. Allen Churchill, now senior minister at Dominion Chalmers United. Dr. Churchill created the Ottawa Summer School of Theology, and I was able to continue my post-graduate studies. He chaired the Ottawa Billy Graham Mission committee in 1998. Brian served on the committee as the prayer coordinator, a lifetime ministry highlight. During these years, Brian also completed a doctor of ministry focusing on preaching, at Gordon Conwell Seminary, Boston, Massachusetts. The ministry highlight for me during our Ottawa years was neighbourhood evangelism—offering numerous studies and seeing Jesus reveal his identity to others. I also ventured into the field of education— teaching accounting one evening a week at Algonquin College. Although there were many joys,

Carol Stewart

the Ottawa years were difficult for me. I'm glad the Lord helped me be a stay-at-home mom, but I felt far from my calling.

I entered the next chapter of life weary and skeptical. Who would think the Lord would use a traditional, declining church in Woodstock, Ontario, to renew my passion for leadership and evangelism? Brian was lead pastor at Oxford Baptist Church from 1998 to 2007. Shortly after we arrived, I was asked to join a new church leadership structure as the deacon of evangelism, along with another woman, Donna Lazenby. The church embraced the Alpha course, as we saw people coming to the Lord. We learned to look outward with women's events and Christmas, Easter and summer ministry opportunities. As a deacon, I was on the church board of elders and deacons. I was often involved in planning and recruiting for the board. Before long, I was co-chair with an elder and entirely accepted by fellow leaders! In 2005, I joined my husband on the staff team at Oxford, serving as the administrator and coordinator of adult ministries for our final two years in Woodstock.

During these years, I taught accounting part-time at Fanshawe College, usually at their Woodstock campus. In 2000, I opened my first email account. I again picked up my seminary studies, mainly at Heritage Seminary in Cambridge: systematic theology with Dr. Stan Fowler and Old Testament theology with Dr. David Barker were notable favourites. In 2005, I completed a master of theological studies (MTS), seventeen years after I started.

I was invited to join the boards of Heritage College and Seminary and FEB International (2001–2006). The Fellowship had numerous boards, which functioned more like committees. The national council (the legal board of directors) was comprised of leaders from geographic regions and key ministries, such as international missions. When the chair of FEB International suddenly stepped down, the executive group, including President Terry Cuthbert, encouraged me to become chair. This made me the first and only woman on the national council. Not everyone was happy to have a woman serving at this leadership level. During this season, the gender war heated up. Some pastors wanted a firm limitation on the role of women in church leadership. For three years, various factions brought forward motions for a vote at the national convention. In the first two years, the motions were narrowly defeated. In Montreal in 2003, those desiring a restriction were successful, and the following phrase was added to the bylaws, "the pastoral office in the church is reserved for qualified men." There are numerous issues with the interpretation and application of the bylaw, but the spirit of limitation remains, and the bylaw has been in place for over twenty years.

It was a bleak time for me and a divided time in the Fellowship. I was asked to join the search committee for a new president. Brian Baxter served admirably as interim president for two years. After searching far and wide, we invited a governance expert and seasoned leader from America, Dr. John Kaiser, to become president in 2005. John quickly removed the many layers of bureaucracy that hindered timely and effective decision-making at the national level, but the process alienated some leaders.

In 2007, Brian accepted a call to become lead pastor at Parkland Fellowship in Surrey, British Columbia. With two teenagers, it was a high-risk move from Ontario to BC, but one confirmed by the Lord. God opened an incredible door for me to join the accounting faculty full-time at Kwantlen Polytechnic University (KPU). We were a vibrant team of over thirty accounting instructors. The following year, I was elected chair of the department. Seeing this team become more effective as we undertook a program review and implemented new initiatives was fun. It was also a crazy number of hours of work. After three years, I pulled back, but mentored and supported the new department chairs. I served on various university committees and the senate. In 2016 I was humbled and honoured to receive a KPU Distinguished Service Award.

Parkland Fellowship grew and implemented two Sunday morning services. In 2013, we ambitiously sent a missionary couple to India and planted a new church in Surrey. Both initiatives and some financial stress and staff tensions stretched the church to its limits. By 2015, Brian was finishing twenty-five years of non-stop full-time pastoral ministry. He resigned from Parkland, and after a four-month break, he accepted an interim position at NorthStar Fellowship Church in Quesnel, BC, that lasted for seven months in 2016. We drove Highway 97 many times, and occasionally took a flight with Central Mountain Air.

Brian and I enjoy travelling. The Lord blessed us with many opportunities to travel for missions, including to visit many Fellowship missionaries. In 1988, we visited the Brunos in Rome, the Kesslers in Paris and attended the European conference in Switzerland. We took young adult teams from Willowdale (North York) to Belgium to work alongside the Flietstras in 1989 and from Alta Vista (Ottawa) to Spain, working with the Francis family in 1994. We served at Amsterdam 2000, the Billy Graham Congress on Evangelism. In 2001, an Oxford (Woodstock) team visited Caracas, Venezuela. In 2008, we were humbled to be guests and speakers at the European conference in northern France. In 2015, we visited the Vannadils in Ooty, India.

At Parkland, I served as the chair of the missions committee for many years, and in our final two years, I initiated a finance committee. In 2009, I joined the board of WINGS, a FEB Pacific transition housing ministry for women and children fleeing domestic violence. Before long, I rejoined the Fellowship's national council. Under the vision and leadership of President Steven Jones and Administrator Rob Cole, I became a founding member and chair of the Fellowship Foundation. In 2016, I remained on the board but stepped away from being chair when Brian accepted his next full-time position as lead pastor at a Mennonite Brethren church, The Life Centre, in Abbotsford.

On a beautiful sunny Tuesday morning, June 19, 2018, I was driving to work when a semi-truck loaded with 50,000 pounds of extra-long steel pipe lost control going around a curve. The load broke loose and came flying at my Toyota Camry, pushing the car backward off the road and crushing me in the vehicle. Quite miraculously, I survived. I blacked out. When I awoke, I could see the blue sky and recall thinking, "I can see. This is good." But I could not move; every corner of my body screamed with pain. I cried out, "Oh, Lord!" I immediately felt the encouragement of the Lord's presence. It took firefighters about an hour to cut me out of the vehicle. The noise of their equipment was deafening. I begged for something for pain, but the accident site was too precarious for paramedics. At one point, I thought I was being led up and away into the warm, bright, beautiful presence of Jesus in eternity.

I was airlifted to Vancouver General Hospital. After x-rays, I was placed into the care of three surgical teams with a list of twenty-two injuries from head to toe, including degloving (scalped), neck fracture, six broken ribs, left open (through the skin) elbow fracture, left open femur (thigh bone) fracture, left tibia (shinbone) fracture, right patella (kneecap) fracture, right foot fracture, and other minor fractures and injuries. Miraculously, I did not sustain brain, spinal or significant organ damage. And I did not bleed out at the scene! After thirteen hours of surgery that first day, and another seven hours a week later, it was time to experience the miracle of healing. At age fifty-five, my body produced a lot of new bone and responded to medications, rest and various treatments. I was in the hospital for fifteen weeks. At ten weeks, my orthopedic surgeon said, "Let's get you up and walking." It took a month of in-hospital high-intensity therapy to re-learn to balance and walk. The loving embrace of family and friends through this unexpected and challenging season was immensely comforting. Brian was at the hospital every day. Family and friends from far and near came to visit. Many people prayed for my recovery and provided much-needed encouragement.

All of the broken bones were mending except one—a nasty femur fracture just above the knee. I was only able to walk by relying on a steel rod that surgeons had inserted; it could break if I fell. Surgeons wanted to go at it again. Seven months after the accident, in January 2019, I had another major surgery, followed by another ten weeks in a wheelchair. The bone healed! However, the metal plate outside the femur from knee to hip caused pain and limited knee function. I was expecting another major surgery to remove the plate when the COVID pandemic hit. Ultimately, this elective surgery was delayed until February 2022. The Lord blessed me with a great employer who provided disability income and car insurance that covered recovery costs. I am deeply grateful for brilliant surgeons, therapists and many amazing people in the healthcare system.

My work at KPU and volunteer commitments came to a full and sudden stop. I was several weeks into teaching four courses during the summer semester, including the inaugural offering of the capstone course in strategy and governance for our post-baccalaureate program. I served on three boards: InterVarsity Christian Fellowship (IVCF), the Fellowship Foundation and WINGS. My fabulous colleagues took over all my teaching responsibilities, and I resigned from the three boards. Accepting that I would never return to the levels of productivity that I enjoyed before the accident was a process. I grieved for all that had been lost and eventually learned to be thankful for a further deepening of my experience of knowing God. Later, I returned to part-time teaching, just one course per semester. The Lord revealed a new depth to his presence and peace in my life. Such faithfulness, lovingkindness and compassion are hard to describe. "Yea, though I walk through the valley of the shadow of death, I will fear no evil, For You are with me; Your rod and Your staff, they comfort me" (Psalm 23:4 NKJV).

On September 2, 2024, I was introduced to my first grandchild, Norah Jeanette Stewart. Being alive to see this day and feel the mighty rush of intense love and attachment to this tiny little girl is a treasured gift from the Lord. Lingering limitations from the car accident have changed my life. Still, I am more appreciative of the gift of life, more willing to accept and enjoy each day, and more convinced than ever of a beautiful encounter with Jesus when this earthly journey ends.

Submitted by Carol Stewart, CPA

24 /

Rev. Pierre Tang

Hong Kong, British Colony (1973–1993): An unsettled journey

I was born in the bustling city of Hong Kong in 1973 and spent my first eighteen years there. My childhood was far from happy. My parents quarrelled constantly, and their conflicts often escalated into enormous fights. My father's bad habits and his business failures added to the turmoil. My mother became depressed and suicidal, often threatening to jump from our high-rise condo.

My father's business ventures, including a travel agency, ended in bankruptcy, leaving us in financial distress. I vividly remember gangsters hired by loan sharks to vandalize our home and bailiffs recording our possessions for foreclosure. At the age of ten, I had to visit relatives to borrow money on behalf of my father. These experiences left me feeling ashamed, insecure and lacking self-confidence. My mother was strict and frequently disciplined me with a "feather duster," leaving red marks on my skin. I was often punished for failing in school, and one traumatic event involved my mother kicking me out of the house for six hours, forcing me to wander around in my underpants.

Throughout my childhood, I viewed Christianity as a Western religion unsuitable for Chinese people. My family practiced Feng Shui (a fortune-telling practice) and worshipped Asian idols. I often visited temples, praying for wealth and harmony. In grade 7, I became interested in Feng Shui and mystical rituals. However, in grade 9, I met hardworking classmates who inspired me to study hard. I eventually ranked second out of 250 students and passed the exam to enter the prestigious St. Paul's Co-educational College.

My first year at St. Paul's was challenging, but with dedication and the help of a private tutor, I improved my English and academic performance. It was here that I re-encountered Christianity. The outstanding Christian students and loving teachers attracted me to join the school's Christian Fellowship. At nineteen, I accepted Christ as my personal Saviour.

Madison, Wisconsin (1993–1999): First love of God

In the summer of 1993, I embarked on a life-changing journey from Hong Kong to the United States, to begin my undergraduate studies at the University of Wisconsin-Madison. Majoring in political science, focusing on international relations, I found Madison's vibrant campus life and diverse student community exhilarating. I was delighted by the array of elective courses available, allowing me to delve into African storytelling, vocal singing, art history and Egyptian history. These courses broadened my horizons, sharpened my critical thinking skills and polished my spoken English.

My church life began in Madison, where I joined the Madison Chinese Christian Church, the only Chinese church in town. This non-denominational church brought together students from Hong Kong, Taiwan and mainland China. After my baptism on Thanksgiving Day in 1994, I became very active in the church, participating in Sunday school, prayer meetings, seminars and discipleship training sessions. Eventually, I served as a Bible study leader and the chairperson of the student fellowship.

In my second year of university, I took a short-term mission trip to a remote Mexican village, witnessing the gospel's transformative power firsthand. The villagers' eagerness to learn about Jesus and the profound impact of the gospel on their lives deeply moved me. This experience inspired me to commit to full-time ministry during a mission conference, where I felt the Holy Spirit urging me to follow God's calling.

Wendy, a supportive friend from high school, was the first to congratulate me on my decision to pursue full-time ministry. We began dating in 1995 and enjoyed our campus church life together. My mentor, Rev. Rolando Gan, prepared me for seminary studies by having me work as a janitor at the church for a year, teaching me humility and gratitude for God's provisions. Later, I worked part-time as a church assistant while studying full-time at the university.

During my fourth year, my mother, who was recovering from thyroid cancer surgery, came to live with me in Wisconsin. Despite her initial skepticism, she eventually embraced Christianity and received baptism. Upon graduation, I faced challenges in pursuing seminary studies, including my mother's disapproval and the responsibility of caring for her. While working as a paralegal at a law firm, I realized that only Jesus could bring true hope and salvation.

After self-reflection and spiritual renewal, I decided to apply to the seminary. With Wendy's encouragement and the guidance of Rev. Thomas Chan of Montreal Chinese Alliance Church, I chose to attend the Canadian Theological Seminary in Regina, Saskatchewan. This decision began a new chapter in my spiritual journey as I sought to follow God's calling and serve him faithfully.

Regina, Saskatchewan (1999–2002): Wilderness adventure

In the summer of 1999, I took a significant step forward in my spiritual journey by entering the Canadian Theological Seminary (CTS) in Regina, Saskatchewan. Though Regina is the capital of Saskatchewan, it felt like a small, quiet city, nestled in the Canadian Prairies. The seminary community embraced me with love and encouragement, making me feel welcome and included, despite being a Chinese student. This inclusive environment was perfect for me to confront my shameful childhood, overcome my lack of self-confidence and address my doubts about my ministry calling.

The Personal Ministry Integration (PMI) program at the seminary was transformative. Each semester, we delved into sexuality, habit formation, conflict management and ministry preparation. This program helped me understand myself better, and to integrate biblical and theological knowledge into real-life ministry situations. Through PMI, I experienced healing from my broken childhood and found emotional stability. Most importantly, I embraced integrity and honesty as the cornerstones of my pastoral ministry. The peaceful environment in Regina allowed me to eliminate distractions and truly felt God's presence in my life.

While in Regina, I became an active member at Regina Chinese Alliance Church. I taught my first Sunday school class, joined the church choir and served as a youth fellowship counsellor. The church provided financial support through bursaries and scholarships, strengthening my faith in Christ and reassuring me of my calling to become a pastor. In my third year of studies, I took on the role of dormitory superintendent, overseeing high school students from mainland China. Initially, I struggled with their behaviour, but over time, I built meaningful friendships with them and even led three of them to Christ. This experience helped me regain confidence and realize that God could use me to bring others closer to him.

In 2002 I graduated from CTS with a master of divinity in pastoral ministry. My days as a seminary student were a healing journey, equipping me with biblical knowledge and pastoral skills and helping me regain self-confidence and assurance of my calling to serve God.

Toronto, Ontario (2002–2007): A dream has come true

Upon graduating from seminary in 2002, I moved to Toronto to become the assistant pastor of Scarborough Chinese Alliance Church, where I completed my internship. I was pleasantly surprised when the church called me, even though they did not immediately need a new pastor. I was genuinely grateful for their kingdom-minded attitude, as they called me to continue training as a servant for God's kingdom.

Three months after starting my new role, I married Wendy. Her parents had been living in Toronto since 1995, and they helped us settle down quickly. It felt like a dream come true. I had finished wandering in the wilderness and arrived in the promised land. Wendy proved to be a loving and supportive partner in my ministry. She completed her masters in musicology and library and information science and worked as a professional librarian. With stable incomes, I felt more secure and no longer worried about financial struggles.

Scarborough Chinese Alliance Church was a large church, with about 1,400 adult members. Rev. Wing Lee was my direct supervisor, and I enjoyed a broad spectrum of ministries, including teaching, preaching, visitation, counselling, officiating funerals, administrative work, youth ministry and evangelism. The church felt like home to me, as most congregants were immigrants from Hong Kong, sharing the same language, culture and traditions. Ministry seemed straightforward, as I already thoroughly understood the congregants' culture.

The church allowed me to fulfill my calling as a pastor and teacher. I had numerous opportunities to teach the Word of God and shepherd the people, particularly the youth and seniors. Wendy also enjoyed her involvement in worship teams, using her musical gifts to serve the congregants and compose music for evangelistic events. We had a supportive network of coworkers and a close circle of friends. In the summer of 2004, I was ordained after submitting sermon recordings, doctrinal papers and book reports, and completing a three-hour interview. Wendy helped me rehearse for the interview, and the process strongly affirmed my calling as a pastor. I still vividly remember the joy of passing the interview and the following celebrations.

A few months after my ordination, our son Ivan was born. His name means "gift of God," and he indeed was a gift, as Wendy had a difficult pregnancy due to her previous radioactive treatment for Graves' disease. We were deeply thankful that Ivan was healthy and weighed over eight pounds at birth. Because of my unhappy childhood, I was conscious of being a good father and protecting my family. I wanted to ensure my marriage was full of love and my family was my top priority. I believed that God blessed me because I had been a faithful servant. I was absorbed in my sweet dream for a few years until 2007.

Lost in transition (2007–2015): A broken dream

In 2007, my life took an unexpected turn. One ordinary working day, I received a shocking phone call from my uncle, whom I hadn't been in touch with for years. He informed me that my mother's cancer had returned and was terminal. This news threw me into emotional turmoil. I felt responsible for looking after her, but I also feared reconnecting with her would jeopardize my ministry and expose my family's issues to the church. Despite my fears, I decided to visit my mother in Wisconsin. Wendy was pregnant with our second son, Matteo, and couldn't travel due to her health. So, I took our toddler, Ivan, and made the trip alone. When I saw my mother, the ice melted instantly. We spent the next few months reconciling and cherishing our time together. By God's grace, our relationship was healed, and she gave me her blessing before passing away.

Around the same time, my ministry supervisor, Rev. Wing Lee, unexpectedly resigned from Scarborough Chinese Alliance Church. This left the church in chaos, with endless meetings and no clear direction. I lost both my mother and my mentor in a short span, but instead of grieving, I threw myself into work, becoming a workaholic and craving approval from others. I took on the unfinished building project left by Wing Lee, hoping to honour his legacy. By God's grace, the project progressed well, and in 2010, it was nearing completion. Around this time, Rev. Michael Tsang from North York (Chinese) Baptist Church invited me to consider serving as the Cantonese sub-congregational lead pastor. Initially hesitant, I prayed and eventually sensed God's calling to take up the challenge.

In February 2011, my family and I moved to North York (Chinese) Baptist Church. As the congregation's lead pastor, I used my spiritual gifts in preaching and shepherding while also helping with their building project. Despite the challenges, I continued to seek God's guidance and remained committed to my ministry.

Discernment in progress (2015–2019): Loss of sight

The year 2015 marked a significant turning point in my life. Wendy's grandmother, who had dementia, passed away, and her grandfather's unexpected death followed this due to an accident in Hong Kong. Wendy travelled back to Hong Kong with her parents but fell seriously ill while there. She experienced fever and diarrhea, which the doctor initially diagnosed as acute gastritis. However, the medication did not help, and Wendy's condition worsened due to anxiety and emotional distress.

I travelled to Hong Kong to care for Wendy, who had not eaten or slept properly for over a week. Seeing her suffer was heart-wrenching. I cared for her until she was well enough to return to Canada. During this time, I questioned whether I needed to quit ministry to take care of Wendy and our two children. Wendy took a three-month medical leave from work, and her recovery was slow. She was later diagnosed with fibromyalgia, which led her to quit her job at the library.

In March 2016, we travelled to Colombia for a short-term mission trip, which helped Wendy regain confidence and faith in God. However, during this trip, I noticed a problem with my eyesight. An ophthalmologist performed eye surgery on me, but I developed antimetropia, a condition where the two eyes have unequal refractive power. Reading became tiring and demanding, and I struggled with my ministry

Pierre, Matteo, Ivan and Wendy Tang.

work. I even considered quitting and applying for a job at a coffee shop. Around the same time, my dad faced financial issues, and his wife blamed me for not sending enough money. Her words shook my faith and made me question my ability to continue in ministry. North York (Chinese) Baptist Church was searching for a new senior pastor, but I hesitated to apply due to my poor eyesight and emotional struggles.

By God's grace, Wendy and I started regular mentoring sessions with a seasoned missionary. These sessions were transformative, helping me understand God better and gain assurance as a follower of Christ. Eventually, I accepted the role of senior pastor at North York (Chinese) Baptist Church. As the senior pastor, I faced challenges in meeting people's expectations and resolving church conflicts. I realized I had been serving as a blind pastor, focusing on church structure and politics rather than a deeper relationship with God. I needed to discern my next steps and cast a vision for the church.

One day, while reading the story of Jesus healing the blind man, I was reminded of the lyrics from "Amazing Grace": "I once was lost but now am found, was blind, but now I see." I needed to rest in God and find clarity in my ministry.

A new destination (2019–present): Forgive and let go
In 2019, my father had a stroke, prompting me to take a trip to Hong Kong to support him. This incident made me deeply reflect on my childhood

experiences and ultimately forgive my father. He finally acknowledged the pain I had endured due to his broken relationship with my mother, bringing me immense relief. He also accepted Jesus as his Saviour and received baptism. Forgiving my parents was a critical milestone in my journey toward a deeper relationship with God. I also needed to forgive myself. Our God is forgiving and teaches us to forgive others seventy times seven (Matthew 18:21–22).

At North York (Chinese) Baptist Church, the diverse sub-congregations present opportunities and challenges in shepherding. The Cantonese-speaking congregation consists of immigrants from Hong Kong; the Mandarin-speaking congregation consists of people from mainland China; and the English-speaking congregation consists of the next generation of local-born Chinese. This diversity requires a nuanced approach to ministry, addressing each group's unique needs and cultural differences. Embracing a posture of repentance allows me to approach each group with humility, acknowledging my limitations and seeking God's wisdom in serving them effectively.

For many years, church conflicts constantly reminded me of my parents. The feelings of abandonment and the fear of disharmony could easily lead me into distress. Learning that God has not abandoned me has been a lifelong lesson. It was not my fault that my parents had a broken relationship, nor was it my fault when church conflicts remained unresolved. I needed the assurance that our God is welcoming, loving and compassionate. The love of God motivated me to let go of issues I had no control over. I forgave the people who hurt me because God also loved and forgave me.

Shepherding became overwhelming when more people were distressed due to the COVID pandemic. People's expectations and demands arose when their spiritual and emotional needs were unmet. I loved these people and felt deeply for them. At the same time, I knew it was not wise to take this up alone, so I relied heavily on teamwork. However, the uncertainties and abrupt changes brought about by the pandemic made everything much more challenging to achieve. I gradually realized that people's expectations had significantly burdened me. I felt overwhelmed.

Church conflicts often reminded me of my parents' quarrels, and people's expectations echoed my parents' strict demands. Even when I did nothing wrong, I would feel a deep sense of guilt and shame. I often perceived people's expectations as God's expectations. Within a year, I began to show symptoms of burnout. However, God did not forsake me. In my journey to find a deeper relationship with my Father God, he directed me to rest in him. The board of deacons granted me a three-month leave of absence.

In 2020, I spent two days on a personal retreat in the middle of the pandemic. Those two days were filled with prayer, confession, reflection and Scripture reading. I prayed for God's guidance and read Lamentations. God spoke to me through the following passage: "I called on your name, O LORD, from the depths of the pit; you heard my plea, 'Do not close your ear to my cry for help!' You came near when I called on you; you said, 'Do not fear!'" (Lamentations 3:55–57 ESV). God comforted me and showed me a key to breaking through my relationship struggles with him.

As I prepared to leave the retreat site the next day, I told God about my fears of fulfilling people's expectations. If God's expectations were different from people's expectations, what would they be? As I stood still, birds began to sing, and the following Bible verse came to me: "Fear not, therefore; you are of more value than many sparrows" (Matthew 10:31). What was God's instruction? He did not ask me to work for him. Instead, he wanted me to know I was precious in his eyes. If there is an expectation from God, it is to let go of working for him and enjoy his presence. The Lord has set me free.

Since the summer of 2023, my right eye has been partially blind due to the loosening of the lens, and I have to wear sunglasses all the time, even while preaching. Despite this permanent physical weakness, I have found peace, hope and a profound sense of God's presence through prayers. These moments testify to the strength and grace our heavenly Father can provide. In moments of weakness, I have also found a renewed sense of repentance, recognizing my need for God's grace and mercy. This process has taught me to lean not on my understanding but on God's infinite wisdom and love.

Epilogue

This is not the end of my story. As I continue to experience spiritual growth and help churches become more kingdom-minded, I hope my journey can bless those around me. For years, I have carried the burden of false guilt and shame. I've realized how conflicts and demands have impacted my spiritual well-being, relationship with God and connection with others. These struggles have often clouded my vision of God's goodness.

Resting in God allows me to cultivate a deeper relationship and live a life that pleases him. Spending more time with God offers me fresh perspectives on ministry. "For my thoughts are not your thoughts, neither are your ways my ways, declares the LORD" (Isaiah 55:8). God's perspective differs from ours.

I hope my brief autobiography brings hope and encouragement to those seeking a deeper relationship with God. Renewing my relationship with him has helped me conquer my fears. I now better understand where my fears stem from and what they signify. God is a living and active presence in my life. Though there will always be challenges, we can find peace in his presence.

Jesus said, "I have said these things to you, that in me you may have peace. In the world you will have tribulation. But take heart; I have overcome the world" (John 16:33).

Submitted by Rev. Pierre Tang

25 /

Dr. Jack A Taylor

T he martyrdom of Jim Elliot, Nate Saint, Ed McCully, Peter Fleming and Roger Youderian by a band of Huaorani warriors in Ecuador, exactly one month before I was born has impacted our family for four generations. Some of my earliest steps occurred on the trails of that same jungle when my parents accepted the call of God to take the good news to those who had never heard.

I was born on February 8, 1956, in the Grace Hospital in Vancouver to Charles and Sheila Taylor, recent graduates of Briercrest Bible College in Caronport, Saskatchewan. They infused the love of the world into my veins, as I watched them wrestle with language, culture, relationships, snakes and numerous changes out of their control. They also brought me to personal faith in Jesus through their faithful teaching and prayer.

The only access to our remote station, nestled in a valley, was by plane (DC-3). Some of my earliest memories involve watching the pilot drop tiny parachutes, with gifts attached, over the jungle so the children would clear the grassy runway and make it safe for him to land. A large boa caught swallowing one of our piglets ended up as a show-and-tell skin, along with a python found slithering through the grass in front of our home. It was a life of adventure.

With some challenges, come change. Our family accepted the responsibility for a church plant among Mexicans in Del Rio, Texas. My earliest classroom experiences came here, and my family expanded to three boys (Jack, Steve, Bryan) and a girl (my only sister Kathy was born in Ecuador). It was in Texas that I felt an urge to one day become a missionary in Kenya, East Africa. This was a call my future wife Gayle was having at the same age in Vancouver, Canada.

Partway through elementary school, I returned to Vancouver with my family. My youngest brother Gerry was born. We settled into Mount Pleasant Baptist (where I was baptized), before transitioning into Faith Baptist during my mid-teens. Pastor Doug Harris would become a significant pastor, mentor and guide for the youth with his call to "stay special for the Lord" and to commit ourselves to living out the *agape* love of God. A good number of pastors, missionaries and church leaders rose from that group of teens at Faith. Through the encouragement of mutual friends, Gayle and I were brought together and were married on April 30, 1977. I was twenty-one, and she was twenty. Our life motto became "Together is our favourite place."

Before I was married, I enjoyed working for several summers in Telegraph Cove's sawmill. During one stint, I was part of a crew that hauled a portable building from Beaver Cove onto a barge, and then down to Port McNeil for the establishment of a new church plant. Other jobs included working in the Vancouver Public Library, various painting gigs, doing custodial work for Faith Fellowship Baptist, cleaning furniture places and embossing door jambs in a factory. It all eventually accumulated to become an engagement ring for the love of my life.

I had planned to become a doctor and started my journey toward med school. During my first year, I played college rugby as a winger. During one tackle, the cartilage in both knees was torn badly, and my knees locked up. I had surgery to totally remove the cartilage and, after the second knee operation, was told I would be in a wheelchair by the time

I was twenty-eight. The surgeries happened during my finals, setting me back on grades. I had severe stomach reactions at that time, and a physician informed me that I would never be able to do what it took to become a doctor.

This news devastated me. While I was praying, the thought of going to Northwest Baptist Bible College filled my mind. I tried to shake it off for several days, then did what every mature believer knows not to do. I made a fleece. "God, if someone says to me, 'Are you going to Northwest this fall,' and they say it by Sunday night, then I'll sign up." I was a youth leader, and nothing was said Friday at youth. Saturday had special family meetings and nothing. Sunday School, Sunday morning and evening services came and went. Then, the college and career group had one last meeting, which also came and went. As I bent over to put on my shoes and leave, one of the most unlikely individuals in the group stepped through the crowd and said, "Jack, are you going to Northwest this fall?"

There was no doubt God had started his lessons on being desperately dependent. There were just three weeks until the start of school, so I applied with no expectation of a reply. An acceptance came back two days before the start date. I showed up and signed up for one year. I was married after my second year. By God's grace, I finished four years, with teaching from Dr. Don Carson, Dr. Herb Sturhahn, Dr. Frank Anderson, Dr. Harold Dressler, Dr. Vern Middleton, Rev. Don Hill and other great professors. Gayle supported me all the way with her bookkeeping work at a dairy. I received my bachelor of theology, and on the night of graduation, Dr. Harold Dressler said, "You must become a preacher."

I honed my preaching skills on a tour of BC and Alberta with the Northwest College Quartet, and learned to appreciate the diversity of smaller churches scattered throughout our land. The friendly welcome and supportive encouragement for our school and our team kept us going day after day.

My wife kindly informed me after my graduation that she would not be a pastor's wife, so becoming a preacher was not an option. We were missionaries. I pivoted to taking my teaching degree and went back to school. Fortunately, my wife has a close relationship with God, and he nudged her to adjust her heart. Eventually, she informed me that if God was still calling me to the pastorate, she would support me. I finished my education course and applied to seminary at Northwest. Rev. Campbell Henderson stopped by the seminary and asked me to join him at Oakridge

Baptist. I am deeply indebted to the men and women who believed in what God was doing in me and through me. We made lifetime friends through our ministry at Oakridge.

Gayle typed every word of my masters dissertation on a manual type-writer, having to ensure there were no more than three fixed typos on any given page. By the time I finished my dissertation, we had applied and been accepted by the African Inland Mission (AIM) for Kenya. Our son, Richard, was born in 1980. At orientation for AIM in New York, I was hit by a soccer ball in the eye and suffered a detached retina. The surgery to repair my eye delayed us six weeks, but by the time my name was called for graduation again, we were already in Kenya.

In Kijabe, Kenya, at the Rift Valley Academy, we inherited a dorm of twenty-eight grade 9 and 10 boys; I taught five classes that needed preparation, coached numerous sports over time and engaged in com-munity outreach. In 1982, our daughter Michelle was born, and in 1985, our daughter Laura was born. After five years, I became the chaplain and counsellor for the school, plus the activity coordinator and outreach director, while still teaching and coaching.

Discipling world changers, along with strugglers, kept us humbled and encouraged. Teaching and counselling became a passion. Training was a joy. Baptizing those who were serious about their faith kept us focused. Reaching out to meet the real needs of the community kept us balanced. For some reason, I gained a collection of eleven tortoises. The largest of these came from a young man who showed up at my door with his specimen in a wheelbarrow. He said his mother had died, and he couldn't afford a coffin. He wondered if I would buy the tortoise so he could bury his mother. I checked. It wasn't a scam.

Azusa Pacific University started a unique program where professors came on campus during our summer break to teach masters level courses to missionaries. I engaged in studies and earned my masters in counsel-ling and human resource development in 1985. I added my PhD in 1991, through a similar arrangement with Trinity Evangelical Seminary. There was not a lot of sleep during those years or during any of our eighteen years of ministry there.

The years 1995 to 1996 were a pivotal time for me, as we took on a home assignment. Arriving in September 1995, I looked out on the city of Vancouver and told God, "I don't know who I am here anymore, God. I know who I am and what I can do in Kenya, but Vancouver is even more of a challenge. Can you do anything with me here?"

A few weeks later, as I drove around listening to the radio, an announcement came on. One of the college youths I had cared for at Oakridge Baptist Church was fulfilling a dream we had often talked about. She was opening a hospice for children with life-limiting challenges. I phoned her up to congratulate her. She told me that everything was ready to go except for one thing: she needed a chaplain who had his PhD, who

Gayle & Jack Taylor

was familiar with faiths of many kinds, who could train staff in spiritual care and who had done funerals for children. I had a PhD, had taught world religions for years, consistently trained 110 staff at the mission school and had only recently done funerals for the adopted children of a missionary doctor. I told her I was available for only a year, and she told me she only needed someone for a year—to launch the hospice and get everyone trained. I went for an interview and spent that home assignment training and loving staff, supporting parents, performing a wedding and conducting funerals for children of First Nations, for Muslims, Hindus and Catholics. Canuck Place was a testimony to God's mercy.

In addition to that, I was asked by Pastor Joe Russell to help him out with taking a group of street kids and forming them into a youth group. I rallied the ladies at Oakridge Baptist to make food, and a group that started with four youths grew to thirty-five. In God's providence, as we neared the end of our year in Vancouver, we were at 95 per cent support and needed 100 per cent to go back. Pastor Joe rallied the youth on our last night with them to pledge babysitting money, bottle collecting money, etc. Each youth wrote down what they would trust God for to support us. By $5, we met our goal.

Back in Kenya, we re-engaged in our roles. Gayle had worked for years as a bookkeeper at the school, and God would use this later for our well-being. On an outreach trip, I became ill and was given antibiotics. A woman who shared my birthday also became sick on that same weekend, climbing a different mountain. She was given malaria medicine, but within ten days, she died. (We both had ticks, but I was given the right medication because the doctors were unsure what was wrong, and she was given malaria medication because doctors thought they knew what was wrong). I still have the tick mark on my calf to show God's mercy. She became one of many memorial and funeral services I conducted for missionaries and their children.

Kenya was a lesson in desperate dependence. AIM is a faith mission, so we lived month by month, trusting God and his people to hear him and respond to him. We had people praying when one of our dorm boys was eaten by a crocodile; when Gayle got hepatitis and I was consistently sick; when our dog died of tick fever; when cape buffalos camped out on our front lawn; when Gayle's parents arrived in the middle of a coup attempt; when violent break-ins in our area arrived at our house; when carjackings took the life of a fellow missionary; and when a pilot, who was the parent of a grade 12 student, was shot down after his wife had already been killed in a car accident, leaving his daughter an orphan on Easter morning. We spoke the hope of resurrection into so many lives in so many situations, and we, too, lived by that hope.

We shared adventures after being charged by buffalos, elephants and a rhino. We marvelled at the provisions of God in sparing me in motorcycle incidents, in meeting numerous financial needs shortly before we knew what was coming and in allowing us to enjoy some of the best scenery and the best people on the planet. It was in Kenya that we helped establish the 12 tasks (see 12tasks.org) to help our three children go through a rite of passage to orient them toward adulthood. Again, we found lifetime friends and supportive colleagues who provided all the sense of family we were missing at home.

God was teaching us the lesson that every part of our experience prepares us for what is next, and when the time is right, he will move us on because he leads in the right paths for his own name's sake. Our son Richard graduated and had a difficult first year at university. As our eighteenth year in Kenya approached, I was stricken by malaria and tick fever. I began to collapse and had to be carried to my classroom. Doctors suggested a two-year rest in Canada to recover. At the same time, our support was cut in half.

Arriving back in Vancouver, we took time as a family to pray and discern what God was asking of us. We shared the issue with our children, separated for several hours, and then reassembled to debrief what we'd heard from God. We each had separate verses and promptings brought to mind, but the common message, despite tears, was that it was time to return to Vancouver. This confirmed the encouragement of Pastor Doug Harris, who was back at Faith Baptist and who told us he knew God's next steps for us. We returned to Kenya for a final six months and wrapped up our work there.

In 1999, we began our ministry at Faith Fellowship Baptist Church. The vision team wanted to transition to becoming a multicultural and multi-generational congregation. There was little diversity in the church family, so I brought in a few others to brainstorm. I preached weekly on the idea that heaven included every tribe, tongue and nation, and we could get a taste of heaven now by welcoming others. The five of us on the visioning team envisioned a community operating a daycare for new Canadians and single parents, a foodbank, an ESL class and homes for refugees. I instituted Circle of Nations Day, where every culture brought tastes from their home culture, wore garb from their home country, paraded their flags, read Scripture in their language and shared music in their heart tongue.

At the same time, I was approached by Larry Nelson from Baptist Housing to start a ministry to build up families. I partnered with Dr. John Auxier from Trinity Western University to establish Smarter Families Canada: a workshop, training and support ministry that would be absorbed into the master of counselling program at Trinity. Leading the hymn sing at Shannon Oaks, a cornerstone of the Baptist Housing group located next door to Faith Baptist, expanded my relationships with many veterans of the faith who had blazed the trail before me.

Joy Manuel, a Pakistani woman attending Willingdon Mennonite Brethren Church, was one of the individuals I called on to assist in dreaming about creating a multicultural community. She had run daycares for twenty years and understood the need for childcare. She demonstrated incredible faith by declaring that she was willing to step down and start our childcare program as long as God kept a roof over her head and bread on her table. She provided leadership and training for that ministry for over twenty years. She was awarded the Multicultural Award by the city of Vancouver in 2009 for her work. Over 850 families have been helped by New Hope Childcare.

I was assigned the task of overseeing the launch of the New Hope Community Services Society, which provided housing for refugees. We started renting two homes, but I wrote a grant request for $635,000 to purchase a home and was awarded the money. Other grants from World Vision, Status of Women and the Baptist Foundation kept us strong and viable. In 2014, New Hope Community Services made the decision to relocate to Surrey and purchased the first of our apartment buildings, to provide secure, safe and affordable shelter for newcomers. Over 850 refugees have now been welcomed and cared for through this ministry.

More than any of our efforts, the refugee ministry changed the complexion and culture of Faith Fellowship Baptist Church. Older saints became Canadian mothers to refugees. Our prayer requests changed. We heard the news differently as people of other nations joined us. Iran, Nigeria, Liberia, Iraq, Afghanistan, Mexico, Columbia, North Korea, Pakistan, Sierra Leone, Congo, Libya, China, the Philippines and dozens more countries were now represented among us. Their issues were now of concern to us. I stepped in as a witness for refugees at their hearings to advocate for their right to remain here. God story after God story encouraged us.

Gayle continued to make life in the city manageable by working part-time at the Vancouver Hebrew Academy. Her work with Orthodox Jews exposed us to Shabbat meals, Orthodox weddings, bar mitzvahs, bat mitzvahs, kosher foods, synagogues, rabbinical relationships and more, while my work with refugees exposed us to halal foods, mosques, dialogues with Imams, Ramadan, numerous Middle Eastern restaurants and intense political awareness. Meanwhile, the church was growing into a family of seventy nations or more.

Despite the changing cultures making up the congregation, the *agape* culture established early on by Pastor Doug Harris continued to thrive, as we learned to share a multitude of greeting styles, greeting languages and food flavours. Faith was energized when Fellowship International and the Fellowship Pacific Region agreed to allocate the support for Mark and Catherine Buhler to develop cross-cultural ministry to Vancouver, based from our church. I had worked for years with Mark in Kenya and knew our heart for the nations would provide a strong chemistry for our team vision. No longer did we have ham at Easter and turkey alone at Thanksgiving.

Each month, we celebrated by having different cultures and geographical areas host meals with their own special tastes. Outreach into the community involved international catering, food banks, bread ministries and more. Eventually, we began a tutoring ministry in partnership with Vancouver Urban Ministries for children with learning challenges. This is another ministry I was privileged to help encourage into existence. Peter Park joined our team with his focus on First Nations ministry, and this broadened our heart for the world even more. His focus on reaching the bands of Lillooet and Lytton through collaborative multicultural teams helped establish a coalition of partners to reach into British Columbia's interior. Our reconciliation service was made even more meaningful because of this connection.

While life for the church in Vancouver was bubbling with energy, we didn't forget about the opportunities elsewhere. My son and his family were active doing work among schools in Rwanda, through the Wellspring Foundation for Education he had cofounded. My daughter and her family worked in Uganda with street boys and orphans, through a ministry she established called Humera Homes. Several times, we sent teams to these countries to assist in specific ministry projects. Other supported missionaries were in Japan, Ethiopia, Colombia, Niger, Brazil and other countries.

Board governance took up space in my schedule through my investment in the Faith board, the New Hope board, the national board of the Fellowship and the national board of the African Inland Mission. Consulting with other organizations taking up this governance model was a privilege. While others dislike meetings, I found them a stimulating place for relationship building. I learned early on that any lasting ministry involved forming partnerships, building teams and working collaboratively. Still, it was clear when the time came to pass on the reins to Pastor Jeremy MacDonald.

Writing became a passion in 2011 while I was debriefing our time in Kenya with my daughters. I published my first novel (*One Last Wave*) based on genuine Kenyan/Canadian adventures and the challenge of re-entry into a home culture for missionaries and their children. This grew into a trilogy, which led to several other trilogies through the years. I also wrote for *Light* magazine. In 2019, I was awarded the Harvey Mackey Journalism Prize. In 2020, my book, *The Cross Maker*, was awarded the Historical Novel of the Year. In 2021, *The Persian Prince* was awarded the Castle Quay Publishing Award for best Canadian Manuscript (jackataylor.com). I was privileged to write for *Thrive* magazine on behalf of the Fellowship. The book, *12 Tasks* (12tasks.org), was designed to help parents orient adolescents toward adulthood, using the program we had established with our own children. The book, *When Ministry and Marriage Collide—Honest Conversations on Thriving Through Conflict*, was designed to assist ministry leaders, volunteers, non-profit leaders and missionaries with practical tools when tensions arose between life in ministry and life at home. There have been seventeen books published at the time of this writing.

Coming home from the mission field meant few resources, and Faith Fellowship agreed on a cost-sharing for a home where they bought 19/31 of a home and let us own 12/31 of the home. The house was $310,000 when purchased in 2001 and sold for $1,848,000 in 2024 upon my retirement. Our 12/31 allowed us to co-purchase a house in Maple Ridge, BC, with my daughter Michelle, her husband Tyler, and their four children. Whether on the field, in the city or now in retirement, we have seen God's faithful provision. His words, "Fear not," are balm to us in all situations.

Upon retiring from ministry, I repositioned myself at The Ridge Church in Maple Ridge, BC. I credentialed as a marriage and relationship coach and started 1heartcoaching to support married leaders. My wife and I launched marriage workshops. I also joined my son in his work, training leaders in Rwanda. I am the academic liaison between Kurumbuka Leadership Solutions and Trinity Western University, helping leaders from sixteen African countries who are working to get their masters in leadership at the university here.

My life started with a focus on missions, and it will likely end that way. In the meantime, the world has come to us, and I have done all I can to celebrate that wonder of God's grace.

Submitted by Dr. Jack Taylor

26 /

Rev. Dr. Russell Job (RJ) Umandap

I f you'd told me thirty-five years ago that I'd be contributing this chapter to the Trailblazer series of the Fellowship of Evangelical Baptist Churches in Canada, I might have asked you what you were smoking. I was in the Philippines studying chemistry, absolutely unwilling to be a pastor. I had actually prayed, "God, if you want me to be a pastor, make me fail my university entrance exams so I'd have to go to Bible college," while arrogantly confident that would never happen. Nonetheless, God patiently pursued me, graciously broke my stubborn resistance and providentially prepared me for ministry. He even used my mistakes and my attempts to escape his will to lead me to his purposes.

My grandparents were Baptists; my parents were Baptists; I attended a Baptist church before I was even born. When I was seven years old, in 1978, the Lord brought me to himself through the witness of my mother. I was baptized the following year by Rev. Dave Boehning at Manila Baptist Church in the Philippines. Being baptized by an American missionary was just part of my Westernized upbringing. I was educated almost exclusively in Christian schools, heavily influenced by North American culture until high school. That made me an outsider in the heavily Spanish Roman Catholic culture of my homeland,[1] but it was part of God preparing me for ministry.

Despite all the godly influences around me, I was desperately trying to live on my own terms, unaware of my selfishness. I would talk about following God's leading, but I had my life planned out by my senior year at the University of the Philippines. I would graduate with honours and teach at the university while I applied to graduate programs in North America. I would get a PhD and spend the rest of my life teaching and doing research. Everything was going according to plan, until I failed to complete my undergraduate thesis on time. I did graduate a year later, but the Lord used that failure to begin to humble me and make me rethink my goals. I ended up teaching chemistry at Grace Christian High School, a Chinese school in Manila, for two years. That was my first exposure to cross-cultural ministry. After that, I worked in water treatment sales. I had no clue what the Lord wanted for me, but the pay was good, the work was challenging, and it allowed me to serve in the church.

I didn't realize I was trying to bribe God to leave my career alone by serving in the church, until I was preparing to preach on Philippians 2:5–11 in 1996. I understood that Jesus' obedience meant that he did nothing but the will of the Father. I saw that acknowledging the lordship of Christ meant I had to give up all my dreams and ambitions and embrace the Father's will for me, regardless of the cost. Paul's words in Philippians 3:7–9 have always resonated with me:

> But whatever were gains to me I now consider loss for the sake of Christ. What is more, I consider everything a loss because of the surpassing worth of knowing Christ Jesus my Lord, for whose sake I have lost all things. I consider them garbage, that I may gain Christ

---

[1] It has been said that Philippine culture is the product of 400 years in a convent followed by forty years in Hollywood, since the Philippines was colonized by Spain and was under American rule before it became independent.

and be found in him, not having a righteousness of my own that comes from the law, but that which is through faith in Christ—the righteousness that comes from God on the basis of faith.

It was time to experience the truth of those words. In July 1997, the Lord led me to work at a water treatment company in Florida. In my first week on the job, my boss asked me to go to Jamaica for three weeks. I was still jet-lagged, so I thought I was getting a vacation. However, when I got to Kingston, Jamaica, I found out I'd be spending at least six months monitoring a project at a power plant. Knowing I'd be stuck in Jamaica for a while, I started looking for a church, and the Lord led me to Grace Reformed Baptist Church (GRBC).

By that time, I was emotionally, physically and spiritually burned out. I had been functioning as a deacon, teaching adult Sunday school, preaching occasionally, playing the piano and conducting the choir. All of these responsibilities came on top of a stressful job that had me working an average of fifty hours a week. My church in the Philippines, Fairview Fundamental Baptist Church, had split three times in ten years. I had gone from being a perplexed spectator to being an active participant in these conflicts. Going to church had become a burden. I was so busy serving that worship was no longer a delight. My first three months attending GRBC gave me much-needed rest and refreshment, as the church unreservedly embraced me as a brother in Christ.

I began to recognize that I didn't want to stay at that water treatment company. As I earnestly sought the Lord's guidance, I realized I loved being in Jamaica because of the church. I had always shrugged off suggestions that I become a pastor. But as I looked back over my career path, I realized I had always found my professional pursuits unfulfilling because my heart was always in serving the Lord in the church, even when church life was burdensome and frustrating. I concluded that the Lord wanted me in pastoral ministry and that I would never be content until I obeyed him. I consulted my pastor in Jamaica, my parents and my former piano teacher, a wise lady who had become a valued adviser. Part of me still wanted them to tell me I wasn't cut out to be a pastor, but they all encouraged me to go into pastoral ministry. My pastor in Jamaica even told me he wanted me to take over for him when I graduated. So, I went to Toronto Baptist Seminary (TBS), trusting God to provide for me and to guide my steps.

I entered TBS in September 1999 with barely a year's worth of tuition, but the Lord provided for me every step of the way. My aunt in Scarborough gave me free board and lodging. Jarvis Street Baptist Church (JSBC) asked me to lead its college and career group and covered half of the tuition for my second year. GRBC brought me back to Jamaica as a summer intern, and covered the other half of my second-year tuition. Pastor Eliezer Catanus of First Filipino Baptist Church (FFBC) hired me as a summer intern after my second year, which paid for most of my final year. He also gave me the privilege of preaching regularly at FFBC during my three years at TBS. The generosity of FFBC went beyond providing for my financial needs. They gave me much-needed ministry experience and even catered our wedding! That was my first experience of life in the Fellowship.

I'd gone to TBS intending to return to Jamaica. Knowing the culture in Jamaica, I knew I had to get married. My problem was that I didn't know any girl who'd marry me. Thankfully, the Lord also had that covered. I joined a ministry team of students representing TBS at Midland Park Baptist Church and accompanied Joelle Ambroisine, a student from the French island of Martinique, as she sang. The following day, she told me I would be her permanent pianist. One thing led to another, and we got married on April 6, 2002, between the last day of class and our first day of final exams.

Joelle and I moved to Jamaica in November 2002, after two pastoral internships in Pennsylvania. The plan was for me to work alongside my old pastor till he retired. Then, I would pastor GRBC till a young man who'd grown up in the church was ready to replace me.

The Lord blessed us with Zachary Calvin (born in 2003) and Johann Samuel (born in 2005), our Jamaican "Frenchipinos" and gave us the privilege of being "parents" to young adults in the church. However, I found ministry in Jamaica so frustrating that I found myself celebrating(?) my birthdays, wishing I was dead. God graciously sustained me through those four years as he taught me patience and perseverance. I left Jamaica in January 2007, disappointed I hadn't accomplished my plan. Thankfully, God's plans are better than mine. After I left, the church eventually ordained Boysie Williams, a man I'd identified as a potential elder, to be its pastor. I visited the church in 2023 and saw the fruit of his faithful labour firsthand. He was truly God's man for the job.

I had left Jamaica to serve as an assistant pastor at Jarvis Street Baptist Church (JSBC). I was responsible for caring for the congregation, overseeing the worship ministry[2] and serving as managing editor of *The Gospel Witness*. Working in that multi-ethnic church environment gave me a functional template for the work God would give me at my next church. God was also at work when myasthenia gravis[3] forced me to take an 18-month break from ministry (2008–2009). He

RJ Umandap

taught me the importance of a loving church community, as my role changed from providing care to receiving care. In the midst of my frustration at not being able to work, God taught me to find my satisfaction in the sufficiency of Christ. I began to learn that my worth wasn't based on my ministry. *Jesus* is my righteousness; *he* defines my worth. He enabled me to experience his words to Paul, "My grace is sufficient for you, for my power is made perfect in weakness" (2 Corinthians 12:9). A dear friend wrote me, "I know God has something special for you. He loves you for he chastens those whom he loves, and we suffer to equip us for ministry and increase our hopes of heaven." Little did I know how true his words would prove to be.

God graciously restored my strength, and I was able to return to work in 2010. However, in the midst of my excitement at being able to return to JSBC, the Lord turned my heart to Living Hope Baptist Church (LHBC). I came to LHBC in January 2011, as the associate pastor and became the lead pastor in 2013 after Pastor Glenn Diel retired. LHBC started in 1998 as a church plant of FFBC. They had hoped to become a multiethnic church, but they hadn't made significant progress. They did

---

2 I'm not a very good musician, but being a one-eyed, short-sighted man in the kingdom of the blind has its advantages. My career in music ministry officially ended when the head of the worship team at Living Hope Baptist Church very kindly thanked me for playing the piano for the worship service and asked me never to do it again. I'm grateful for her candour and continuing friendship.

3 Myasthenia gravis is an autoimmune disease that results in severe muscle weakness. There is no cure, but its effects can be managed by medication.

have a significant number of second-generation young adults eager for change. When I became lead pastor, they helped drive the transformation of LHBC.[4]

Ethnic churches form out of a longing for home. Immigrating to a foreign land can be traumatic. You're starting life from scratch, adrift in a society you don't fully understand. People don't understand you and your strange accent; your qualifications are not recognized; people don't respect your past achievements. Going to church with people from your home country is like going home without the jet lag or paying $1,500 for airfare. You're in a bubble where you are *somebody*. Ethnic church is your safe place, but if it lets "other people" in, you're thrust back into the society from which you're seeking refuge.

At LHBC, we recognized that we needed to reflect the diversity of heaven if we were to be a faithful kingdom outpost in Toronto. As the gospel took root in our hearts, we understood that our worth comes not from our accomplishments, cars, houses or degrees, but from being in Christ. Our faith-union with Christ binds us to other believers as citizens of heaven and members of God's household. It enables us to embrace them, regardless of ethnicity, language and social status. *Christ* is our unshakeable refuge who gives us joy to endure the pain of losing our safe place.

When comfort and security are the underlying motives (consciously or unconsciously) for being in church, complacency tends to set in. Refocusing on the gospel, challenged *everyone* in the church to grow. Our older members began to acknowledge there was much they still needed to learn. Our younger members became more aware of the need to preserve unity by caring for those outside their peer group. The older members graciously ceded leadership to our younger adults, recognizing that our young adults had a better understanding of the changes we needed to make to reach out to people in Toronto, and were better equipped to implement those changes. They allowed them to make theologically-driven changes to the way we did things, and accepted the discomfort involved. The young adults helped us examine our habits and practices in light of Scripture and helped us recognize the unintended messages we were communicating. In everything, they consistently worked for the greater good of the whole body, recognizing that leadership means self-giving service.

---

4 I've adapted material I previously published on the TGC Canada website, https:// ca.thegospelcoalition.org/article/5-things-weve-learned-as-we-transition-from-an-ethnic-to-a-multicultural-church/. Used with permission.

Not only did we become a healthier church, but the Lord also expanded our ministry. We joined Morningstar Christian Fellowship's initiative to train pastors in the Philippines through LeadersFormation. We supported Église du Plateau, Montreal, through the Fellowship's 7x7 program. We came alongside Liberty Grace Church (where I also served as an external elder), by providing a music team once a month. We joined a quarterly joint worship service with other Fellowship churches in Toronto. Ennerdale Road Baptist Church and Christie Street Baptist Church started joining our youth retreats. These initiatives helped us embrace "the other" and experience the joy and beauty of being part of the Fellowship.

As we gained confidence engaging outside the Filipino community, the Lord enabled us to build connections with the Lakeshore community. Highlights of those years were helping with Youth Unlimited's Lakeshore Soccer League, holding summer basketball clinics and joining our neighbourhood's annual street party. Our annual vacation Bible school was filled with unchurched kids from the community. People in our neighbourhood began to consider LHBC a benefit to the community. By 2018, I could see we had turned a corner, as members of the church began to make non-Filipinos feel welcome. Even the stress test that was COVID demonstrated the congregation's growth in godliness. We were united in following government-mandated restrictions because we recognized that ignoring the restrictions would have negated our ten-year investment in building relationships with the Lakeshore Village community. So, for the sake of the gospel, we endured, as we longed for gathered worship. (It didn't hurt that a significant number of our congregation were healthcare workers or lived with healthcare workers.) God faithfully sustained us through those difficult times we'd all rather forget. By God's grace, LHBC is now a multiethnic church, faithfully reaching out to the Lakeshore community.

Worn out from leading LHBC's efforts to become a Christ-centred, gospel-driven, kingdom-focused multiethnic congregation, I took a sabbatical in February 2020. I also needed to seek God's guidance as LHBC entered the next phase of its life. As I came to the end of my sabbatical, I was refreshed but perplexed because God had not given me a fresh vision for the church.

Then, COVID happened. Once again, God had given me what I needed, not what I wanted. As we anticipated the easing of restrictions in 2021, I began to sense God was leading me out of LHBC. I was interested in an anglophone church in Quebec, but Tim Strickland of FEB Central convinced me to contact Crestwicke Baptist Church. I'd seen their posting, but I was hesitant to consider Crestwicke. Guelph and Toronto have very different cultures. LHBC was twenty years old and focused on its neighbourhood; Crestwicke is almost 100 years old and considers the whole city its place of ministry. Crestwicke seemed to be a highly intellectual church of theology geeks; when I was interviewed at LHBC, no one asked a single question about theology.

Much to my surprise, the search committee decided to recommend me to the congregation in exactly one month.[5] Trusting the Lord was leading me to Crestwicke, I started in January 2022. I've been at Crestwicke for three years, and it's been a joy to be a part of a loving, welcoming congregation, with a delightful sense of humour. We love theology, and we are serious about putting it into practice. Our Canadian Frenchipino, Daniel Alister (born in 2017), is benefiting from the church's vibrant children's ministry. Joelle, Zachary and Johann are serving in various church ministries. The church is growing, and it's been a privilege to showcase God's multicoloured wisdom as we worship together. The Lord has been opening opportunities for the church to minister to people in the city, and I'm excited for what he has in store for us as we seek to be a basecamp for believers, a lighthouse for the lost.

God has been using my time at Crestwicke to challenge me in ways beyond my imagination. The church has allowed me to serve on the FEB Central regional board and the Fellowship's Affirmation of Faith committee, which have both been stretching and humbling experiences. Working alongside godly elders and deacons has been helping me grow and develop as a pastor, a leader, a husband and father, and a follower of Christ. I'm grateful God has been patiently leading me into his purposes for me. I don't know what the future holds, but by God's grace, "I press on toward the goal to win the prize for which God has called me heavenward in Christ Jesus" (Philippians 3:14). *Soli Deo Gloria!*

Submitted by Rev. Dr. Russell Job (RJ) Umandap

---

5 The search committee received my application on September 1, and by September 30 (after three interviews), they were scheduling me to preach at Crestwicke so the congregation could vote on calling me.

the fellowship
BAPTIST PRESS

The Fellowship Baptist Press is a ministry of the Fellowship of Evangelical Baptist Churches in Canada (fellowship.ca), a movement of over 500 Evangelical Baptist churches in Canada—united through our faith in Christ working nationally and beyond our borders.

fellowshipbaptistpress.com

www.ingramcontent.com/pod-product-compliance
Lightning Source LLC
Jackson TN
JSHW070949061025
92093JS00003B/6